REGULATING HEALTHCARE

STATE OF HEALTH SERIES

Edited by Chris Ham, Professor of Health Policy and Management at the University of Birmingham and Director of the Strategy Unit at the Department of Health.

REGULATING HEALTHCARE
A Prescription for
Improvement?

Kieran Walshe

Open University Press
Maidenhead · Philadelphia

Open University Press
McGraw-Hill Education
McGraw-Hill House
Shoppenhangers Road
Maidenhead
Berkshire
England
SL6 2QL

email: enquiries@openup.co.uk
world wide web: www.openup.co.uk

and

325 Chestnut Street
Philadelphia, PA 19106, USA

First Published 2003

A catalogue record of this book is available from the British Library

ISBN 0 335 21022 8 (pb)   0 335 21023 6 (hb)

Library of Congress Cataloging-in-Publication Data
CIP data has been applied for

Typeset by RefineCatch Limited, Bungay, Suffolk

Printed and bound in Great Britain by
Marston Book Services Limited, Oxford

To my parents, Joe and Angela Walshe

CONTENTS

SERIES EDITOR'S INTRODUCTION

Health services in many developed countries have come under critical scrutiny in recent years. In part, this is because of increasing expenditure, much of it funded from public sources, and the pressure this has put on governments seeking to control public spending. Also important has been the perception that resources allocated to health services are not always deployed optimally. Thus at a time when the scope for increasing expenditure is extremely limited, there is a need to search for ways of using existing budgets more efficiently. A further concern has been the desire to ensure access to health care of various groups on an equitable basis. In some countries this has been linked to a wish to enhance patient choice and to make service providers more responsive to patients as 'consumers'.

Underlying these specific concerns are several more fundamental developments that have a significant bearing on the performance of health services. Three are worth highlighting. First, there are demographic changes, including the ageing population and the decline in the proportion of the population of working age. These changes will both increase the demand for health care and, at the same time, limit the ability of health services to respond to this demand.

Second, advances in medical science will also give rise to new demands within the health services. These advances cover a range of possibilities, including innovations in surgery, drug therapy, screening and diagnosis. The pace of innovation is likely to quicken, with significant implications for the funding and provision of services.

Third, public expectations of health services are rising, as those who use services demand higher standards of care. In part, this is stimulated by developments within the health service, including the availability of new technology. More fundamentally, it stems from the emergence of a more educated and informed population, with people more accustomed to being treated as consumers rather than patients.

Against this background, policy-makers in several countries are reviewing the future of health services. Those countries which have traditionally relied on a market in health care are making greater use of regulation and planning. Equally, those countries which have traditionally relied on regulation and planning are moving towards a more competitive approach. In no country is there complete satisfaction with existing methods of financing and delivery, and everywhere there is a search for new policy instruments.

The aim of this series is to contribute to debate about the future of health services through an analysis of major issues in health policy. These issues have been chosen because they are both of current interest and of enduring importance. The series is intended to be accessible to students and informed lay readers as well as to specialists working in this field. The aim is to go beyond a textbook approach to health policy analysis and to encourage authors to move debate about their issue forward. In this sense, each book presents a summary of current research and thinking, and an exploration of future policy directions.

Professor Chris Ham
Director of Health Services Management Centre
University of Birmingham

PREFACE

Like it or not, we are living in what might be called the golden age of regulation. Despite the strenuous efforts of some governments to deregulate, circumstances appear to conspire to extend the scope and scale of regulatory intervention in economic, social and commercial life. Regulation spreads like bindweed, regulatory agencies multiply and the regulatory ratchet tightens a little more each year. Healthcare is no exception to this trend, and the last few years have seen a rapid growth in regulation in many countries. Where once we trusted clinical professionals like doctors and nurses, and institutions like hospitals and clinics, now we put our faith increasingly in regulatory agencies and the systems of regulation that they manage.

But does it work? What effect does regulation have on the quality of health services that we, as patients, clients, users and the general public receive? Does healthcare regulation make for better healthcare, does it have costs and harms as well as benefits, and how does it measure up? In an age when evidence-based policy-making is all the rage, and the British Government holds to the tenet that 'what matters is what works', it is timely to ask whether and how regulation works. That, in essence, is the question this book sets out to answer. It does so in two ways. Empirically, it examines the experience of regulating healthcare in the USA and the UK over the last three decades. Theoretically, it draws on a body of regulatory theory – concepts, ideas, models and methods – developed and tested across many regulatory spheres of activity.

This book could not have been written without the generous support and encouragement of the Commonwealth Fund, a private non-profit foundation based in New York that supports research and analysis on a wide spectrum of health policy issues. The Fund runs the long-established international Harkness Fellowship Programme, which gives policy-makers, academics and senior managers and clinicians from the UK, Australia and New Zealand the opportunity to live and work in the USA, learning about and from the US health-care system and undertaking research there. As a Harkness Fellow in 2000–2001, I spent almost a year based at the University of California, Berkeley in the School of Public Health. Not only did this enable me to undertake the research into US healthcare regula-tion which forms an important part of the book, it also gave me the opportunity to work with American scholars, to meet American academics and policy-makers, to experience US healthcare first-hand and to observe the superficially familiar but fundamentally different US culture at close quarters. I owe particular thanks to Karen Davis, Gerry Anderson, Robin Osborn, Beth Lowe and all the staff of the Fund's international programme.

There are many colleagues who, over the last two years, have aided, informed, enlightened, humoured or tolerated my enthusiastic search for truths about regulation. I owe special thanks to Steve Shortell and Tom Rundall at the University of California at Berkeley and Charlene Harrington at the University of California at San Francisco, who were great research collaborators and hosts and helped me at least to begin to understand the US healthcare system; to Chris Ham and John Clark at the University of Birmingham who were unfailingly supportive before, during and after my Harkness Fellowship; and to Joan Higgins and other colleagues in the Manchester Centre for Healthcare Management at Manchester Business School where I now work, and where this book has been completed. My understanding of how healthcare regulation works has been shaped by countless meetings, discussions and interchanges with many people working in regulatory agencies, healthcare organ-izations, government departments and academic institutions on both sides of the Atlantic, and I am thankful to them for their time and their insights. Of course, any errors or omissions in this book remain my responsibility.

Finally, I owe a huge personal debt of gratitude to my wife Catherine and our four children – Siobhan, Ruth, Michael and Daniel – who for months have put up with my sitting in a corner tapping away on my laptop at odd hours of the day and night and leaving piles of papers around the house. They are very pleased that this book is finished, but I am not sure they are going to read it – familial love and loyalty has its limits.

Kieran Walshe

1

INTRODUCTION

This book is about the regulation of healthcare organizations – how and why they are regulated, what forms regulation takes, what regulators do, and how regulation changes their behaviour and impacts on their performance. Although healthcare regulation can serve many purposes, its primary goal is usually performance improvement – make healthcare organizations perform better, provide higher quality health services, or be more effective and efficient in what they do. For that reason, this chapter starts by considering where regulation fits in the context of healthcare performance improvement. It then goes on to provide a brief introduction to the history and development of healthcare regulation and to set out the key issue at the centre of the book – what do we mean by effective healthcare regulation and how do systems of regulation measure up? Finally, the chapter sets out the structure of the rest of the book.

THE CHALLENGE OF PERFORMANCE IMPROVEMENT

Every healthcare system in the developed world is engaged in a continuing search for ways to get healthcare organizations to change and improve. Regardless of how health services are funded, what payment mechanisms are used, or how delivery systems are organized and structured, they have a common challenge of performance improvement. There is plenty of evidence to show that: many healthcare organizations have huge, unrealized opportunities for improvement (Berwick 1996); the quality of healthcare services varies wildly from place to place, from organization to organization, and even within organizations (Brook *et al.* 2000); and necessary change can be difficult and often happens very slowly or even not at all, despite the availability of robust evidence to show what should be done (Ferlie and Shortell 2001; Isles and Sutherland 2001). The practical consequences of all this must be that some patients who turn to healthcare organizations at the time in their lives when they are at their most vulnerable are harmed rather than helped, and that many more get less good care than they could or should receive.

One way to illustrate this problem of poor or variable performance is to review some examples of suboptimal clinical practices that are acknowledged to be commonplace. For instance, Table 1.1, based on work by the UK National Health Service (NHS) Centre for Reviews and Dissemination, lists some well-documented areas in which current clinical practice in many organizations does not match up with known best practice, whether through the underuse of effective healthcare interventions, the overuse of ineffective therapies or the misuse of interventions which may be effective but which are not targeted on the right patients. Although the scale of underuse, overuse and misuse is difficult to estimate, there is little doubt that examples such as these are simply representative of a much wider problem that must result in an enormous waste of healthcare

Table 1.1 The unmet need for changes in clinical practice: examples of overuse, underuse and misuse drawn from reviews by the NHS Centre for Reviews and Dissemination

Overuse	Prophylactic extractions of asymptomatic impacted third molars (wisdom teeth) Screening for prostate cancer Composite and other new materials used for dental fillings in place of traditional amalgam
Underuse	Drug treatment of essential hypertension in older people Smoking cessation through nicotine replacement therapy Compression therapy for venous leg ulcers Cardiac rehabilitation for people with heart disease
Misuse	Pressure-relieving equipment in the prevention of pressure sores Interventions to diagnose and treat gynaecological cancers Selection of hip prostheses in hip replacement surgery Some preschool hearing, speech, language and vision screening tests

Note: These examples are all drawn from the *Effective Health Care Bulletins* issued by the NHS Centre for Reviews and Dissemination and available from its website at http://www.york.ac.uk/inst/crd/

resources and leave many patients less healthy than they need be (Institute of Medicine 1999).

Another, more epidemiological approach to mapping the performance problem is to examine data on the prevalence and consequences of errors or adverse events in healthcare organizations – circumstances in which patients suffer some harm as a result of the care they receive (Walshe 2000a). An Institute of Medicine report published in 2000 in the USA received widespread media attention when it concluded that errors in healthcare organizations were the eighth most common cause of death, killing between 44,000 and 98,000 people each year in the USA, more than breast cancer, AIDS or motor vehicle accidents (Institute of Medicine 2000). A parallel report from the British Government drew similar conclusions (Department of Health 2000a). Based on US and UK studies, it estimated that: between 4 and 10 per cent of inpatient admissions suffered some kind of adverse event; about half of these adverse events were preventable; and the annual costs of additional healthcare provided as a consequence of adverse events could amount to £2 billion. It is clear that many of these errors, in areas like the prescribing and administration of pharmaceuticals, could be prevented, yet their occurrence is often accepted and seen by some as an inevitable consequence of the complexity of modern healthcare (Institute of Medicine 2000).

A third, more qualitative approach to demonstrating that a performance problem exists is to explore instances of major quality failures in healthcare organizations, which sometimes result in a public or other inquiry. In recent years, the NHS has seen a spate of such problems in paediatric cardiac surgery, general practice, cervical screening, gynaecology, radiotherapy, pathology and so on, but there is a long history of quality failures followed by inquiries stretching back at least three decades (Martin 1984). A brief summary of some recent examples of major failure that have been investigated by a formal inquiry is contained in Table 1.2, which demonstrates that although they differ in size, scope and clinical content, they often have much in common. Such inquiries do more than just describe the symptoms of quality failures by documenting the damage done to patients and exposing alarming instances of clinical incompetence, individual misbehaviour or organizational dysfunction. They frequently highlight the underlying common causes and contributing factors that allowed such things to happen, finding: NHS organizations with a protective 'club' culture among professionals, which inhibits criticism or learning; poor or weak clinical and managerial

Table 1.2 Some recent major inquiries into quality failures in the NHS

Year	Issues investigated	Inquiry findings and recommendations
1999	Serious breaches of security and illegal activities at Ashworth High Security Hospital in 1995–96	Allegations of major failings generally supported; problems of dysfunctional management found. Made 58 recommendations, including that Ashworth should close and major changes in high security/forensic psychiatry services should be made
2000	Removal, retention and disposal of human tissues and organs from children after death at the Royal Liverpool Children's Hospital (Alder Hey)	Serious failings in clinical practice and managerial arrangements found. Made 67 recommendations covering changes to NHS/university structures, coroners' role and function, consent arrangements and wider systems for dealing with the bereaved
2000	Serious failures in the clinical practice of Rodney Ledward at the South Kent Hospitals NHS Trust 1990–96	Clinical failings documented and confirmed. Made 103 recommendations for changes to quality systems in the NHS and private sector, and consultant appraisal and disciplinary procedures
2001	The management of the care of children receiving complex cardiac surgical services at the Bristol Royal Infirmary (BRI) between 1984 and 1995	Found serious clinical and organizational failings and concluded that 30–35 more children had died than would have if BRI service had met standards elsewhere. Made 198 recommendations regarding service organization, leadership, safety, professional competence, public involvement and the care of children
2001	The conduct of Dr Harold Shipman, a general practitioner in Hyde, Derbyshire who was convicted in January 2000 of murdering 15 patients	The inquiry commenced in 2001, produced an interim report on the numbers of patients murdered by Dr Shipman in July 2002, and is expected to report in 2003 or 2004

leadership, which fails to address the problems when they occur; and an isolative, inward looking ethos, which rejects advice or opportunities to learn from practice elsewhere (Higgins 2001; Kennedy 2001).

So, given that there seems to be a serious need for performance improvement, why is it difficult to achieve change and improvement in healthcare organizations? Few people would argue that those who work in healthcare organizations – clinical professionals, managers, ancillary workers and others – do not want to do the best they can for patients, or that they are lazy, incompetent and uncaring. In fact, it is much more likely that most people working in healthcare organizations are dedicated, hard-working and conscientious, and that they take great personal and professional pride in the services they provide (Berwick 1989). It is more likely that the problem lies in the highly complex, poorly understood healthcare system – the ways in which healthcare organizations are structured, healthcare processes are set up and managed, and healthcare services are financed and delivered. Improvement, therefore, means changing that system (Berwick 1996).

Over the last two decades, increasing attention has been focused on managing and improving performance and the quality of care in health services, as public and political awareness of the problems of poor performance and of the variations in quality has grown. Healthcare systems and organizations have turned to a variety of what might be termed 'improvement strategies', approaches or methods aimed at promoting, enabling, encouraging or even forcing change and improvement to happen. Regulation is just one of the strategies to be used, and it is worthwhile considering how it compares with some of the other approaches.

There are two main groups of approaches to performance improvement in healthcare organizations, outlined in Table 1.3. *Internal* approaches to improvement work inside the individual healthcare organization or even just in part of it, and focus on bringing about change from within. They often involve the development or adoption of new organizational structures, processes, measurement tools or methods. For example, continuous quality improvement is an internal approach to improvement that uses high-level organizational changes in culture, leadership and direction coupled to lower-level changes in structures and processes to bring about continuous improvement (Blumenthal and Kilo 1998). Process re-engineering or redesign is another example of an internal approach, which uses some well-established techniques for mapping and improving care processes coupled with an ambitious, transformational managerial

Table 1.3 Internal and external approaches to performance improvement in healthcare organizations

	Internal approaches	*External approaches*
Examples	Continuous quality improvement and other whole-system approaches Risk management Benchmarking Re-engineering and process redesign Clinical governance Quality teams and quality circles	Markets and competition Economic incentives and sanctions Publication of performance comparisons or league tables Legislation and civil liability Regulation
Characteristics	Micro-level interventions, used within an individual organization	Macro-level interventions, used at a system or area level across a number of organizations
Advantages	Direct and highly targeted interventions which can be tailored to the organization's needs and which operate very close to the level at which service change happens	Powerful incentives and sanctions which command the attention of organizational leaders and which are certainly capable of driving organizational change
Disadvantages	Pay too little attention to organizational context and environment; ignore institutional, social and economic pressures that shape organizational objectives; often have weak or limited effects because they lack high-level organizational commitment	Pay too little attention to the complexities and subtleties of organizational behaviour; are based on simplistic and naive assumptions about mechanisms of change; often involve universal interventions that are not well matched to individual organization's needs

approach, and which aims to rethink whole service areas and how they work (Locock 2001).

In contrast, *external* approaches to improvement work from outside the healthcare organization, and aim to change its environment in ways that will make it then change its behaviour. For example, increasing competition in a healthcare market by removing barriers to entry or making contracts more contestable may be intended to force healthcare organizations to become more efficient and responsive to purchaser requirements (Luft 1985). Publishing comparative data on healthcare organizations' performance in 'league tables' is another external approach, predicated on the assumption that poor performers will be identified by the process and that pressure from a range of stakeholders (not just purchasers, but patients, professional groups and other healthcare organizations) will force improvement to happen (Marshall *et al.* 2000).

Both approaches have their limitations, because they tend to treat either the organization itself or the environment within which it exists as a 'black box'. The problem with internal approaches to improvement is that they often behave as if the organization exists in isolation from its environment, and ignore the powerful institutional, social and economic pressures that shape organizational objectives. For example, a hospital may have a superb continuous quality improvement programme, but if the purchasers which buy its services are only interested in getting the highest workload for the lowest price possible, then however motivated the organization may be, it will be difficult for it to sustain its commitment to excellence. In another setting, healthcare providers might be striving to collaborate with each other using 'breakthrough' methodologies to learn from best practice elsewhere and bring about improvement, but if they exist in a crowded and highly competitive marketplace, the competitive pressures upon them are likely to prevent the open sharing of any innovations that might confer some competitive advantage, therefore undermining the whole concept of collaborative improvement. Internal approaches to improvement implicitly assume that the organization is not the way it is *because of* the financial, commercial or political environment in which it operates, and that the organization can swim against the tide of that environment if need be. Organizational theory suggests that both assumptions are highly suspect (Cook *et al.* 1983). The rather disappointing progress made by total quality management/ continuous quality improvement in the USA may be explained, at least in part, by a failure to recognize the limits of intra-organizational improvement efforts in an environment that has been at best uninterested and at worst actively hostile towards quality improvement (Shortell *et al.* 1995; Blumenthal and Kilo 1998).

On the other hand, external approaches to improvement often fail because they ignore the complexities and subtleties of organizational behaviour, take little or no account of organizational context and culture, and make naive, universal assumptions about the mechanisms for organizational change. For example, when comparative performance data for hospital mortality have been published in the UK and the USA, it has led hospitals to engage in a prolonged defence of their own performance, and made them find creative and perverse ways to fix the data rather than to bring about real improvement (Berwick and Wald 1990). Similarly, while in theory it is plausible that increasing competition between healthcare organizations will stimulate performance improvement, there is remarkably little evidence that it does, and there are many adverse effects of competitive behaviour that may harm overall performance rather helping to improve it (Light 1998). External approaches to improvement are often 'one size fits all' interventions, which may appear rational at the macro level across a health system but which look arbitrary and inappropriate at the micro level when applied to individual healthcare organizations. For example, if a particular nursing home is failing because of poor leadership and inadequate investment, then subjecting it to greater external pressures through increased competition may simply drive it into insolvency rather than stimulating improvement, thus leaving its residents homeless. One weakness of external approaches to improvement is that they treat all healthcare organizations as if they were the same – with similar expectations, motivations and capabilities. They are often based on naive and simplistic paradigms of organizational and individual behaviour that simply don't work in the complex and messy real world.

The conflict (or complementarity) between external and internal approaches to improvement is perhaps well demonstrated by a common but paradoxical finding. Research suggests that internal approaches to improvement usually work better than external approaches, in the sense that they are more capable of bringing about the complex changes in processes and in clinical practice that are needed for improvement to occur (Merry 1991). However, this research also shows that some organizations are much better than others at using these internal approaches to improvement. In general, well managed and led, stable healthcare organizations are more likely to develop successful internal quality and performance improvement activities than organizations with weak management and poor clinical leadership that are undergoing substantial organizational change (Walshe 1995). This is a paradox because the most significant opportunities for performance improvement probably exist in the latter group of organizations, but they are least able to realize them and make performance improvements. If only internal approaches to improvement are used, those lagging organizations are likely to fall further and further behind. So external approaches to performance improvement are undoubtedly needed, probably alongside internal approaches. Perhaps what might work best is a planned combination of internal and external approaches designed to complement each other.

Regulation is an external approach to performance improvement but with the crucial difference that it can and often does reach inside organizations, and it uses interventions that incorporate elements from some of the internal approaches listed above. For example, a regulator might use external inspection to assess an organization's performance, and could impose incentives and sanctions based on what is found, both of which clearly place it in the external improvement paradigm. However, the focus of its inspection might be the systems for improvement in the organization, and it might tailor its inspection to fit the particular problems or issues of the organization being reviewed, both of which are characteristics of the internal improvement paradigm. It is this capacity of regulation to bridge the divide between internal and external approaches to improvement and, perhaps, to combine the advantages or strengths of both, which makes it an interesting and potentially very powerful tool for performance improvement.

THE RISE OF REGULATION

It is probably helpful to begin by defining what is meant by regulation. The concept is discussed in some detail in Chapter 2, but in brief, the definition which seems both the simplest and most widely used is: 'Regulation is sustained and focused control exercised by a public agency over activities which are valued by a community' (Selznick 1985: 363).

An everyday understanding of regulation would probably encompass the work of such agencies as: the US Food and Drug Administration and its British counterpart, the Food Standards Agency; the UK's Health and Safety Executive and its American cousin, the Occupational Safety and Health Administration; utility regulators who oversee industries like electricity, gas, telephones and water; and transport regulators who oversee airlines, train services and highway safety. It would also probably include regulators who work mainly with public sector or government organizations, like inspectorates for the prison service, fire brigades, social services, schools, universities and so on. In healthcare it would probably include the agencies that inspect or accredit hospitals, nursing homes, health insurers and other healthcare providers. In fact, it is easier to define regulation by enumeration like this, than it is to arrive at a functional definition like Selznick's or to define regulation in terms of its objectives (which are notable by their absence from Selznick's definition).

It is important to set sensible boundaries around the concept of regulation. First, virtually all legislation could be seen as regulation, in the sense that it sets rules which regulate the conduct of people or organizations, but such a wide interpretation makes the concept almost meaningless. Regulation is not legislation, although regulatory agencies are often created by governments and legislatures and they often draw their statutory authority, powers and remit from legislation. One useful distinction is that civil legislation is generally decentralizing, in that it empowers everyone to act on their own behalf. For example, someone who thinks they have been unfairly dismissed can use employment legislation to take their former employer to court. In contrast, regulation is generally centralizing, in that we empower the regulatory agency to act on society's behalf in overseeing some activity. For example, environmental legislation commonly empowers agencies like the Environment Agency in the UK or the Environmental Protection Agency in the USA to act for all of us to do things like prevent pollution, rather than giving us each as individuals the right to sue the polluter.

Secondly, all performance management and oversight could be construed as regulation; then, things like central government directives to local authorities or health authorities, or oversight of the performance of NHS trusts by health authorities, could be labelled regulation. Again, such broad definitions are probably unhelpful. What distinguishes regulation from many and varied mechanisms for performance management is that generally the regulator is a 'third party' to any transaction or inter-organizational relationship. In a market setting, the regulator is a third party to the transaction between buyer and seller, intervening to constrain or frame the transaction and to protect the interests of the buyer or, less commonly, the seller. For example, food labelling and food preparation regulations are there to help the public know what they are buying and to assure them that it is fresh and hygienically produced. The same is true in the regulation of government or public sector organizations. For example, British schools are performance managed by their local education authority, but the Office for Standards in Education is a third party to that performance management relationship, overseeing both the performance of the school and the performance of the local education authority.

Thirdly, it is worth noting that Selznick's definition speaks of a public agency, but not necessarily of government. Much regulation is undertaken by non-governmental organizations of various kinds, often within a framework or with some authority endowed by government or legislation. For example, the Joint Commission on the Accreditation of Healthcare Organizations (JCAHO), which is the dominant force in healthcare accreditation in the USA, is a private sector entity, governed by a board drawn largely from industry stakeholders like professional groups and hospital associations. However, its accreditation decisions are used to decide whether providers can participate in government healthcare programmes like Medicare and Medicaid, which gives them considerable weight and JCAHO substantial authority. But while regulation is not necessarily undertaken by government directly, it is usually undertaken with governmental support or authority, and regulators generally have a mission to protect, promote or support the public interest, however that might be defined or realized.

However it is defined, regulation is a ubiquitous part of modern society. It is difficult to identify many transactions or activities outside the setting of the family or the home that are not, in some way, regulated. Take a train, buy a sandwich, read a newspaper, watch TV, drive a car, go to school, rent a house, take a job, get a haircut, see a doctor, consult a lawyer – in every one of these interactions, the organizations and sometimes the individuals who provide the service are regulated. It was not always so. The earliest examples of regulation relate to trade and date back at least to the 1800s, with the creation of government offices to oversee weights and measures and to prevent foodstuffs and other goods being adulterated (Ogus 1994). In the late nineteenth and early twentieth century, both the UK and the USA developed regulatory agencies to oversee factories, public health, food producers, transportation systems, construction, fire safety, manufacturing standards and other areas of commerce. But regulation really grew most in both countries after the Second World War, particularly in the 1960s and 1970s. In the USA, this was the golden age of government, when many major social programmes (like social security and healthcare provision) were created and regulation was developed or extended in many realms – occupational health and safety, environmental protection, civil rights and anti-discrimination, consumer rights and protection, urban planning and development, health and social care, and so on. In the UK, a rather more gradual but similar progression occurred (Rhodes 1981; Eisner 1994; Ogus 1994).

In the late 1970s and 1980s, both the UK and the USA saw a powerful political backlash against regulation. Regulation was simultaneously and rather contradictorily portrayed as ineffective and susceptible to capture and corruption by some observers (Wilson 1980) and as overbearing, bureaucratic, anti-competitive and stifling of innovation by others (Higgs 1995). In the USA, Ronald Reagan came to power in 1980 and immediately cancelled or suspended scores of regulations, and then set about creating, in the Office of Management and Budget and his own executive office, systems for regulatory review and clearance that were designed to discourage new regulation and to force a more rigorous assessment of the costs and benefits of regulations before they were promulgated (Eisner 1994). In the UK, Margaret Thatcher's Conservative administration in 1979 shared the Reaganite ideological commitment to deregulation and similarly tried to limit new regulation and or simply remove existing regulation (Baldwin and Cave 1999).

In fact, there was more rhetoric than reality in the anti-regulatory politics of the 1980s. Despite the often strong language of deregulation that spoke of removing whole layers of regulation and freeing up organizations to compete and innovate, the reality is that little regulation was removed and, after a short hiatus, new regulatory pressures began to grow (Ayres and Braithwaite 1992). In the USA, there was in fact a tightening and extension of regulation in many areas as diverse as financial services, occupational health and safety, and nursing homes. In the UK, the growing integration of Britain into the European Union brought a raft of new regulatory agencies and regulations that more than made up for any retrenchment elsewhere, but there was also increasing regulation of financial institutions and a huge growth of regulation resulting from the privatization of utilities like gas, water, telephone and electricity companies. These had all effectively been nationalized industries, but as they were turned into conventional, for-profit shareholder-owned entities, the Conservative government created a host of new regulators to oversee their performance, regulate prices and ensure they did not abuse their monopoly or near-monopoly market power (Moran and Prosser 1994; Baldwin and Cave 1999).

In addition, the UK saw a substantial growth in the regulation of public sector or government organizations during the 1980s and

1990s. The Conservative administration created the Audit Commission in 1982 and the National Audit Office in 1983, tasked respectively with overseeing the economy, efficiency and effectiveness of local and central government. Inspectorates were created or enlarged for schools, universities, social services, prisons and other public services (Hood *et al.* 1998). It has been estimated that by the mid-1990s there were 135 different regulators overseeing the performance of the public sector in the UK, spending between them about £770 million a year or 0.3 per cent of total relevant government expenditure. This was double or even quadruple the level of public sector regulation that had existed in 1975 (Hood *et al.* 1999). In both the UK and the USA, conservative administrations have, despite their anti-regulatory rhetoric, been just as prone to regulate as more liberal governments, and the growth of regulation has proceeded more or less unabated for half a century or more. The reasons for this growth are explored in Chapter 2.

In US healthcare, regulation has been endemic for many years (O'Donoghue 1974; Gordon 1980; Greenberg 1991), but the 1990s saw continuing regulatory growth in many areas. The regulation of managed care entities was perhaps the most dramatic example of increasing regulation, as both state and federal legislatures responded to widespread public disquiet about the impact of managed care on the quality of and access to healthcare (Altman *et al.* 1999). Existing regulatory agencies were given greater powers of oversight and, in many states, new managed care regulators were created. But regulation grew in other healthcare sectors too, with the implementation of new federal regulatory requirements for nursing homes (Walshe 2001a), and the continuing extension of both government and non-government regulation of hospitals (Leyerle 1994; Weiner 2000).

In the UK, healthcare organizations within the National Health Service escaped much regulatory attention until the 1980s. As government organizations, they were simply accountable through a straightforward bureaucratic hierarchy to central government and the Secretary of State for Health. At the same time, regulatory oversight over non-governmental healthcare organizations, like private hospitals and nursing homes, was relatively limited (Health Select Committee 1999). There were some government regulators (e.g. the Audit Commission, the Health Advisory Service, the Mental Health Act Commission and the Health Services Commissioner) and non-governmental regulators (e.g. the Royal Colleges overseeing medical education, the King's Fund healthcare accreditation programme and the NEQAS external quality assurance scheme for pathology laboratories), but overall the scope and reach of regulation was quite modest, especially in comparison with the USA (Klein 1987; Day and Klein 1990).

However, since 1997, there has been a rapid and continuing growth in healthcare regulation in the UK, especially in England. The incoming Labour government moved away from a reliance on markets, contracting and competition to drive performance improvement in the National Health Service, but was reluctant to put its faith in traditional bureaucratic direction through the line of control from the Department of Health down to NHS trusts. Instead, it has increasingly turned to regulation, creating new national regulatory agencies like the National Institute for Clinical Excellence, the Commission for Health Improvement, the National Patient Safety Agency and the National Clinical Assessment Authority. It has also launched a complete reform of professional self-regulation for doctors, nurses and other clinical professionals, and instituted a powerful new national regulator for private health-care, the National Care Standards Commission (Walshe 2002).

Indeed, there is an international trend towards the greater use of regulation in healthcare. In Europe, many countries have introduced programmes of external review, inspection or accreditation in the last decade (Klazinga 2000), and the process of economic and social convergence among European Union states has seen an increasing use of regulation at both a national and a European level (European Commission 2001). Both in Europe and elsewhere, healthcare accreditation has grown rapidly in recent years – programmes now exist in over forty countries, with new national initiatives in France, Switzerland, Spain, Israel, Taiwan, Brazil, Hungary, South Africa and several other countries (International Society for Quality in Health Care 1997). Although this book focuses its empirical exploration of healthcare regulation in two countries – the USA and the UK – it should be remembered that much of what is found might equally be noted in studies of other European and Anglophone countries at least, and that many of the lessons to be learned from the US and UK experience have at least some international resonance in other countries.

The continued growth of healthcare regulation on both sides of the Atlantic has engendered an ongoing debate about the costs and benefits of regulation and its impact on the performance of healthcare organizations, which stretches back more than two decades (Gordon 1980; Brennan and Berwick 1996). At times, that debate has seemed distinctly polarized and politicized, and rather evidence-free. On the one hand, some stakeholders argue that regulation has been an important force for improvement, driving change and raising standards over many years (Schyve and O'Leary 1998; AHQA 2000; NCQA 2000). Others, on the other hand, argue that regulation has imposed a substantial and unwarranted burden on healthcare organizations, pushed up costs, inhibited competition, stifled innovation and done little or nothing for the cause of improvement (Goodman 1980; Leyerle 1994; Brennan and Berwick 1996; AHA 2001). A third viewpoint, often espoused by user or consumer groups, is that regulation has been too timid and ineffectual and is largely captured and neutralized by the healthcare industry, and what is needed is more regulation with more aggressive regulatory strategies and greater efforts at enforcement (Dame and Wolfe 1996; Latimer 1997).

In part, the debate has often been polemic, polarized and politicized because, in the absence of good empirical evidence, it is easy for dogma and opinion to hold sway. A more evidence-based, thoughtful and balanced dialogue might be more productive, in which stakeholders in regulation – including healthcare providers, funders, professional groups, regulators, policy-makers, patients and the public – looked for some common ground, based on sound evidence on what works in regulation. There is a growing research literature on healthcare regulation, an extensive literature on regulation in a wide range of other settings, and an established body of literature on general regulatory theory, concepts and models (see the Further Reading section at the end of the book for more details). This book is intended to bring that evidence to bear in asking what constitutes effective regulation and how can the contribution of regulation to performance improvement in healthcare organizations be maximized?

ABOUT THIS BOOK

This book explores how healthcare organizations are regulated and what impact regulation has upon their performance. It does so by bringing together experiences of regulation and research into regulation in healthcare in two countries – the USA and the UK – with a much wider body of literature, research and experience on regulation drawn from other settings. Although there are many obvious similarities between regulation in different countries, industries or settings, there is often little interchange of ideas or experiences. Regulators tend to be highly focused on their own sector or specific remit – healthcare, social care, finance, manufacturing, health and safety or whatever – and to pay little attention to how other regulators work. The 'regulatory community' is fractured and poorly organized and, as a result, intersectoral learning and the transfer of ideas and experience is rather limited (Hood *et al.* 1999).

The practical examples of healthcare regulation described in this book are drawn from two countries – the UK and the USA – which, although they share a largely common language, have little else in common, in healthcare terms at least (Walshe 2001b). The UK National Health Service is a universal, tax-funded and government-run healthcare system that is one of the cheapest to run in the developed world. Although the NHS is sometimes praised for its parsimony and its excellence in some areas such as primary care, it suffers chronic problems of underprovision and offers patients little choice or control. The mismatch of public demand for healthcare and cash-limited supply results in service rationing through a variety of mechanisms, most obviously long waiting lists for elective surgery. In contrast, the USA has a market-led healthcare system in which government, insurers, employers and patients all play some part in funding healthcare and in which healthcare is provided through a bewildering profusion of different types of private and public entities. The US healthcare system is the most expensive to run in the developed world, spending three times as much per citizen as in the UK (Anderson and Hussey 2000). It has an enviable reputation for high quality and technological sophistication, but leaves about 17 per cent of the population, or around 43 million people, with little or no access to healthcare because they do not have health insurance coverage (Davis 2001). It is hugely complicated for patients to navigate, highly bureaucratic and extremely inefficient (Reinhardt 1992).

These very different healthcare systems use regulation in very different ways, but for broadly similar purposes – to improve performance and to make healthcare organizations and professionals accountable for their performance. This book aims to use their experience of regulation and research in both countries to inform the discussion of its central theme – how regulation impacts on organizational performance and what can be done to maximize its effectiveness. To do that, it is structured into four main chapters, bracketed by this introduction and a concluding chapter that attempts to draw together some lessons for the future of regulation.

Chapter 2 sets the wider context for the book by outlining some *key concepts and theories in regulation*. It defines regulation, discusses its causes and describes a framework for analysing systems of regulation that can be used to undertake a structured comparison of different approaches to regulation. It also introduces the ideas of responsive regulation, which appear to offer some attractive solutions to common regulatory problems.

Chapter 3 then describes *how healthcare is regulated in the USA*. It gives a brief overview of the US healthcare system by way of context and outlines the history and development of healthcare regulation. In what is a highly diverse and complex healthcare system, it uses the regulation of three main types of healthcare organization – hospitals, health plans and nursing homes – to describe how US healthcare regulation works. It concludes by reflecting on what regulation has achieved and what the main problems seem to be.

Chapter 4 provides a broadly parallel account of how *healthcare is regulated in the UK*. It sets the context by describing the UK National Health Service and outlining the history and development of regulation. Then, because healthcare regulation in the NHS has changed rapidly in the last few years, it describes first the work of some established regulatory bodies and then looks at the new systems of regulation that have been created in recent times. It offers a separate analysis of the regulation of private healthcare and nursing homes, and concludes by reflecting on the lessons from British healthcare regulation.

Chapter 5 returns to the evaluative framework introduced in Chapter 2, and uses it to *analyse, compare and contrast regulatory practice in healthcare* in the USA and the UK. Each dimension of the framework is discussed in turn, and there is a particular focus on the issues of: direction – how regulators set standards; detection – how regulators measure or monitor performance; and enforcement – how regulators get change to happen.

Chapter 6 tries to draw together *some conclusions* from the book as a whole and uses them to outline lessons for the future of regulation. It discusses the value of intersectoral comparisons and opportunities for learning across the wider regulatory community, develops an analysis of the causes of regulatory failure, and returns to the question around which this book is centred by exploring the traits of effective regulation and outlining some principles that may be useful in improving regulatory effectiveness. It closes by discussing the future of regulation and regulatory reform in healthcare.

Finally, it is worth both noting and explaining why this book does not tackle the business of professional regulation – the regulation of individual healthcare professionals such as doctors, nurses, therapists, pharmacists and so on. Although many of the regulatory issues and approaches discussed in this book are found both in the regulation of healthcare organizations and the regulation of healthcare professionals, and there is much to be learned by comparing regulatory activity in these two areas, there are also many differences. More practically, professional regulation is a huge area and it would not be possible to do justice to it in this book while still covering the field of organizational regulation properly. Professional regulation has been tackled by some other authors in both the USA and the UK (Stacey 1992; Moran and Wood 1993; Jost 1997; Moran 1999).

2

REGULATION: CONCEPTS AND THEORIES

This chapter examines some key concepts and theories in regulation, which provide the foundation for the analyses of healthcare regulation in the USA and England that follow it. Regulatory theory may not, on the face of it, appear to be a particularly exciting subject, but it offers important insights that can help us to understand how healthcare regulation works – or does not work. The chapter begins by exploring the definition of regulation and attempting to bound the concept. It then examines the causes of regulation, looking to economic, social, political and organizational explanations for the development of regulation. Next, the chapter sets out a framework for analysing and comparing regulatory regimes and processes, which helps to highlight similarities and differences and which is used in the rest of the book. The chapter then examines two key areas of regulatory theory – the use of a regulatory model or paradigm on a spectrum from deterrence to compliance, and the relatively recently developed ideas of responsive or smart regulation. The chapter does not attempt to provide a comprehensive account of regulatory theory, a task that others have addressed very successfully (Baldwin and Cave 1999).

DEFINING REGULATION

Some seminal writers on regulation have been remarkably reluctant to subscribe to a definition of regulation (Breyer 1982), regarding the issue as both controversial and something of a distraction from the substantive issues involved in studying regulation. But without a clear definition, arguments about the meaning of the concept and its boundaries are inevitable. For example, Hood *et al.* (1999: 8) adopted a broad interpretation of regulation in government in their study of the UK public sector, based on three characteristics – that one public organization tried to shape the activities of another, with some official mandate, and with a degree of separation from the organization concerned. Others have suggested that such a broad definition encompasses many activities that are really just bureaucratic performance management, and so overstates both the importance of regulation and its growth (Midwinter and McGarvey 2001). Defining regulation is important, because it helps to frame the concept and acts as a starting point for subsequent study and analysis.

Selznick's (1985) brief and neatly worded definition of regulation as 'sustained and focused control exercised by a public agency over activities which are valued by a community' (p. 363) has been widely cited by others and fits the needs of this book. It contains, explicitly or implicitly, the four key characteristics that are central to the nature and purpose of regulation:

- *Formal remit or acknowledged authority.* In any system of regulation, the regulator has to have some kind of formal remit to regulate that is acknowledged by other stakeholders, most obviously the organizations being regulated. That may be based on an explicit legal statute, or it may rely on other non-legal but equally powerful mechanisms, such as market position and influence or professional group leverage.
- *Centralization of oversight.* Regulation represents a centralization of responsibility, power and oversight in the regulator, and a transfer of those things from other stakeholders in the business being regulated. The regulator is regulating on behalf of others, such as corporate purchasers, funders, consumer groups, individual consumers and wider society, who cede some powers to the regulator in exchange for an undertaking, implicit or explicit, that the regulator will act in their interests. Sometimes, because of the nature of the activities being regulated, that centralization of responsibility is necessary because it would not be feasible or practical for the individual stakeholders to act on their own account.
- *Third-party accountability.* As a result of the centralization referred to above, the regulator is always a third party to market transactions or inter-organizational relationships. In a market setting, the regulator is a third party to market transactions,

providing a framework within which they take place and acting to constrain the actions of buyers and sellers. In non-market settings, the regulator is still a third party to the inter-organizational relationships and accountability arrangements. There will always be some kind of reporting, performance management or accountability chain through which an organization is overseen, but the regulator sits outside that chain of command or bureaucratic hierarchy.

- *Action in the public interest.* Perhaps the most difficult – or contestable – core characteristic of regulation is that it is undertaken in the public interest. In other words, the process of regulation is intended to serve some wider societal goals, often established or expressed by government. This does not mean that regulation is necessarily an activity of government – far from it, as much regulation is undertaken by quasi-governmental or non-governmental agencies of one kind or another – but that the objectives of regulatory agencies are expressed in terms of the public interest. Of course, some regulatory theorists would question whether regulation is really undertaken for those reasons, and the public and private interests involved in regulation are discussed further below.

Regulation is also, in academic terms, a contested domain. It has been studied and written about by economists, lawyers, organizational behaviour specialists, sociologists, political scientists and so on, and each group brings the disciplinary baggage and preconceptions of its own field to the subject. So, for example, economists' analyses of regulation have often seen it largely or wholly as an economic instrument, used to tackle economic problems such as failures in competitive markets. They have been less interested in the social component of regulation, even though it is arguably a bigger part of regulatory activity. In contrast, lawyers have often focused on the rule-making processes of regulation and its connection with ideas from administrative law, while political and social scientists have been more concerned with the origins and motivations of the various stakeholders in regulation, its impact on their power and status, and its relationship with wider society. Perhaps the most convincing accounts of the causes and consequences of regulation are those that span some of these disciplinary divides and bring together perspectives from law, economics, political science and organizational theory (Noll 1985).

Many definitions of regulation make reference to two distinct types of regulation – economic regulation and social regulation

(Ogus 1994; Baldwin and Cave 1999). In broad terms, economic regulation aims to control or influence the demand, supply or price of goods or services by regulated organizations. For example, price-setting controls on suppliers of electricity and gas, advertising restrictions on pharmaceutical suppliers and licensing restrictions on the establishment of bus and coach routes are all forms of economic regulation. Social regulation is rather harder to define and is broader in nature. It aims to control or influence the behaviour of regulated organizations in ways that may be only indirectly related to issues of supply, demand and price. Examples of social regulation include licensing and certification requirements for childcare facilities and nursing homes, environmental controls and oversight of pollution, and the regulation of health and safety in the workplace.

THE CAUSES OF REGULATION

It has already been observed that regulation is ubiquitous in modern society, but there are still some areas of business that are much more regulated than others. It has been claimed, with some justification, that healthcare organizations are among the most heavily regulated entities, at least in the USA (Greenberg 1991). The development of regulation, or its causes, can be explained in four main ways – in economic, social, political and organizational terms. Each is discussed in turn below.

Economic causes of regulation

Perhaps the most straightforward rationale for regulation is that most commonly advanced by economists – market failure. In essence, the argument is that markets are the most efficient way to maximize the utility of any goods or services and that they provide the most effective spur to improvement for organizations, through competition. However, in some conditions, the market either works less well or begins to fail (Breyer 1982; Ogus 1994). A list of the commonly cited types of market failure and their effects is set out in Table 2.1, alongside the likely form of regulatory response (Breyer 1982; Baldwin and Cave 1999).

It is immediately evident that many of the conditions of market failure are to be found in abundance in healthcare (Brown 1980). There are often monopolistic suppliers (e.g. large hospital networks or medical groups) and monopsonistic purchasers (e.g. big health plans and health insurers). Both try to use their market power to gain competitive advantage. There are huge information asymmetries in healthcare that generally favour the provider or producer of healthcare, result in a great amount of provider or supplier control over levels of demand, and can mean it is very difficult for healthcare funders, purchasers and users to make sensible, fully informed purchasing decisions. Externalities are commonplace, especially at the interface between healthcare, social care and employment, and can mean that healthcare organizations optimize their own efficiency at the expense of wider society. There are many examples of service scarcity, and coordination or continuity problems, in areas like the provision of healthcare to rural and poor communities, the control of capital developments and the purchase of high-cost technological equipment. Finally, healthcare is often claimed to be a public rather than a private good (that is, something whose availability or provision benefits us all, not just the person or people who use it) and the problem of third-party moral hazard – services being consumed by patients but paid for by insurers or government – is almost universal. In short, even in the most market-oriented healthcare systems like the USA, healthcare markets fit most of the conventional economic criteria for market failure. This may provide quite a credible explanation for the intensity of healthcare regulation in the relatively market-oriented US healthcare system.

Another way to illustrate the difficulties of applying a market-based paradigm in healthcare is to map out the relationships and interactions between different health system stakeholders, as shown in Figure 2.1. Economists' models of markets are founded on a rather straightforward model of transactions between buyers and sellers or providers and consumers, like that shown on the left. But it is difficult to fit health systems into that model. They look more like the model shown on the right, with multiple, interacting and interdependent stakeholders: funders who meet the costs of healthcare, like governments and employers; purchasers like health insurers or health plans; healthcare providers in many shapes and sizes, including both organizations and professionals in groups and as individuals; and, of course, consumers of health services and the wider public.

When markets fail, the regulatory response is usually an economic one, often aimed at promoting or sustaining competition. However, most healthcare regulation is social rather than economic in nature, although there are many examples of economic regulation in

Table 2.1 The main types of market failure, their effects and likely regulatory responses

Type of market failure	Healthcare example	Effects	Regulatory response
Monopoly or monopsony – there are very few sellers or buyers in the market	In some places there are only a few health insurers, plans or hospital groups	Sellers or buyers can manipulate supply and price to make excess profits	Control prices or impose other controls to limit excessive profit-making and promote competition
Information inadequacy or asymmetry – information about goods or services is not available, or is only available to some parties	Patients and healthcare funders often have little information about the clinical quality of service providers and are poorly equipped to judge appropriateness or quality	Buyers can be misled about the quality of goods/services and their needs, and so can make poor purchasing decisions	Make information more widely available and provide it in ways that promote its use by buyers
Externalities – the full costs of services or goods do not fall on the buyer/seller	Poor-quality healthcare or unmet healthcare need result in wider social costs such as benefit payments, lost production, etc.	Buyers and sellers behave perversely because of incentives resulting from cost/price structure	Make the buyer/seller pay the full costs or impose controls to prevent perverse behaviours

Service scarcity, coordination and continuity – supply is limited or constrained by non-market factors	Providing health services to poor or dispersed communities, planning major healthcare capital developments, and making best use of the available healthcare workforce	The supply of essential goods and services may be erratic or incomplete, or there can be considerable duplication and resulting wasted resources and low utilization	Impose controls on service provision and development, aimed at ensuring supply and planning development rationally
Public good and moral hazard – where goods or services are paid for by one group but used by another	Health insurers meet the costs of healthcare but the benefits fall to consumers. There are, therefore, few incentives for consumers to limit their use of health services	No incentives for users/consumers to limit consumption; funders respond by rationing and restricting access, or by imposing co-payments on users	Manage demand/need for services to avoid both excessive usage and improper rationing or restrictions. Impose usage restrictions through access/referral guidelines or thresholds, or waiting lists

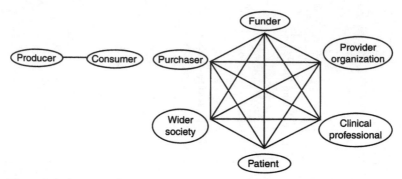

Figure 2.1 A comparison of simple market relationships and health system relationships.

healthcare, like price-setting schemes for pharmaceuticals, certificate of need controls on the building of new hospital facilities, and reimbursement rate-setting arrangements for physician fees and other payments. The fact that most healthcare regulation is social rather than economic in nature suggests that the causes of healthcare regulation are not primarily economic, and other explanations for regulation need to be sought.

Social causes of regulation

Many people do not see healthcare as simply another commodity, to be traded in a market like any other. Some argue that healthcare is a public good, the availability of which benefits all of society not just the individuals who may receive it. Others assert that people have a right to healthcare when they need it, regardless of their individual ability to pay for it at the time. These are statements of moral or social values, and regulation can be seen as a mechanism for implementing the societal objectives or policy goals that arise from values like these. Some of the social goals in healthcare that might precipitate a regulatory response are listed in Table 2.2, alongside some examples of potential regulatory interventions aimed at promoting those social goals.

It is evident from this analysis that much of the regulation of healthcare that we see around us can be cast as an instrument of social policy (rather than economic policy), aimed at supporting or pursuing social goals, not promoting competition.

Table 2.2 The use of regulation to realize social goals

Social values	Linked societal objectives or policy goals	Potential uses of regulation
Equity and fairness	Everyone should have access to healthcare according to clinical need rather than ability to pay	Regulator prevents healthcare organizations from refusing access or coverage to individuals or groups such as those with low incomes or high health needs
Diversity	Healthcare services should cater appropriately for different ethnic groups, geographic areas or cultures and not discriminate	Regulator requires healthcare organizations to provide services tailored to groups' needs, or in particular geographic locations
Social solidarity	The costs of healthcare should be spread across all members of society and not fall unduly on a few	Regulator makes coverage compulsory, and prohibits or prevents risk stratification or differentiation by healthcare organizations
Accountability	Powerful corporate and professional interests should be held to account for their actions	Regulation is used to make organizations and professions accountable and regulator is given powers to address performance problems
Freedom of information	People should have a right to access healthcare information about themselves and information about health services	Regulator may require healthcare organizations to provide access to personal information and to publish data on services and performance
Paternalism	People may not make sensible, informed decisions about healthcare matters	Regulator monitors and manages performance and quality to ensure acceptable standards on behalf of users/ consumers
Privacy	People should have a right to keep their own healthcare information private and to control how it is used by healthcare organizations	Regulator requires healthcare organizations to meet privacy or data protection standards, and prohibits data transfer/ sharing

Political causes of regulation

Political scientists often explain the growth of regulation in political rather than economic or social terms. For example, some would argue that, over recent decades, the nature of political accountability has changed. In the past, straightforward notions of elective political accountability saw governments as ultimately accountable to the electorate, and government services and departments accountable to the public in the same way. But the increasing scale and complexity of government makes this kind of accountability less and less meaningful, as the connection between service performance and elected representatives becomes more and more distant (Day and Klein 1987; Power 1997). Although local councils may, to some extent, still be held to account in this way for their management of services like education, social care, transport and the like, central government cannot really be argued to be accountable in this way except at the most macro level. Similarly, corporations were once seen as straightforwardly accountable to their shareholders, but the sheer size of many corporations, and the extent to which their ownership is vested in major institutional shareholders like banks and pension funds, means that they are rarely held to account by shareholders directly. Company boards enjoy remarkable latitude and are only really taken to task by their shareholders if something goes seriously wrong. In both cases, regulation provides another, parallel or supplemental mechanism for accountability. It might be argued that in both the private and public sector, we have moved from a simple, democratic model of accountability (whether it is electors or shareholders who are voting) to a stakeholder model of accountability, in which regulation is used to make public and private sector organizations accountable to a wide range of stakeholders, including consumers and users, trading partners and competitors, staff groups and professional bodies, funders and payers, and so on (Ham 1999; Klein 2001b).

Another political explanation for increased regulation relates to the diminishing place in many countries for direct state control. In the UK and Europe, the last two decades have seen a substantial reduction in state or government ownership in many areas, and its replacement by private ownership and provision. For example, utilities like gas, water, electricity, telephones, buses, trains and many others have been privatized, with commercial, shareholder-owned companies taking over the assets and running these businesses for profit (Moran and Prosser 1994). In areas more traditionally seen as the province of the public sector, such as housing and education, a similar though less dramatic transfer from government to the private or independent sector has taken place. The rise of what has been called the 'new public management' (Ferlie *et al.* 1996), bringing private sector approaches to management into the public sector, has resulted in many public sector organizations being managed more proactively and given more local freedom and autonomy with reduced central or local government involvement and control. And in healthcare, while the role and contribution of the private, for-profit sector has often been politically controversial, the reality is that, in the UK and many other countries, a mixed model of private and public provision exists and there has been some significant growth in the extent of private sector healthcare provision (Scott 2001).

It could be argued that increasing regulation has been one of the results of this trend away from public ownership. Majone (1994) coined the term the 'regulatory state' to describe the replacement of direct state control through ownership by indirect control through the regulation of entities such as commercial companies, mutually owned organizations, charities and so on. For politicians, regulation may be a convenient mechanism for distancing themselves from some of the unpleasant and controversial issues involved in direct ownership or control, while actually sustaining or even increasing their scope to influence the behaviour of regulated organizations.

For much of the last two decades, there has been overt political hostility towards increasing regulation in both the USA and the UK. In the 1980s, regulation was seen as ineffective, susceptible to corruption and capture, anti-competitive and bureaucratic. Governments in the USA and the UK set about deregulation with considerable ideological enthusiasm. In practice, although the growth of regulation may have been put on hold for a while, regulation did grow even under these governments, which had appeared so committed to dismantling current regulation. It could be argued that the political value and advantages of regulation outweighed the ideological arguments ranged against it, and that the failure even of governments opposed to regulation to halt its steady expansion suggests that regulation is politically attractive and, perhaps, even necessary.

A third approach to the political analysis of regulation relates particularly to the assertion, made earlier in discussing the definition of regulation, that it is in the 'public interest'. This assumes that a common societal view of the public interest can be established (which may be difficult, as different interest groups may assert conflicting versions of what they see as the public interest) and that regulators will act in a disinterested, objective and public-spirited manner and have no 'interests' of their own. A range of 'interest group' theories have emerged to challenge this rather idealistic view of the public interest. They argue that regulation is often the product of negotiations or struggles for power between powerful interest groups, such as corporate groups, professions, political parties and consumer groups (Francis 1993). They also assert that regulators have a distinct self-interest in the business of regulation, just like regulated organizations, and that the result is often what has been termed 'regulatory capture', in which regulated organizations and regulators collaborate to serve each others' interests rather than any public interest and the interests of consumers or users are set aside (Baldwin and Cave 1999). Some theorists have argued that regulation has a momentum, a logic and a life cycle of its own (Bardach and Kagan 1982) in which regulatory systems or structures are first established in response to public and political concern, often sparked by particular events or failures; that they grow and develop in part because it is in the self-interest both of regulators and those who create them to find things for them to regulate; and that they are gradually captured by provider or producer groups as political interest in their work diminishes (Bernstein 1955).

Organizational causes of regulation

There are several explanations of regulation which are rooted in an understanding of organizations and organizational theory, and which may be particularly useful in explaining how organizations respond to being regulated. In fact, it can be misleading to talk of how an organization responds to regulation, because regulation may be welcomed by some parts of an organization while being met with disinterest or even hostility by others. For example, the health and safety department in a factory may welcome health and safety inspections because they provide a way to get their objectives achieved, while operational managers may be more antipathetic towards health and safety inspections because they get in the way of achieving production targets. In more general terms, external regulation may change power balances and relationships within organizations.

One organizational cause of regulation may be the strength or weakness of internal hierarchies or managerial arrangements. In general terms, it can be argued that organizations with strong internal structures may have less need of regulation than those with weak internal structures. In organizations that have relatively weak or loose managerial hierarchies, external regulation may confer legitimacy on the actions of some actors within the organization and be used to pursue corporate objectives that could otherwise meet with resistance. Healthcare organizations can be seen as having relatively weak internal hierarchies and structures – they have strong professional groups and a culture that resists managerialism and corporacy, tending instead to emphasize individualism and professionalism. Regulation may be a mechanism for giving those who lead or manage such 'weak' organizations greater internal power within those organizations.

A second organizational cause of regulation may be to do with the size of the organizations being regulated. Very large organizations with complex, multilayered bureaucracies may be difficult to run effectively and efficiently through a conventional hierarchical structure. The UK National Health Service is a good example: if it is seen as a single organization, it is a huge undertaking, spending over £50 billion a year and with over a million staff. The managerial challenges of directing such a massive and complex enterprise are considerable, and it can be argued that the Department of Health is not equipped either organizationally or politically to do it. Regulation may provide an alternative or supplementary mechanism for performance management, in which the very large organization is treated as a network, chain or set of smaller organizations. From this perspective, the NHS would be seen not as one organization but as a network or confederation of about 1000 NHS organizations – trusts, health authorities and so on. Rather than the Department of Health attempting to direct and performance manage the health service through a traditional bureaucratic hierarchy, regulatory bodies or agencies are created that take on much of that task of performance management, working to an overall strategy that is set centrally (Ham 1999; Walshe 2002).

RESEARCHING REGULATION: A FRAMEWORK FOR EVALUATION

It is immediately apparent that there are often large differences in the regulatory arrangements in different sectors and settings. Regulation is highly diverse in terms of the structures and systems put in place, the processes and procedures used, and the impact or outcomes produced. That diversity is both a challenge and an opportunity for researchers. On the one hand, it makes comparing regulatory regimes complex, because they can be different and similar in many separate ways. On the other hand, it provides many opportunities for natural experiments, in which the relationships between different regulatory approaches, structures, systems, processes and interventions can be explored and their impact, outcomes and effectiveness can be studied.

This book uses a framework for evaluating regulation developed by Walshe and Shortell (submitted) that builds on the work of several other authors (Scrivens 1995; Walsh and Walshe 1998; Hood *et al.* 1999). It divides the business of regulation into seven main areas for evaluation, which are listed and defined briefly in Table 2.3.

The intention of the framework is to facilitate comparisons between different approaches to regulation, either by regulators working in the same area (such as healthcare in the UK or in the USA) or by regulators working in quite different sectors and settings. Although its primary purpose is conceptual, it can be used to develop more quantitative measures of regulatory approach or performance. Four of the areas in the framework – regulating organization, regulatory goals/objectives, scope of regulation and regulatory model – are essentially concerned with the environment or context for regulation. The other three areas in the framework – regulatory direction, regulatory detection and regulatory enforcement – are primarily concerned with the process of regulation itself and how it is done. In each area of the framework, there are several distinct issues or elements to any comparison:

- *Regulating organization.* This area is mainly concerned with the constitution, governance and accountability of the regulator. Regulation is often undertaken by a government agency, but it can also be provided by independent, non-governmental organizations. It is helpful to consider what kind of organization takes on the role of regulator. It is important, in particular, to review what formal remit or legal authority it has and from where it derives, and to whom and how is it accountable for its regulatory activities through its governance or reporting arrangements.
- *Regulatory goals or objectives.* Regulation can be used to address a wide range of problems or needs, as discussed above, and different needs are likely to result in quite different forms of regulation. Of course, the goals or objectives of regulation may not be explicitly

Table 2.3 A framework for evaluating regulation

Characteristic	Description
Regulating organization	The constitution, nature, formal remit or mandate, legal powers and authority, governance and reporting or accountability arrangements of the regulating organization
Regulatory goals/objectives	The purpose of regulation and how clearly or explicitly it is stated
Scope of regulation	The forms or types of organization that are subject to regulation (horizontal scope) and the range of functions or activities within those organizations that are regulated (vertical scope)
Regulatory model	The extent to which the regulating organization's philosophy, strategy and methods are oriented towards deterrence or compliance
Direction	The methods used to communicate regulatory requirements or directions to regulated organizations
Detection	The methods used to measure and monitor the performance of regulated organizations to determine whether they comply with regulatory requirements or directions
Enforcement	The methods used to persuade, influence or force regulated organizations to make changes to comply with regulatory requirements or directions

stated, but it is more feasible to determine the extent to which they are achieved if they have been defined at some point. It is therefore helpful to consider what the goals or objective of regulation are, and how clearly or explicitly they are specified. Several common goals or objectives can be identified – most obviously, the improvement of performance, but also the provision of assurance to stakeholders that services meet certain standards, and the establishment of a mechanism for holding organizations or individuals properly to account.

- *Scope of regulation.* Defining the scope of regulation involves determining both what types or forms of organization are subject to regulation and establishing which of their functions or activities are regulated; these two dimensions can be referred to as horizontal and vertical scope. Both can vary – for example, a regulator may have authority over some organizations but not others (such as privately owned hospitals but not publicly owned ones, or nursing homes which receive government funding but not those which do not). Within an organization, the regulatory remit can be confined to a narrow range of functions (e.g. particular clinical service areas, or specific matters like health and safety or risk management) or can be much broader and allow the regulator to undertake a more general review of organizational performance.

- *Regulatory model.* Regulators can be described as either deterrence- or compliance-oriented (Reiss 1984). Deterrence regulators see the organizations they regulate as 'amoral calculators', out to get what they can, and only likely to conform with regulation if they are forced to do so. They tend to have distant, formal and rather adversarial relationships with the organizations they regulate, and to make extensive use of formal sanctions and penalties. In contrast, compliance regulators see the organizations they regulate as fundamentally good and well-intentioned, and likely to comply with regulations if they can. They have closer and more friendly relationships with the organizations they regulate, are often involved in support or educational activities, and only use formal sanctions or penalties as a last resort. In practice, regulators often use a mixture of deterrence and compliance strategies. Each has different advantages and disadvantages, and different circumstances may require different approaches.

- *Direction.* All regulators need to communicate their requirements or expectations to the organizations they regulate, a process called 'direction'. Many regulators use some form of written standards, guidelines or regulations as their primary approach to direction, although some do not. The development and maintenance of valid, reliable and acceptable standards can be a major component of regulatory activity.

- *Detection.* Regulators need mechanisms that allow them to measure and monitor the performance of the organizations they regulate, a process called 'detection'. There are several detection methods that regulators can apply, such as undertaking regular surveys or inspections, responding to complaints or problems with focused investigations, and monitoring performance on a continuing basis through a range of data sources.

- *Enforcement*. This refers to the methods that regulators use to persuade, influence or make the organizations they regulate to change. Some regulators have few formal enforcement methods and make great use of persuasion and informal influence. Others have significant incentives or sanctions available, such as the imposition of financial penalties, placing restrictions on the organization's activities, requiring certain actions to be taken and, ultimately, organizational delicensing or closure. Regulators often use the disclosure or publication of their findings as an enforcement strategy.

This framework is used to structure the analyses of healthcare regulation in Chapters 3 and 4, and each of the components of the framework is discussed in some detail in Chapter 5.

REGULATORY MODELS: DETERRENCE AND COMPLIANCE

Regulation is a socially constructed task – how regulators approach their role and function appears to be highly culturally dependent, and similar regulatory problems result in quite different regulatory solutions in different countries, for example (Kagan and Axelrad 2000; Braithwaite and Drahos 2000). There are many components to that social construction, but what has been called the regulatory model or paradigm – how regulators think about their mission and the organizations they regulate – appears to be especially important in explaining the differences in regulatory approach that are often apparent.

Two models of regulation are often described: deterrence and compliance (Reiss 1984). In many ways, they represent two ends of a spectrum of regulatory behaviour, and most real-world examples of regulation fall somewhere in between. Deterrence regulators see the organizations they regulate as 'amoral calculators' (Kagan 1984) – out to get what they can, and perfectly willing to behave badly if they can get away with it and doing so would benefit them. They believe that regulated organizations are dominated by their own self-interest and have to be watched carefully and forced to behave properly. Deterrence regulators tend to make extensive use of formal standards and inspections, and routinely resort to sanctions or penalties for non-compliance. They usually have poor and antagonistic relationships with the organizations they regulate, who resent them and seek ways to neutralize or avoid the regulatory process.

In contrast, compliance regulators see the organizations they regulate as 'good-hearted compliers' – generally sharing the regulator's objectives and worthy of trust and support. When things go wrong, they see the problem more as a product of unfortunate circumstances and sometimes of incompetence rather than a sign of wilful opposition. Compliance regulators often focus on providing guidance, support and advice to regulated organizations and are slow to use sanctions or penalties, which are seen very much as a last resort. They usually have good and friendly relationships with the organizations they regulate, who regard them as partners.

Some of the other characteristics of deterrence and compliance regulation are set out in Table 2.4. It can be seen that deterrence regulation is more commonly found in sectors where regulators have limited contact with individual regulated organizations because there are many of them, or where there is a strong entrepreneurial, business culture. Compliance regulation is more common in sectors where regulators only have to deal with a small number of organizations and are able to build a longitudinal relationship with each one, or where there is a strong ethical or professional culture.

It is wrong to see either the compliance or deterrence model as inherently better or worse than the other – each has distinct advantages and disadvantages. For example, the deterrence approach is very effective at getting regulated organizations to take regulation seriously and to respond to regulatory directions. It may be a good way to secure speedy change. However, it tends to be costly to implement and sustain, and it can produce a range of perverse behaviours by regulated organizations such as creative compliance (in which they comply with regulatory directions superficially but little really changes) and resistance and subversion (in which they act individually or in concert to try to undermine the regulatory process). More fundamentally, deterrence regulation may be seen as running counter to the wider theoretical understanding of organizations and of how change and improvement happen, and particularly to most of the ideas that underlie theories of quality improvement.

The compliance approach tends to be better at securing the cooperation and support of regulated organizations, and building a longer-term commitment to improvement. It is less costly (although not necessarily cheap) and less prone to the perverse behaviours described above. However, when compliance regulation encounters individual regulated organizations which do not really buy into the aims of regulation, and which are prepared to circumvent or contravene the spirit and even the letter of regulation, it is relatively powerless to cope. Even if relatively few such 'rogue' regulated organizations exist, they can run rings around the regulator, demotivating the majority of well-behaved regulated organizations who then see little advantage in being well-behaved, thus bringing the process of regulation into disrepute. A second problem is that compliance regulation may seem to be (and, indeed, may actually be) a rather cosy and comfortable approach for both the regulator and the regulated organizations – to the disadvantage of the consumers or the general public whom regulation was supposed to protect. Compliance regulation may, in fact, result in a consensual and con-flict-adverse relationship between regulators and regulated organizations which is excessively normative, defining acceptable standards of performance largely in terms of what already happens, and offering little challenge to the existing way of doing things. To others, this may appear to be a form of regulatory capture that works, ultimately, against the public interest, which regulation is meant to serve.

The deterrence–compliance model is, of course, simplistic. Regulated organizations vary widely in their behaviour – few are wholly 'amoral calculators' or 'good-hearted compliers' and they may exhibit either or even both forms of behaviour, depending on the circumstances or context (Kagan 1984). Similarly, regulators are rarely wholly deterrence- or compliance-oriented in their approach, although individual regulators do tend to exhibit a consistent pattern of behaviour over time. It has been observed that even when a regulator has an overtly deterrence-oriented strategic approach, its operational realization is often more compliance-oriented than it might at first appear, because of the 'street level' realities of working life for regulatory staff and those with whom they interact (Lipsky 1983; Hawkins and Thomas 1984). However, it is worth considering the interaction between regulatory model and regulated organization behaviour, particularly when there is a mismatch between them, as Table 2.5 shows.

It can be seen that compliance regulation probably results in both the most effective and most ineffective regulatory regimes. When matched with regulated organizations that are compliance-minded, it clearly has many advantages and may be the most effective approach to adopt, but when organizations are 'amoral calculators', it is likely

Table 2.4 Deterrence and compliance models of regulation

	Deterrence	Compliance
Settings in which the model is most often found	Where regulator deals with a large number of small organizations, heterogeneous in nature, and with a strong business culture (private sector, competitive, profit-maximizing, risk-taking, etc.)	Where regulator deals with a small number of large organizations, homogeneous in nature, and with a strong ethical culture (public sector, professionalism, voluntarism, not-for-profit organizations, etc.)
Regulator's view of regulated organizations	Amoral calculators, out to get all they can, untrustworthy	Mostly good and well-intentioned, if not always competent
Regulated organizations' view of the regulatory agency	Policeman, enforcer – feared and often respected, usually disliked	Consultant, supporter – not seen as a threat or problem, may be respected and liked
Temporal perspective	Retrospective (identify, investigate and deal with problems when they have happened)	Prospective (aim to prevent problems occurring through early intervention and support)
Use of regulatory standards and inspection	Many, detailed and explicit written standards, often with statutory force; highly standards-focused approach to inspection and enforcement	May have detailed written standards and policies often accompanied by guidance on implementation; standards play a less prominent role in interactions with regulated organizations
Enforcement and use of sanctions or penalties	Part of routine practice, valued for deterring both those penalized and other regulated organizations	Seen as the last resort, used only when persuasion has been exhausted

Provision of advice and support to regulated organizations	Not part of the regulator's role – seen as risking regulatory capture and conflict of interest with policing and punishing role	Essential part of regulator's role – valued as an opportunity to understand, build cooperative relationships and influence performance
Relationship between regulator and regulated organizations	Distant, formal and adversarial	Close, friendly and cooperative
Costs of regulation	High cost to both regulator and regulated organizations, in inspection and enforcement	Lower costs, particularly in inspection and enforcement, although costs to regulator of providing advice and support to regulated organizations can be higher
Likely advantages	Regulated organizations pay attention to regulator, take it seriously and respond readily to its initiatives	Regulators and regulated organizations work together on improvement and collaborate effectively; costs of regulation are minimized
Likely disadvantages	Creative compliance, resistance and lobbying by regulated organizations are likely to subvert purpose of regulation; very high costs of sustained inspection and enforcement that are required	Regulation may lack teeth and be seen as weak with limited ability to make unwelcome changes happen in regulated organizations; regulator may be seen as too close to or allied with the organizations it regulates

Table 2.5 The interaction of regulatory model and regulated organization behaviour

Regulated organization behaviour	Regulatory model	
	Compliance	Deterrence
'Amoral calculator', focused on its own aims or agenda and will ignore regulation to gain advantage	Regulated organization 'runs rings around' regulator; breaches of regulation are frequent and go unchecked, and aims of regulation are not achieved	Regulated organization takes regulation very seriously and exhibits compliance – or the appearance of compliance. However, may find creative ways to avoid or evade regulation and seek to subvert it
'Good-hearted complier', supports aims of regulation and is generally willing to comply	Regulator and regulated organization work in partnership and bring about improvements, but close cooperation between them may be viewed with suspicion by other stakeholders	Regulated organization takes regulation very seriously and tries hard to comply, but resents regulatory behaviour and sees that there is little benefit to it being a 'good-hearted complier'.

to fail. On the other hand, deterrence regulation probably produces rather more consistent results, regardless of the actual orientation of the regulated organization, with the advantages and disadvantages spelt out above. Table 2.5 also suggests that the two characteristics – regulatory model and regulated organization behaviour – may be interdependent. For example, when a regulator takes a deterrence approach to regulation, there are few if any advantages to regulated organizations behaving like a 'good-hearted complier'. In fact, compliance-minded organizations are likely to feel resentful and offended when they are subjected to an aggressive and adversarial regime of deterrence regulation, wondering what they have done to deserve such treatment. Over time, the deterrence model may prove to be self-fulfilling, in that it may lead regulated organizations to take a self-interested, defensive and adversarial approach to regulation, becoming more like the 'amoral calculators' that deterrence regulation expects. More speculatively, it has been suggested that the compliance model can also influence the attitudes of regulated organizations by appealing to their better nature and setting expectations of public-spiritedness to which they may then feel some obligation. In other words, compliance regulation might help to establish a culture in which non-compliance becomes less socially acceptable, and so 'amoral calculator' behaviours are reduced or hidden (Bardach and Kagan 1982; Ayres and Braithwaite 1992).

BEYOND DETERRENCE AND COMPLIANCE: RESPONSIVE REGULATION

In the 1990s, a new approach to regulation emerged among regulatory theorists that attempted to move beyond the longstanding and rather polarized debate between advocates of regulation and deregulation, and ideas of deterrence versus compliance. Termed 'responsive' or 'smart' regulation (Ayres and Braithwaite 1992; Gunningham *et al.* 1998), it is a pragmatic attempt to escape these long-established dichotomies and to replace them with an approach to regulation that is highly flexible, situationally specific and adaptable. Responsive regulation can be characterized as being founded on six main ideas or concepts: contingency, hierarchy, flexibility, tripartism, parsimony and empowerment. Each of these is defined and discussed in more detail below.

Contingency

Contingency is the core concept of responsive regulation. Responsive regulation eschews the use of 'one size fits all' approaches, in which a uniform regulatory methodology is applied consistently (or even rigidly) to all regulated organizations, regardless of their status or behaviour. Such approaches are often used in the name of fairness and transparency, but their universality comes at a price. Using the same regulatory methods with every organization is rather like giving everyone in the population exactly the same healthcare services regardless of their health status or health needs. It is at best a strategy that wastes regulatory resources. More seriously, since regulatory interventions can do harm as well as good, it can diminish or even eliminate the net benefits of regulation.

Instead, responsive regulation emphasizes the idea of contingency – making the nature of the regulatory regime highly contingent on the behaviour of individual regulated organizations. In this way, high-performing organizations are deliberately treated differently from low-performing organizations, and 'amoral calculators' are dealt with differently from 'good-hearted compliers'. In so doing, responsive regulation recognizes the diversity that exists between and even within regulated organizations. A contingent approach creates its own performance incentives, since regulated organizations know that good performance will be rewarded by, for example, greater regulatory freedom.

The use of a contingent approach presupposes that regulatory methods have discriminatory power; in other words, that regulators can tell the difference between different behaviours by regulated organizations. This may not always be straightforward, since the process of assessment can be subjective, and organizations' behaviours can be heterogeneous within the organization and vary over time. For example, a regulator must be able to distinguish between deliberate, wilful flouting of regulatory directions and infringements that result from a lack of organizational capacity and capability to comply, and treat them differently. It must be able to deal with organizations in which some parts are performing very well while others are performing badly. And its approach must be able to detect and respond to significant changes in performance (either positive or negative) while not being triggered falsely by non-significant changes or by 'noise' in the assessment process. In other words, responsive regulation requires more sensitive and specific measurement tools.

Hierarchy

Responsive regulation makes full use of a hierarchy of regulatory methods or interventions in each of the three domains of direction, detection and enforcement. This hierarchy is often presented as a pyramid, as in Figure 2.2, which sets out an example for regulatory enforcement.

The aim is to provide the regulator with a full suite of regulatory interventions that can be used responsively and tailored to the needs and behaviours of individual regulated organizations. The interventions at the bottom of the pyramid are generally those that are used most frequently and involve the least intervention. As the pyramid is ascended, the interventions become more serious and significant, more expensive in time and other resources to the regulator and the regulated organization, and are expected to be used on smaller and smaller numbers of regulated organizations. At the top of the pyramid are the 'nuclear interventions' that should be used

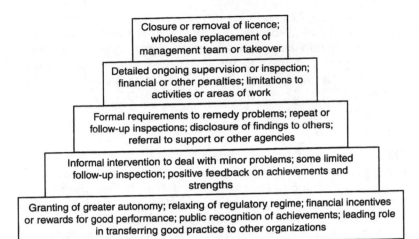

Figure 2.2 A hierarchy of regulatory enforcement.

very rarely, in the most serious cases of poor performance. In a hierarchy such as this, it is expected that most regulatory activity with regulated organizations takes place on the lower levels; if more than a few organizations are being dealt with on the higher levels, the regulatory workload quickly becomes very high and difficult to sustain, since those interventions tend to be lengthy and costly to deploy.

Advocates of responsive regulation argue that it is important for regulators to have a complete hierarchy of regulatory interventions available to them, and are able and willing to use them. Three common problems result from a lack of such a hierarchy of intervention. First, some regulators have only high-level interventions available to them like closure or removal of licence. In practice, these enforcement interventions are so serious that it is hardly ever appropriate to use them, and the regulator might just as well have no interventions at all. Secondly, some regulators have only low-level interventions available to them, such as follow-up inspection or the publication of regulatory findings. In practice, they are then not able to deal with serious performance issues because they lack clout. For regulated organizations, their interventions become a peripheral annoyance but nothing more than that. Thirdly, some regulators are locked in by legislation or by custom and precedent to particular levels in the hierarchy, which means they fail to respond sufficiently to differences in regulated organizations' behaviour and performance.

In describing the idea of hierarchy, Ayres and Braithwaite (1992) argued that the most effective regulator is a 'benign big gun' – able to develop friendly relationships with regulated organizations; seen to be tolerant and understanding, but also known to be tough when necessary; and willing to use its enforcement powers to the full if need be.

Flexibility

The two preceding traits – contingency and hierarchy – both demand that regulators are able to be flexible or adaptable in their approach to regulation, tailoring their interventions to fit the behaviour of regulated organizations and moving freely up and down the hierarchy of regulatory interventions as appropriate. However, this need for flexibility conflicts with two common regulatory imperatives – consistency and transparency. It is often argued that systems of regulation should be fair and consistent in their treatment of regulated organizations so that no-one is disadvantaged, and that the methods they use should be entirely transparent so that everyone (and particularly regulated organizations) can see how assessments are made and judgements are arrived at. However, the practical result of these laudable aims is that all too often regulators' hands are tied by highly prescriptive, explicitly defined rules and standards which attempt to codify the whole regulatory process and which, consequently, leave little or no room for regulators to exercise discretion or judgement. Because it is very difficult to write standards and measures that suit all regulated organizations, such explicit approaches tend to compromise the validity of regulatory tools in exchange for attempting to increase their reliability and consistency.

It appears that there is a trade-off here, between regulatory flexibility and validity on the one hand, and regulatory consistency, reliability and transparency on the other. Advocates of responsive regulation would argue that effective regulation has to have flexibility, and that an undue focus on consistency and transparency may actually harm regulatory effectiveness. Some would go further and assert that an obsessive search for greater consistency and transparency expressed, for instance, through explicitly defined and very detailed regulatory procedures and standards, is ultimately self-defeating because such approaches create as many measurement problems and difficulties as they solve for regulators (Braithwaite and Braithwaite 1995).

Tripartism

The relationship between a regulator and a regulated organization is not simply bilateral. There are many other stakeholders with an interest or involvement in the regulated organization's performance. Advocates of responsive regulation suggest that regulatory arrangements should be designed to make use of or co-opt these other groups to the purposes of regulation, an approach that is termed 'tripartism'. For example, workers in a manufacturing organization have a strong self-interest in good workplace safety arrangements, thus occupational safety and health regulations often require manufacturers to have some kind of formal employee involvement and representation in workplace safety structures and processes. In this way, workers and their representatives are brought into the regulatory process, where they can be an important source of information to the regulator and can help to promote regulatory compliance. Regulatory agencies have very limited resources in comparison with the organizations that they regulate, and even the most intensive approaches to regulatory oversight are unlikely to allow regulators to oversee directly more than a very small proportion of the activities they regulate. Tripartism provides a mechanism by which regulators can extend their oversight over regulated organizations, by using other stakeholders as informants, and can secure greater regulatory compliance by using those stakeholders to pressure regulated organizations to change.

Another way to use the idea of tripartism is to consider the regulatory process as simply one of a much wider set of influences or pressures on regulated organizations, and to examine how those influences interact. For example, an organization may have to respond to regulatory demands, while also competing in the marketplace, and dealing with rising consumer expectations and meeting employee demands. It is unlikely that all of these different influences will always coincide, or be aligned. Some conflict is probably inevitable, but it is worth considering how organizations will behave when regulatory pressures conflict with other influences, how they will reconcile these conflicting demands and which pressures or influences will prevail.

It could be argued that regulation is most effective when the requirements or objectives of regulatory agencies are aligned with other influences on the behaviour of regulated organizations. For example, regulatory compliance with environmental health standards among food producers is generally good, because the producers recognize that any significant outbreak in food-related disease can result in major harm to their commercial interests, such as loss of market share, reduced consumer confidence and esteem, and damage to their public image and reputation. Enthoven (1980) argued for a 'procompetitive' approach to regulation in market situations, in which, as far as possible, the regulatory regime is designed to reinforce or complement existing market incentive structures or influences on regulated organizations. Gunningham *et al.* (1998) put a similar case for seeking 'win–win' regulatory solutions in which regulation achieves its objectives but also has some business benefits for the regulated organization.

Parsimony

The principle of parsimony is straightforward – regulatory regimes should be designed to use the least intrusive and cheapest possible regulatory interventions to achieve their objectives. There are two reasons to promote a parsimonious approach. First, and most obviously, it is desirable to minimize the costs of regulation to the regulator and to regulated organizations. In practice, regulators often have few incentives to keep their costs down, because those costs are borne either from public funds or by fees or payments from regulated organizations and there are usually no competitive pressures upon them. Indeed, it could be argued that regulators have built-in incentives to expand and extend regulation and so increase regulatory costs. In contrast, regulated organizations have strong incentives to minimize the costs of regulation, but they often argue that too little account is taken of the wider costs of regulation when regulatory regimes are being designed or developed. A parsimonious approach can help to control regulatory expansion and demonstrate that the costs of regulation are seen as an important factor in regulatory policy-making. Secondly, experience suggests that regulation is often fraught with unanticipated problems and unintended consequences (Dunlop 1980; Breyer 1982; Ayres and Braithwaite 1992). Ambitious attempts to establish comprehensive systems of regulation often fail because of these problems, which may simply reflect the complexity of the systems and organizations being regulated and the limited understanding we have of how they work. For this reason, a more parsimonious, cautious and incremental approach to regulatory design is advocated, in which regulatory methods and interventions are deployed more carefully and their potential side-effects and adverse or unintended consequences are minimized.

The concept of parsimony can also be helpful in making fundamental decisions about whether or not to regulate an activity at all and, if so, what kind of regulatory regime is needed. Alternative strategies might be able to be used to achieve the same goals as regulation through, for example, strengthening consumer information or consumers' legal rights. But even if regulation is seen as necessary, a parsimonious approach would first consider the use of self-regulation as the least intrusive and cheapest possible regulatory mechanism. It would then consider options such as enforced self-regulation (in which self-regulation is strengthened by some degree of external oversight of the regulatory process) or partial regulation (in which some but not all entities or activities are regulated). Only if these other approaches do not or would not work, should the use of what might be termed a traditional system of regulation be considered, and even then the idea of parsimony should continue to influence decisions about regulatory design and development (Ayres and Braithwaite 1992).

Empowerment

If the purpose of regulation is to improve organizational performance, it makes little sense for regulation to bring about improvement in some organizations but to act as a barrier to improvement in others. Yet this is exactly what regulation often appears to do – by setting a 'floor' or 'safety net' of minimum standards which may help poorly performing organizations to improve, but which may do nothing to promote improvement in organizations that already perform well, and may even act as a barrier to innovation and so to improvement. The idea of empowerment is that regulation should be designed to support improvement across the spectrum of performance, not just to set minimum expectations which become accepted norms. Regulators should aim to enable or empower organizations to do well, rather than impose requirements that may constrain or limit what they do.

Empowerment is a difficult concept to put into practice, although it is clear that some of the other features of responsive regulation, such as contingency and hierarchy, serve its purposes. Two key concerns can be identified. First, empowerment means that regulation should be designed around the long-term goal of performance improvement, rather than the achievement of short-term regulatory objectives. For example, sanctioning an organization for a regulatory breach may force them into immediate compliance, but create resentment or ill-feeling that makes it less likely that they will be a good regulatory citizen in future. Secondly, empowerment means that the likely benefits and harms of regulatory interventions need to be assessed, taking into account their impact on all regulated organizations. For example, introducing a regulation that brings about some improvement in a tiny proportion of organizations at the cost of deterring or hindering innovation at many other regulated organizations should be seen clearly to be a mistake.

Testing responsive regulation

The ideas of responsive or smart regulation are intellectually attractive and coherent, and have an intuitive appeal and an almost self-evident nature which make it tempting to believe that they must be right. However, if responsive regulation is such a good idea, why aren't there more responsive regulators out there? In practice, few regulators live up to the ideals of responsive or smart regulation, and many regulatory regimes fly in the face of this theoretical wisdom. For whatever reason, there is little empirical evidence to support the case for responsive regulation, and many participants or stakeholders in healthcare regulation would be deeply sceptical about whether it would work. The next two chapters examine healthcare regulation in the USA and the UK and illustrate the complex practical realities of making regulation work. Hopefully, they will help both to illuminate the theories that have been outlined in this chapter and to provide an empirical foundation for some further consideration of responsive regulation in Chapter 5.

3

REGULATING HEALTHCARE IN THE UNITED STATES

This chapter describes the development of healthcare regulation in the USA, provides an overview of the current systems of regulation and explores in some detail the use of regulation and its impact on performance in three areas – hospitals, health plans and nursing homes. However, to set the material on regulation in context, the chapter begins by providing an overview of the US healthcare system.

AMERICAN HEALTHCARE AND THE RISE OF REGULATION

The US healthcare system is certainly the largest and probably the most complex healthcare system in the world. To the outsider, it is a baffling, ever-changing and evolving landscape, which appears to defy mapping or structured description, let alone analysis (Davies and Marshall 2000; Walshe 2001b). Table 3.1 provides a simplified overview of the way that US healthcare is funded and delivered, which helps to illustrate its complexity.

The USA spends far more than any other country on healthcare, both in absolute terms (about three times as much per person as the UK, for example, and more than twice as much as the OECD average) and as a proportion of the country's income. About half that money comes from government; the other half comes from employers (providing health insurance for their employees and their families) and directly from patients themselves (Iglehart 1999a; Anderson and Hussey 2000). Because the system is insurance-based,

Table 3.1 An overview of the US healthcare system

Expenditure	The USA spends about $1.2 trillion per annum on healthcare for its 270 million population, much more per capita than any other OECD country both in real terms ($4178 per person per annum) and as a proportion of GDP (13.6%)
Funding sources	Government (at state and federal level) funds healthcare for those aged over 65 through Medicare (20% of all health spending) and for the very poor through Medicaid (14% of all health spending). Private health insurance purchased either by employers or by individuals directly represents 33% of health expenditure. Other public and some private schemes provide a further 16% of funds, and the rest (17%) comes directly from patients in out-of-pocket payments
Coverage	Public insurance schemes (Medicare, Medicaid, etc.) cover 25% of the population; private health insurance covers 58% of the population; 17% (about 44 million people) have no coverage at all and, therefore, have very limited access to health services. Benefits and services included in insurance schemes vary widely – most schemes cover inpatient and outpatient care, but cover for behavioural health care, prescription drugs and dental care is more limited
Delivery	The healthcare system is huge – around 1200 private insurers or health plans, 730,000 doctors, 6000 hospitals, 17,000 nursing homes – and complex. There is a mixture of public, private, for-profit and not-for-profit institutions. Healthcare insurers contract with healthcare providers to provide services using both fee-for-service and capitated contracts. There are some integrated healthcare provider organizations but in most places provision is quite fragmented
Usage	Among the lowest number of hospital beds per population in OECD. Very low acute hospital admission rates (0.7 days per person per annum) and lengths of stay (mean 6.0 days) but very high costs ($1204 per day – five times the OECD median). Among the fewest physician visits per capita (6.0) and average numbers of physicians (2.7 per 1000 population), but per capita spending on physicians is the highest in OECD ($849 per annum). More coronary bypasses, hysterectomies, dialysis and other acute or high-tech interventions than most other OECD countries

Table 3.1—*continued*

Health statistics	Life expectancy at birth of 79.4 years for females and 73.9 years for males. Infant mortality rate 7.2 per 1000 births, one of the highest in OECD. Highest premature mortality rates in OECD mainly due to high death rates in young adult population. Highest incidence of prostate and breast cancer in OECD, but among the lowest mortality

Sources: Anderson and Hussey (2000), Walshe (2001b).

coverage is variable. Most people of working age are covered by employer insurance, although they tend to be low users of health services. Government insurance programmes like Medicare and Medicaid cover the elderly, the chronically sick and the very poor (Iglehart 1999b,c). However, 17 per cent of the population (44 million people) have no health insurance. If they fall sick, they have to pay directly for care; if they are unable to do so, they rely on the charity of healthcare providers. The uninsured are predominantly those on low incomes, in poorly paid jobs with no employer health cover, and those from non-white ethnic groups (Davis 2001). Even for those who have insurance of some kind, access to healthcare is often limited by what their insurance covers. For example, Medicare does not provide prescription drugs for the elderly except as part of a hospital admission, so many elderly people spend a substantial proportion of their income on pharmaceuticals. Many insurance policies have high co-payment rates or an annual ceiling on benefits. Some exclude or reduce cover for certain types of care, such as mental health services (Kuttner 1999a,b).

Health services are provided by a bewildering variety of private, public, profit and not-for-profit organizations. For example, of America's 6000 acute hospitals, some are run for profit by companies listed on the stock exchange that often own or manage a large hospital network; others are independent not-for-profit institutions, often run by or linked to a philanthropic organization such as a church or charity; and some are public organizations funded or run by government at a city, county, state or federal level. The same is true of health plans and health insurers. Some, like the Blue Cross and Blue Shield networks, have existed for decades and were founded as not-for-profit institutions, although parts of them have since been converted into commercial, for-profit organizations. Others have always been investor-owned, public-listed companies. Some of the largest health plans, like the Federal Employees Health Benefits

Program (FEHBP), are government run. There is also much diversity and variation in the way that doctors interact with health-care providers and health plans. Although some physicians are directly employed in hospitals or other healthcare facilities, most work independently either as self-employed practitioners or as part of a medical group or association that brings together a number of physicians, sometimes in a single specialty area but often across a number of specialties. These medical groups contract with hospitals and health insurers to provide physician services. There are some more integrated models – single organizations that provide a full range of health services in primary and secondary care from one, integrated network in a way more akin to the UK National Health Service – such as Kaiser Permanente in California and Group Health Cooperative in Seattle (Shortell *et al.* 2000; Feachem *et al.* 2002). However, these integrated delivery models are the exception rather than the rule in most places. Although the USA spends so much more than other countries on healthcare, it does not necessarily consume a lot more health services. Indeed, the data suggest that utilization rates for hospitals, prescribed pharmaceuticals, physician visits and other services are quite moderate. The USA spends more because the unit costs of healthcare are much higher, in part because of the wasteful and bureaucratic way the system works (Reinhardt 1992).

Over the last two decades, there have been huge changes in the way that healthcare is provided in the USA – driven by market competition, rising costs, technological advances, increased patient expectations and widespread public and political concern about healthcare. Some of these changes are outlined in Table 3.2. Perhaps the most important shift has been the rise of managed care. Traditional fee-for-service-based health insurance (where the insurer just pays a hospital or physician for providing care to an insured person after the event has occurred) has increasingly been sup-planted over the last twenty years by a variety of mechanisms often termed 'managed care'. Managed care organizations come in all shapes and sizes, but they generally attempt to manage the provision of care much more proactively than a traditional insurer, so as to keep costs down and assure quality. They often pay providers a capitated fee per patient instead of paying for services provided, with the aim of discouraging overuse; prevent direct access to specialists, making patients see a primary care physician first; limit patients to using particular physicians or hospitals that are part of their network; and require providers to follow guidelines on treatment,

Table 3.2 A brief chronology of health policy changes in the USA, 1980–2002

1980–92 Republican (Ronald Reagan and George Bush)	When Ronald Reagan came to power, American healthcare was dominated by the traditional, insured, fee-for-service model. The 1980s and early 1990s saw huge cost pressures, to which government responded initially with the introduction of prospective payment systems to control costs. The spiralling cost of healthcare led to the rise of managed care organizations and a host of associated reforms such as capitation payment and risk-sharing for providers, utilization review, gatekeeping and clinical protocols or guidelines. The economic pressures also led to increasing integration and consolidation of healthcare delivery, and saw an expansion of commercial, for-profit health plans and providers at the expense of not-for-profit entities. Government-funded programmes like Medicare and Medicaid were not immune to these changes. By the early 1990s, healthcare cost inflation was back under control, but considerable public concern and disquiet about quality, cost and access issues had been generated
1992–2000 Democrat (Bill Clinton)	Healthcare reform was a leading issue in the 1992 election, and President Clinton ambitiously promised reform proposals in his first 100 days. A hugely complex reform package was eventually assembled that would have delivered universal coverage and capped healthcare costs, but it ran into sustained political opposition from many – insurers, pharmaceutical companies and the business lobby – who stood to lose out. No legislation was passed and the Democrats lost control of Congress in the 1994 mid-term elections as a result. Subsequently, efforts focused on more incremental changes like the SCHIP programme to provide health insurance to the children of uninsured adults, and a healthcare Bill of Rights to protect patients' interests (which has yet to make it to the statute book). Federal budgetary reforms in the mid-1990s cut Medicare hospital reimbursement very significantly and drove major consolidations among providers. Managed care continued to expand, although the economic boom of the late 1990s lessened the pressure to control healthcare cost inflation

Table 3.2—*continued*

2001–2002 Republican (George W. Bush)	Since his very narrow victory in the 2000 election, the administration of President George W. Bush has paid little attention to health policy and made almost no progress on the issues that were featured in the election – Medicare reform, the development of a prescription drug benefit within Medicare, and the expansion of the SCHIP programme's coverage of the uninsured. The agenda has instead been dominated by domestic economic problems and the international 'war on terrorism'

prescribing, referral and so on (Robinson and Steiner 1998; Weiner *et al.* 2001). Managed care expanded dramatically in the 1990s, mainly because it was seen as an effective way to contain rising healthcare costs (Robinson 1999). It was a financial success but a political failure as patients and politicians reacted angrily to the way it constrained access to healthcare (Robinson 2001a).

To the average American citizen, US healthcare was traditionally a source of some pride, because of its justified reputation for technological excellence and for pioneering new treatments (Iglehart 1999a). Once, it was not unusual for Americans to claim they had 'the best healthcare in the world' and to see few lessons for themselves in the way that other countries organized healthcare (Brown 1998). But the seismic changes in the US healthcare system over the last two decades have shaken that confidence. Surveys show that Americans are increasingly dissatisfied with their healthcare system, frustrated by its complexity and bureaucracy, concerned about its high costs, angered by its failure to provide access to healthcare for many people, unsure of how to make it work better, and distrustful of the healthcare industry's and of government's motivations and capacity to change it (Donelan *et al.* 1999). The last major attempt at reform during the first Clinton administration in 1992–96 began with widespread popular support but ended in political catastrophe for the Democrats, produced no real change at all, and now serves as a constant reminder to US politicians of the risks and potential problems involved in tackling the apparently intractable issue of healthcare reform (Johnson and Broder 1996). In comparison with other developed countries, the US healthcare system is costly, inequitable and inefficient – a controversial World Health Organization report (2000) on health systems performance placed the US 37th out of 190 countries and bottom of the developed world (WHO 2000). However, in many ways, the healthcare system simply reflects wider American cultural and social values, such as a love of individual freedom, a belief in markets and competition, a distrust of big government and a tolerance of inequity (Walshe 2001b).

Healthcare regulation in the USA is as complex – and sometimes as baffling – as the healthcare system it regulates. There is a long and varied history of healthcare regulation in the USA, by both private (or non-governmental) and public (or governmental) agencies. The private or non-governmental regulation of US healthcare by accrediting organizations like the Joint Commission for the Accreditation of Healthcare Organizations (JCAHO) began about 80 years ago (Roberts *et al.* 1987); there are now at least 25 non-governmental organizations involved in accrediting various types of healthcare organization. The regulation of hospitals and other healthcare organizations by state governments first became common in the post-war period, but has expanded dramatically over the last three decades (Hackey 1998). Practices vary widely from state to state but, for example, California's state government now recognizes and regulates 30 different types of healthcare entities. Federal involvement in regulating hospitals and nursing homes began with the advent of the Medicare and Medicaid programmes in 1965, and grew as the regulation of other types of healthcare organization (such as health maintenance organizations, clinical laboratories, home healthcare agencies and so on) was developed. The current regulatory environment is complex, with a combination of non-governmental, state and federal government regulatory arrangements that cover a wide range of different types of healthcare organization: insurers, health plans, hospitals, clinics, laboratories, medical groups, nursing homes, home healthcare agencies and so on. The regulatory arrangements for three key entities discussed in this chapter – health insurers and health plans, hospitals and nursing homes – are summarized in Table 3.3. Because state regulatory arrangements vary widely from state to state, Table 3.3 cites regulatory arrangements in California as an example.

There are many links and interdependencies between the systems of regulation shown in Table 3.3, both horizontally (across the non-governmental, state and federal regulatory arrangements for a given type of healthcare entity) and vertically (across different types of healthcare entity). For example, the regulation of hospitals by JCAHO is deemed under federal legislation to satisfy the Health Care Financing Administration's (HCFA) requirements for

Table 3.3 A summary of regulatory arrangements in US healthcare

	Non-governmental regulation	State regulation in California	Federal regulation
Hospitals	Accreditation programmes operated by the Joint Commission on the Accreditation of Healthcare Organizations (JCAHO) and some other accreditation organizations	Licensing and certification by state Department of Health Services	Health Care Financing Administration (HCFA) regulation and oversight of Medicare/Medicaid for hospitals. Medicare peer review organization network oversight of hospitals
Health plans	Accreditation programmes operated by JCAHO, the National Committee for Quality Assurance and some other accreditation organizations	Licensing and oversight of health maintenance organizations by state Department of Managed Health Care; of preferred provider organizations by state Department of Insurance; of Medicaid health plans by Department of Health Services	HCFA regulation and oversight of Medicare Choice plans HCFA oversight of some aspects of some plans under the Health Maintenance Organization Act 1973, the Employee Retirement Income Security Act 1974, the Health Insurance Portability and Accountability Act 1996 and other federal legislation Medicare peer review organization network oversight of plans
Nursing homes	Accreditation programmes operated by JCAHO and some other accreditation organizations	Licensing and certification by state Department of Health Services	HCFA regulation and oversight of Medicare/Medicaid for nursing homes Medicare peer review organization network oversight of nursing homes Long-term care ombudsman programme

Medicare participation, and the federal regulations for nursing homes are implemented by state government agencies on behalf of HCFA. Some of the regulators work across many different types of healthcare entity, like JCAHO, which accredits health plans, hospitals and nursing homes and a number of other types of health-care organization; or like the federally funded network of Medicare peer review organizations, which interact with plans, hospitals and nursing homes and other entities that participate in Medicare.

For an individual healthcare organization, such as a hospital or a health insurer, the regulatory picture appears to be crowded with organizations that seek to oversee what they do. The American Hospitals Association has reported that hospitals have to deal with up to 30 different regulatory bodies just in the federal government and that, as a result, up to 50 per cent of doctors' and nurses' time is spent on paperwork or data collection mandated by various outside agencies including regulators, rather than on caring for patients (AHA 2001). Studies have shown that US hospitals have very high administrative costs compared with those elsewhere, accounting for 25 per cent of all costs on average, which must be partially a result of the regulatory burden. On the face of it, there is some justification for longstanding claims that American healthcare organizations are among the most heavily regulated entities in the world (Levin 1980).

But if regulation is ubiquitous in US healthcare, it is far from uncontroversial. Some argue that regulation has been an important force for improvement in US healthcare, driving change and raising standards over many years (Schyve and O'Leary 1998; AHQA 2000; NCQA 2000). Other commentators assert that the regulation of healthcare organizations imposes a substantial and unwarranted bureaucratic burden upon them, raises costs, acts as a barrier to entry to the healthcare marketplace, stifles innovation and improve-ment, and has other negative effects (Goodman 1980; Leyerle 1994; Brennan and Berwick 1996; AHA 2001). Still others charac-terize healthcare regulation as timid and often ineffectual, and argue that more aggressive regulatory strategies and greater efforts at enforcement are needed (Dame and Wolfe 1996; Latimer 1997).

REGULATING HOSPITALS

The Joint Commission on the Accreditation of Healthcare Organizations (JCAHO), a private, non-governmental organization, is the dominant force in the regulation of US hospitals. Although, as Table 3.3 shows, there are also important governmental regulators, at a state and federal level they make extensive use of JCAHO's accreditation process in their regulatory mechanisms. For this reason, it makes sense first to explain how JCAHO hospital accreditation works, and then to describe state and federal governmental regulation.

JCAHO hospital accreditation

The Joint Commission on the Accreditation of Healthcare Organizations (JCAHO) has accreditation programmes for a wide range of entities, including health plans, nursing homes, home healthcare agencies and so on, but its hospital accreditation programme is by far its largest and longest established activity. The organization was created in 1951 as the Joint Commission for the Accreditation of Hospitals and was originally established to take over the running of an accreditation programme which had begun life in the 1920s as the Hospital Standardization Programme and been hosted for its first three decades by the American College of Surgeons (Schyve and O'Leary 1998). An analysis of JCAHO's hospital accreditation programme is set out in Table 3.4, using the evaluative framework introduced in Chapter 2 (see Table 2.3).

As Table 3.4 shows, JCAHO is a non-governmental, not-for-profit organization, led by a board of governors whose make-up reflects the organization's antecedents. Most members of the board are representatives of healthcare industry or professional groups, such as the American Hospitals Association, the American Medical Association and the American College of Surgeons. For this reason, some other stakeholders (such as patient groups, health insurers and health plan associations) see JCAHO as being effectively controlled by the organizations which it is there to regulate and as being insufficiently independent of them. It is certainly true that in the past, when JCAHO has been faced with making decisions about the development of its hospital accreditation programme, which might impose new costs or regulatory requirements on hospitals, board members have been influential in reining in regulatory action (Leyerle 1994; Wiener 2000).

Although JCAHO is a private organization, with no formal ties or accountability to government, its hospital accreditation programme plays a very important role in the federal regulation of hospitals. When the huge federally funded Medicare and Medicaid programmes were established in the 1960s, the legislation imposed a

Table 3.4 A regulatory analysis of JCAHO hospital accreditation

Characteristic	Analysis of JCAHO accreditation of hospitals
Regulating organization	Joint Commission on the Accreditation of Healthcare organizations. JCAHO is an independent, private sector, not-for-profit organization and has no formal legal powers or authority over hospitals. It was established in 1952, originally to run an accreditation programme for hospitals that had been in existence since the 1920s. It is governed by a board dominated by representatives of the American Hospitals Association, American Medical Association, American College of Surgeons and similar groups. However, because JCAHO's accreditation programme for hospitals has 'deemed status' under federal Medicare/Medicaid legislation, accreditation is effectively mandatory for most acute hospitals
Regulatory goals/objectives	JCAHO's stated mission is 'to continuously improve the safety and quality of care provided to the public through the provision of health care accreditation and related services that support performance improvement in health care organizations'
Scope of regulation	JCAHO accredits many types of healthcare organization, but this analysis focuses on their accreditation of hospitals. About 4500 hospitals (or 80% of the total) have accreditation. JCAHO's oversight covers almost all areas of hospital performance
Regulatory model	Generally compliance-oriented, with enforcement used as a last resort. Major focus on the educational and developmental dimension of the accreditation process. Emphasis placed on quality improvement
Direction	JCAHO maintains an extensive accreditation manual for hospitals, which contains over 500 standards organized around 15 main areas. For each standard there is detailed guidance on its intent, implementation and assessment
Detection	Three-yearly accreditation surveys of hospitals, usually involving a 4–5 day visit to the organization by a three-person surveyor team. Visit is preceded by months of preparatory activity and followed by a report that describes compliance with the standards and identifies any recommendations for improvement

Table 3.4—*continued*

Characteristic	Analysis of JCAHO accreditation of hospitals
Enforcement	Over 95% of hospitals achieve full accreditation, although many have follow-up reports or visits to check on implementation of recommendations. Denial of accreditation is the only formal sanction, and it is used very rarely (in less than 1% of cases). A limited summary of each accreditation report is available to the public on paper and via the JCAHO website, but the full document is confidential to the hospital

certification process on participating hospitals that had to demonstrate their suitability to admit and care for Medicare/Medicaid
patients. However, hospitals could do this in one of two ways,
either by undergoing inspection by the Health Care Financing
Administration, which administered the two programmes, or by
undergoing JCAHO accreditation. In the terminology, JCAHO
accreditation was 'deemed' to meet the requirements for certification. This deemed status has been an enormously powerful incentive
for hospitals to get and keep JCAHO accreditation, and accounts for
the fact that about 80 per cent of US acute hospitals (and virtually
all major hospitals) are JCAHO accredited. Many state governments have followed the federal lead, as have many private health
insurers and health plans who require hospitals to have JCAHO
accreditation to participate in their networks. Accreditation by
JCAHO has thus become a necessary part of doing business for
hospitals – mandatory in all but name.

The JCAHO largely adopts a compliance approach to regulation.
It places great stress on its role in education and development, and
expresses its mission in terms of quality and performance improvement. Its closeness to the industry it regulates would make it difficult
for JCAHO to be more deterrence-oriented, but in any case the
professionally dominated provider-led culture of JCAHO is antithetical to the ideas of the deterrence model. Interestingly, although
JCAHO is clearly a compliance regulator, it is not necessarily seen
as such by the hospitals it regulates, who frequently complain about
the regulatory burden of accreditation, the costs of the process –
both in fees and in preparation for accreditation – and the changes
in practice which it forces upon them, not all of which they see as
necessary or a high priority.

Regulatory direction is provided through its *Comprehensive Accreditation Manual for Hospitals* (JCAHO 1996), a formidable 725 page loose-leaf manual that documents in considerable detail the system of over 500 standards organized around 15 main areas; the manual also describes how the accreditation process works and how accreditation decisions are made. The accreditation standards used to be based around individual departments or service areas in a hospital, such as radiology, pathology and surgery. In the early 1990s, JCAHO undertook a fundamental revision of its accreditation standards, reducing the numbers of standards and moving to a system of standards based around key organizational functions, rather than departments. The 15 areas are listed in Table 3.5, which shows that five are focused on particular patient processes like assessment and treatment, six are essentially organizational functions like leadership, and four relate to what JCAHO regards as key structures, such as governance arrangements and medical staff management.

Each of these areas then breaks down into many separate standards. Behind each of those standards lies a detailed statement of its purpose or intent, a series of examples of how organizations might comply with it, a description of the evidence that could be used to demonstrate compliance, and a definition of how compliance with the standard should be scored. This detailed specification

Table 3.5 An overview of JCAHO's accreditation standards for hospitals

Patient-focused functions	Patient rights and organizational ethics Assessment of patients Care of patients Education Continuum of care
Organization functions	Improving organizational performance Leadership Management of the environment of care Management of human resources Management of information Surveillance, prevention and control of infection
Structures with functions	Governance Management Medical staff Nursing

Table 3.6 An example JCAHO accreditation standard

Standard area	Improving organization performance. This area contains 33 standards, of which one is . . .
Standard	PI.1 states that 'The hospital has a planned, systematic, hospital wide approach to process design and performance measurement, assessment and improvement'
Intent and examples	Defines the purpose or intent of the standard, saying that 'performance improvement activities are most effective when they are planned, systematic and organization-wide and when all appropriate individuals and professions work collaboratively to implement them. Too often, performance improvement efforts are isolated within specific departments, units or professions. Collaboration on performance improvement activities enables an organization to plan and provide systematic organization-wide improvement'
Evidence of performance	Manual offers examples of the kinds of evidence which can be used to assess compliance with this standard – such as discussions with leaders and staff, planning documents, meeting minutes and training materials
Scoring	All standards are scored on a scale from 1 (substantial compliance) to 5 (non-compliance). For this standard a score of 1 (yes), 3 (yes but the approach is not hospital wide), 4 (yes but the approach is not planned and systematic) or 5 (no) is possible. Anything apart from a score of 1 would result in recommendations for change or conditions being placed on accreditation

of the accreditation standards is demonstrated in Table 3.6 for a simple example standard concerned with organization performance improvement.

The JCAHO standards are developed and updated continuously – the accreditation manual is revised each year, new standards are often added and existing ones are changed in the light of experience. There is a well-established and quite intensive process for producing new standards, which involves extensive consultation with other bodies and leading experts, may draw in an external task force, and moves relatively cautiously from definition to piloting and field testing before standards are incorporated fully into the accreditation process.

The primary mechanism for regulatory detection is periodic inspection. Hospitals are generally accredited against the JCAHO standards once every 3 years, through a visit by a team of JCAHO surveyors. Since the early 1990s, JCAHO has been making efforts to move towards a more continuous process for monitoring hospitals' performance, through the ongoing collection of quality indicators and other data and through pilot programmes in which hospitals have ongoing contact with surveyors between surveys. It has even considered reducing the interval between surveys from 3 years, but the triennial survey remains the foundation of its accreditation programme (JCAHO 2000).

Hospitals know when their accreditation visit will take place well in advance and are encouraged to prepare for it very carefully by testing their own compliance with the standards and making changes before the visit itself. The JCAHO surveyor team will usually include a physician, a nurse and a hospital manager, and some effort is made to match team skills to the characteristics of the hospital being surveyed. About 10 per cent of surveyors are full-time JCAHO staff, about 40 per cent are part time staff and about 50 per cent are intermittent surveyors who generally spent a quarter of their time on surveys. Most part-time and intermittent surveyors have other jobs – either working in a hospital or in consultancy – or are retired. All surveyors are required to have at least 5 years experience of senior management in hospitals and to undertake a 2 week training programme followed by several 'preceptored' surveys.

The timetable for a JCAHO accreditation visit is very demanding, both for the survey team and for the hospital. Most take about a week, with the surveyors spending time visiting departments and services, interviewing staff, reviewing documents and reports, looking directly at the records of care, and meeting together frequently to share their findings. They do not directly review performance standard by standard, but use the information they gather to fill in an assessment matrix as they go. Their findings are automatically aggregated and scored using a laptop computer, so that at the end of the visit they can give the hospital some immediate interim feedback. For the hospital, the visit is the culmination of 12 months preparatory work and an investment of hundreds of thousands of dollars of staff time and effort. They make a huge effort to create a favourable impression and to present the best face of their organization possible (Wiener 2000).

After the visit, it takes 2–3 months for the formal accreditation report and decision to be made. Most hospitals receive full accreditation or accreditation with 'Type 1 recommendations', which means there are some specific changes required by JCAHO which they must report back on in writing within 6 months. A small number receive conditional accreditation, which indicates that there is some non-compliance with the accreditation standards and usually results in a follow-up or repeat survey a few months later. About 3 per cent of hospitals are provisionally denied accreditation, which means that unless they rectify the problems identified by the survey, accreditation will be withdrawn on a given date in the future. Of the 1700 hospitals surveyed each year, only a handful (between 5 and 10) actually lose accreditation. The accreditation report itself is a confidential document between JCAHO and the hospital concerned, but the accreditation decision and an abbreviated summary report are made public and are available through JCAHO's website.

There is little consensus among stakeholders in the JCAHO accreditation process about whether it works or how useful it is, and there is a remarkable absence of empirical evaluation studies that might provide some foundation for a rational debate. For example, research examining the relationship between JCAHO accreditation results and other measures of hospital performance (Hadley and McGurrin 1988; Jessee and Schranz 1990; HCIA/JCAHO 1993) has struggled to find any meaningful association. A recent Office of the Inspector General investigation of hospital regulation concluded that the JCAHO accreditation process mattered greatly to hospitals and was effective in prompting some improvement, but was insufficiently searching to identify or deal with many quality problems (OIG 1999a). Some consumer groups have been persistent critics of JCAHO, alleging that the accreditation process is organized for the benefit of hospitals, not patients, and that it fails persistently to uncover and deal with poor-quality healthcare (Dame and Wolfe 1996). Table 3.7 uses the same evaluative framework as Table 3.4 to summarize the main alleged benefits and disbenefits of JCAHO accreditation, and demonstrates just how difficult it is to draw firm conclusions about the value of JCAHO's accreditation programme.

However, it is clear that JCAHO's hospital accreditation programme involves a substantial investment of resources. For a hospital, the accreditation fees charged by JCAHO amount to several tens of thousands of dollars. However, the main costs of accreditation are in the process of preparation and the survey itself, with several hospitals estimating that they spend at least ten times that – between a quarter and half a million dollars – on preparing for and then undergoing accreditation (Rockwell *et al.* 1993). On that basis, the total costs to the healthcare system of JCAHO hospital accreditation probably lie between $425 and $850 million a year. A substantial regulatory industry has grown up in the USA around JCAHO; these consultants and advisers will help your organization to prepare for its accreditation visit, tell you how to interpret the often very complex accreditation standards, know what 'hot topics' are the focus of attention for JCAHO at present and keep you informed, understand the common causes of Type 1 recommendations and help you avoid them, and even collate a database of information on individual accreditation surveyors and will advise you on their personal characteristics and foibles. Hospital quality managers who are tasked with leading their organization's preparation for the accreditation process invest a huge amount of effort in the process of preparation, and exchange information regularly through formal and informal networks. Table 3.8 offers some examples of this kind of exchange in action, drawn from a public email discussion list called JCAHO-WATCH, which give some indication of how accreditation looks and feels from their perspective.

State and federal regulation of hospitals

The Joint Commission on the Accreditation of Healthcare Organizations (JCAHO) is only one part of a complex network of hospital regulation, as Table 3.3 shows. Federal and state governmental regulatory agencies also play an important part in hospital regulation. The regulation of hospitals and other healthcare organizations by state governments first became common in the post-war period, but has expanded dramatically over the last three decades (Hackey 1998). Practices vary widely from state to state but, for example, California's state government now recognizes and regulates 30 different types of healthcare entities. Federal government involvement in regulating hospitals and nursing homes began with the advent of the Medicare and Medicaid programmes in 1965, and grew as the regulation of other types of healthcare organizations (such as health maintenance organizations, clinical laboratories and home healthcare agencies) was developed.

At a federal level, the Centers for Medicare and Medicaid Services (CMS, which used to be called the Health Care Financing Administration) is the government agency charged by Congress with overseeing these two huge federal healthcare programmes, which

Table 3.7 An analysis of the perceived benefits and disbenefits of JCAHO's hospital accreditation programme

Characteristic	Perceived benefits	Perceived disbenefits
Regulating organization	JCAHO's non-governmental status allows it to move more quickly than governmental regulators in updating standards, and to invest more in the regulatory process; it also gives JCAHO necessary independence and 'honest broker' status. Formal links to professions and to hospitals via JCAHO board help to secure their support for, and involvement in, regulation.	JCAHO is insufficiently accountable to government and to stakeholders; it is seen as being captured by the professions and the hospital industry, and dominated by their agenda and concerns. The sheer size of JCAHO makes it slow and bureaucratic to deal with and not very responsive to customer needs
Regulatory goals/ objectives	The focus on quality improvement emphasized throughout JCAHO's hospital accreditation programme provides a core objective to which all stakeholders can subscribe and on which they can agree, creating common ground. It helps to avoid deterrence model behaviours on both sides	JCAHO's concern with quality improvement is laudable but it gives insufficient attention to dealing with quality problems and failing hospitals. Others would also argue that JCAHO's corporate espousal of quality improvement is not reflected on the ground, where a quality assurance/ control model is more evident
Scope of regulation	Accreditation is voluntary – no hospital has to undergo it because there are always other ways to get certified to participate in Medicare/Medicaid. The high level of participation in accreditation, therefore, shows that hospitals value the process for its benefits to them	Hospitals participate because they have to – it's effectively mandatory because alternative routes to Medicare/ Medicaid participation are even less attractive. If JCAHO did not have 'deemed status' for Medicare/Medicaid and participation depended on the value of accreditation to the market and to individual organizations, many hospitals would just not take part

Regulatory model	Compliance-oriented approach is seen to be well-suited to professional culture of hospitals and to quality improvement goals of accreditation. It maximizes cooperation and disclosure by hospitals	Compliance-oriented approach is seen as evidence of regulatory capture and a barrier to tough enforcement. It allows poor hospitals to get away with continuing non-compliance for years
Direction	JCAHO accreditation standards are seen to be well-developed and very up to date. JCAHO invests heavily in standards development, and is good at involving professionals and experts in the process	The accreditation standards are produced by professional consensus and are not evidence-based. They often represent a trade-off between what is needed and what JCAHO stakeholders are willing to concede, and tend to be normative. There are far too many standards, they are long and complex, and difficult to measure
Detection	The JCAHO triennial survey, supported by ongoing data monitoring and interim or follow-up accreditation visits, provides a strong strategic impetus for quality improvement in hospitals. Surveyors are well-regarded as experts in their fields and well-trained for the job. The standards provide a framework and ensure consistency	The triennial survey cycle distorts hospital behaviour, with a 'ramp up' of preparation beforehand and a relaxation and return to normal afterwards. Surveyors are often out of touch with current practice, and different surveyors take different approaches, meaning that inter-surveyor reliability/comparability is poor. It is impossible to assess 500 standards adequately in a survey visit. Because of all the preparation, the survey visit becomes a ritualized performance on both sides and does not give a realistic picture of the organization being surveyed
Enforcement	The low denial rate for accreditation is a mark of success, showing that the compliance approach works. Most problems are dealt with through Type 1 recommendations, which hospitals take very seriously	The low denial rate for accreditation shows that JCAHO is not doing its job properly in identifying poorly performing hospitals. JCAHO has too few intermediate sanctions below denial and is very reluctant to use this ultimate sanction, hence it lacks sufficient enforcement powers

Table 3.8 Examples of information exchanged by email between hospital quality managers on the JCAHO accreditation process

'JCAHO will be at our facility June 18–20. We have done the following: We created a JCAHO employee reference manual with common questions and answers this was given to all of the staff, we had a JCAHO bee (a spelling bee), where we ask a question and if you answer incorrectly you sit down and the next person can answer, we had mandatory classes on infection control, PI, EOC, documentation, Med administration and patient rights, we are having a JCAHO carnival featuring the functions, every week we had someone in the cafeteria asking staff questions, weekly a poster is distributed with information such as Who's Who, what is a sentinel event, how to use a fire extinguisher, we conducted mock surveys, mock patient interviews and coaching sessions for each area. We have a contest called second set of eyes where staff that finds clinical equipment not dated or vials, ointments etc not dated receive a coupon for a free dessert. With every pay check JCAHO questions and answers are in the newsletter. We also send info via email. No wonder I am tired. Hopefully it will all pay off'

'Just had [name deleted] last week (96, no type I's). Incredibly thorough, you think he's just scanning documents but he's not, he's read and remembered every word. He also is very grounded in reality as he still runs his own lab and his own consulting business on consolidating labs. He showed us how to save money on our next survey and wrote those suggestions on our application. We had him scheduled for three full days and he said he could easily have finished in just one but hung out for two anyway. He did permit fixing of things during the survey which I have been told they're not supposed to do. Loves good ol' home cookin' so if you've got those type restaurants in your area, take him out to lunch. he's from New York and was looking for chicken fried steak and gravy, fried chicken etc. good luck'

'[name deleted] is one the easiest surveyors out there. He just glances at things. What he really looks for is attractive women. So if you have any make sure that they are very visible wherever he goes.'

'We recently (5/23) came through our visit with JCAHO and did great, but almost got into trouble because of redundant documentation. Our forms for admission assessment, med-surg flow chart, multidisciplinary plan of care and patient teaching record have been modified over the years and have multiple areas where documentation is redundant resulting in patient and staff dissatisfaction. I would appreciate it if anyone was would be willing to share their forms. My fax is [number deleted]. Re our survey: Our surveyors were [names deleted]. I spent most of my time with [name deleted]. She was great. She managed to put the staff at ease almost instantly, so they were really able to talk about their patients and their practice. Although very thorough, the staff seemed very comfortable going through charts with her. She was very professional and spent some time on each unit talking about the valuable and difficult services provided by staff. Truly the best survey I have ever had to pleasure to participate in!!!'

'We had our 5 day survey last week . . . four surveyors for four days and two surveyors for one additional day. I was pleased with the results of the survey. We will have some type 1s to respond to but they are few and far between. I'll be more than happy to share the final report results once I receive them. Right now, the surveyors flagged a few items on the report for evaluation by the computer central office. I am hopeful, as are they, that these will receive more favorable scores than those generated by the computer program. I must say that surveyor variability is alive and well. As a perfect example of this, we had modified our approach to age-specific competency validation from that used during our previous survey on the advice of those previous surveyors and subsequent consultants. Last week, during the competency review, the nurse and administrative surveyor both commented on how we really should be documenting competency validation the way we did 3 years ago instead of the way we are doing it now . . . even though they found no fault with the way we are approaching it now. Since I was on my fourth day with these two, I shared politely why we had modified our approach. They still insisted that we should revert back to our previous methodology'

Source: JCAHO-WATCH email discussion list.

provide healthcare coverage for the elderly and the very poor. The CMS sets out its 'conditions of participation' for Medicare and Medicaid, a set of regulations with which hospitals that admit Medicare and Medicaid patients are required to comply. The CMS does not itself survey many hospitals to check their compliance with the conditions of participation. It delegates this task in two ways. First, hospitals with JCAHO accreditation are legally deemed to have fulfilled the conditions of participation and so do not need to be surveyed. Secondly, it contracts with state government agencies that license and certify health facilities in each state to undertake these surveys on its behalf. This is complex because, at a state level, those agencies are also mandated by state legislatures to set standards for licensure which hospitals are required to meet to do business in the state, and to survey hospitals to make sure that they comply with those requirements too. Some states accept JCAHO accreditation as sufficient evidence of compliance, but most have some additional or separate regulatory requirements of their own. There is one further piece to the jigsaw, a federally funded network of Medicare peer review organizations. There is usually one peer review organization in each state although some work across two or more states. The Medicare peer review organizations were first established in the 1970s, with federal funding from the Medicare programme and a remit to oversee quality and utilization in all healthcare providers funded by Medicare (not only hospitals, but also outpatient care, nursing homes, home healthcare agencies and so on). Most Medicare peer review organizations are not-for-profit organizations; they work under contract to CMS to fufil an agreed work programme, which mainly consists of a combination of topic-focused projects, on-going quality monitoring and complaints investigations. If this network of government regulatory activity sounds complex, in practice it is complex. Table 3.9 uses the evaluative framework again to compare the three main governmental regulators of hospitals which we have described – CMS, state licensing and certification agencies, and Medicare peer review organizations. Because arrangements at a state level vary widely, it presents data from the largest state, California.

Again, there are widely differing views about how effective these systems of hospital regulation are in improving performance or dealing with performance failures. A recent evaluation of the systems for hospital regulation undertaken by the Department of Health and Human Service's Office of the Inspector General examined the work of state agencies and the CMS as well as the

Table 3.9 A comparative regulatory analysis of government regulation of hospitals in the USA

Characteristic	Centers for Medicare and Medicaid Services (CMS)	State licensing and certification (L&C) agency – the California Department of Health Services, Licensing and Certification Division	Medicare peer review organization (PRO) network
Regulating organization	A federal government agency that oversees a $476 billion annual budget and is responsible to the Secretary of State for Health and Human Services and to Congress	Part of the state government, accountable to the governor and to the state legislature. However, Medicare/Medicaid certification is carried out under a contract with CMS, who fund these activities	A network of private organizations (about one per state) under contract with CMS to provide Medicare quality improvement services set out in a rolling 'scope of work' programme
Regulatory goals/ objectives	'CMS develops Conditions of Participation (CoPs) that health care organizations must meet to participate in the Medicare and Medicaid programs. These standards are used to improve quality and protect the health and safety of beneficiaries'	L&C 'promotes the highest quality of medical care in community settings and facilities' and aims 'to improve access to care and assure quality of care'. To this end it 'operate[s] a responsive, uniform enforcement program in accordance with state licensing and federal certification requirements'	Defined in law as 'to protect Medicare beneficiaries and ensure the quality of their healthcare while at the same time safeguarding the integrity of the Medicare program'

continued

Table 3.9—*continued*

Characteristic	Centers for Medicare and Medicaid Services (CMS)	State licensing and certification (L&C) agency – the California Department of Health Services, Licensing and Certification Division	Medicare peer review organization (PRO) network
Scope of regulation	CMS has a huge remit, of which hospital regulation is a relatively small part. Apart from administering Medicare/Medicaid, it also implements numerous other federal healthcare initiatives and responsibilities	The Department of Health Services (DHS) licenses and certifies 30 different types of healthcare organization, as well as dealing with a host of other public health and health financing issues	PROs oversee all services provided within Medicare – not just limited to hospitals but also nursing homes, home healthcare agencies, etc. Hospitals do not have to take part in PRO quality projects but are all subject to PRO oversight of complaints/fraud
Regulatory model	Relatively deterrence-oriented approach, focused on inspecting hospitals, identifying deficiencies and imposing sanctions – although as noted below, those sanctions are rarely enforced	Largely deterrence-oriented approach – inevitably, since DHS is working for CMS and using its rules and processes	Until the early 1990s, PROs had a relatively adversarial and deterrence-oriented approach to hospitals and physicians. A review of the PRO programme led to a major change, towards a compliance-based quality improvement model, although PROs still have some functions like fraud and abuse prevention which fit better in a deterrence model

Direction	CMS conditions for participation in Medicare/Medicaid for hospitals set out in Federal Register (42 CFR 482.11–482.57). Standards have not been comprehensively reviewed since mid-1980s and are out of date	DHS uses the CMS *State Operations Manual*, which defines in comprehensive detail how to use and interpret the Medicare/Medicaid conditions of participation. Also has its own standards, set out in title 22 division 5 of state law, which are generally higher and more up to date	PROs do not set explicit standards for compliance by hospitals
Detection	CMS undertakes some validation surveys of its own, but relies mostly on state survey agencies and JCAHO accreditation. There is no specific interval for hospital surveys	DHS has its own survey process, which is coordinated with the JCAHO accreditation process so that the two survey teams visit at the same time and try to coordinate their work	PROs work with hospitals on quality improvement projects in key topic areas identified by CMS; they also investigate complaints and examine problems of fraud
Enforcement	Wide range of sanctions available, from denial of payment, imposition of financial penalties up to removal from Medicare/Medicaid. In practice, sanctions are rarely implemented	DHS has a similar range of sanctions available to it, up to and including delicensing. State agencies vary in how toughly they use enforcement measures – California has a relatively assertive approach to enforcement	PROs make relatively little use of sanctions, although in the past they used sanctioning extensively. It is now seen as unhelpful to their collaborative, quality improvement focused approach

Sources: CMS website at http://www.hcfa.gov/cop/default.asp accessed 25 April 2002; DHS website at http://www.dhs.cahwnet.gov/ accessed 25 April 2002; AHQA website at http://www.ahqa.org accessed 25 April 2002.

Joint Commission on the Accreditation of Healthcare Organizations (OIG 1999a). At the same time, the Medicare Payment Advisory Commission was tasked with reviewing a range of perceived problems in Medicare, including the systems for regulation and quality assurance (MedPAC 2000). These two reports identify a number of issues.

First, there is a fundamental conflict between the largely deterrence-oriented approach of CMS and the state survey agencies on the one hand, and the mainly compliance-oriented approach of JCAHO on the other, made more acute by the fact that JCAHO's deemed status means it is effectively regulating hospitals on behalf of CMS and the states, but doing so in a very different way. The Office of the Inspector General warns of the dangers of 'collegiality' and argues that the JCAHO process is unlikely to detect substandard patterns of care. It suggests that a more regulatory approach is necessary to protect patients from failures in the standard of care, and proposes that CMS should do more to oversee the work of JCAHO and hold it to account (OIG 1999a).

Secondly, the CMS conditions of participation are hopelessly out of date (MedPAC 2000). The last full revision was undertaken in 1986; attempts to update them in the late 1990s have made little progress, for two reasons. The rule-making procedure followed by federal agencies under the Administrative Procedure Act (Rosenbloom 1994) is a very slow and bureaucratic process, involving the publication of proposed regulations in the Federal Register, a period for public comment and then a process of revision before the final rule is issued. The Health Care Financing Administration, as CMS was then known, did issue a proposed revision to the hospital conditions of participation in 1997 and received 60,000 public comments. The final rules have yet to be issued. In addition, CMS has many other responsibilities mandated by Congress and the government, which tend to take priority over tasks like regulatory revision and updating. The agency is overwhelmed with work and has too few staff and limited resources with which to do its job (Iglehart 2001).

Thirdly, both the Medicare Payment Advisory Commission and the Office of the Inspector General point out that while JCAHO-accredited hospitals are surveyed every 3 years, those hospitals which are not JCAHO accredited but which instead undergo inspection by CMS and the state survey agencies have no set survey interval, and the mean time between surveys has been rising. The CMS only funded state survey agencies to survey 10 per cent of hospitals in 1998, a policy which, if continued, would result in each hospital being surveyed only once every 10 years on average. Both the Medicare Payment Advisory Commission and the Office of the Inspector General suggest that the state survey agencies are underfunded and need more resources to fulfil their regulatory mandate and inspect hospitals more frequently, although they also suggest that the inspection process should be more targeted, with providers whose compliance is poor facing increased scrutiny.

Fourthly, while the Medicare/Medicaid conditions of participation give CMS and the state survey agencies considerable apparent powers to sanction providers who fail to comply by imposing financial penalties and even terminating their participation in Medicare/Medicaid, in practice these sanctions don't work very well. There is a lack of effective intermediate sanctions and the sanctioning process is slow and laborious. Providers can tie sanctions up with appeals, and they get a grace period in which they can come into compliance and avoid the sanction, but then lapse afterwards, a phenomenon known as temporary compliance. Providers' past history of compliance cannot be taken into account, so persistent poor performers and those with good compliance records get treated the same. The ultimate sanction of decertification is rarely if ever used (no hospitals were decertified in 1999).

Fifthly, both reports point out that there is a lack of openness in hospital regulation, since the CMS and state survey agency reports on hospitals are not published, and suggest that these reports should be more widely available and could be used to provide information to consumers.

Medicare Peer Review Organizations programme

The history of the network of peer review organizations (PROs) provides an object lesson in the problems and challenges of regulation. They were first established in 1974 as professional standards review organizations (PSROs) to provide a professionally led, federally funded stimulus for quality improvement within Medicare. Many of the first PSROs were set up by state medical societies and other professional associations (Sanazaro 1974). Their original contracts required them to use a standards-based approach, working with hospitals to set standards and then audit compliance. This resulted in a huge volume of standard-setting and criterion-based audit, but it was soon perceived to be producing relatively little actual change or improvement (Komaroff 1978; Sanazaro and Worth 1978). The PSROs came to be seen as a bureaucratic imposition on hospitals, which added little value to Medicare.

In the early 1980s, Congress restructured PSROs to form a much smaller number of PROs, with a very different and more overtly regulatory mandate. The PROs were tasked with directly reviewing the quality of care given to Medicare beneficiaries by hospitals. They did this by undertaking reviews of a sample of all admissions, looking for problems or deficiencies in the quality of care. When problems were found, hospitals and physicians were notified and, depending on the seriousness of the issue, payment could be reduced or denied, the patient could be informed, and the providers could be instructed to take corrective action. This approach was enormously unpopular with hospitals. It imposed large costs upon them, as they had to provide copies of patients' medical records for review and many felt they had to undertake parallel internal reviews of some or even all admissions in an attempt to detect any problems before the PRO. The system for raising and investigating problems was adversarial and punitive, hospitals often complained that PRO reviewers were inexpert and did not understand the cases they reviewed, while PRO reviewers often believed that hospitals were unwilling to acknowledge problems existed or to tackle them (Institute of Medicine 1990; Feldman and Rundall 1993). The PROs took a largely deterrence-oriented approach to their mission and, as a result, the relationships between PROs and hospitals were often very poor.

In 1992, the job of the PRO network was changed once again, in recognition of these problems and in response to an influential Institute of Medicine report on the Medicare PRO programme and quality assurance (Institute of Medicine 1990; Jencks and Wilensky 1992). Although they kept their names, they now became tasked with supporting quality improvement in hospitals through a series of collaborative quality improvement projects on specific topics. Currently, hospitals are invited (not compelled) to participate in these quality improvement projects and the PRO plays a facilitative, networking role, helping hospitals to collect data and compare performance (AHQA 1999, 2000). Although the PROs still have some more regulatory responsibilities, undertaking case reviews to detect quality of care problems and to screen for potential fraud and abuse, their whole approach has been changed from deterrence to compliance (AHQA 1999).

Summarizing hospital regulation

The American Hospitals Association believes that US hospitals are over-regulated, a viewpoint with which it is difficult to disagree.

It argues that hospitals have to deal with over 30 different regulatory agencies at the federal government level, let alone further regulation by states and by non-governmental agencies like the Joint Commission on the Accreditation of Healthcare Organizations. It points out that the regulations governing Medicare and Medicaid are very complex (over 130,000 pages of rules and instructions, three times the length of the federal tax code) and cites a host of examples of apparently pointless regulation and burdensome paperwork. In a case study of an elderly patient admitted with a fractured hip after falling, it detailed a welter of forms to fill, records to submit, authorizations to seek and data to collect for various regulators and estimated what proportion of care providers' time was spent on these administrative tasks. In emergency departments it was 50 per cent, in inpatient surgery 37 per cent, in nursing homes 33 per cent and in home health care 44 per cent (AHA 2001).

The overlapping roles and responsibilities of different governmental regulators and the combination of both governmental and non-governmental regulation are very costly, and almost inevitably result in duplications of effort and conflicts of direction between different regulators. Despite this huge investment in regulation, it is remarkably difficult to tell what impact hospital regulation has had on the performance of hospitals or on the quality of healthcare. There have been few evaluative studies that might be used to assess both the costs and benefits of these different regulatory regimes, and to inform future regulatory developments (Walshe and Shortell, submitted).

REGULATING HEALTH PLANS

When straightforward fee-for-service insurance predominated in US healthcare, the regulation of health insurance was primarily a state responsibility, undertaken largely by state agencies which also regulated other forms of insurance and whose primary concern was the financial solvency and stability of insurers. Today, that simple fee-for-service model has been replaced by a variety of different models of managed care – from integrated health maintenance organizations, through point of service and preferred provider organizations, to other kinds of networks – and a range of different funding mechanisms. The distinctions between different types and forms of health plan have become increasingly complex and blurred, and the systems for regulation have, perhaps consequently, grown to be equally complicated, fragmented and difficult to understand and navigate. The questions of who regulates a health plan and how they do it can only be answered if you know who is purchasing the health cover, for whom it is purchased, how it is funded or paid for, and what kind of organization is providing the cover (Fuchs 1997). There are still three main levels of regulation – federal, state and non-governmental – which are summarized in Table 3.4, but at each level there are multiple, overlapping forms of regulatory provision. This section describes each in turn.

Federal regulation of health plans

The Centers for Medicare and Medicaid Services (CMS) is the main federal agency involved in regulating health plans. It does this in two ways. First, as the agency charged with overseeing Medicare and Medicaid, it regulates managed care organizations that serve Medicare and Medicaid beneficiaries. Once, Medicare and Medicaid were both wholly fee-for-service programmes, but in the last decade beneficiaries have been encouraged to move into Medicare and Medicaid managed care programmes, which often provide a bit more cover in exchange for some restrictions on access. Medicare and Medicaid have become among the largest purchasers of managed care. The CMS regulates health plans that contract with Medicare and Medicaid, just as it regulates hospitals, nursing homes and other providers who participate in these programmes (Iglehart 1999b,c, 2001).

Secondly, CMS has responsibility under federal legislation – the Health Maintenance Organization Act 1973 and the Health Insurance Portability and Accountability Act 1996 – for regulating some aspects of all health plans. The Health Maintenance Organization Act 1973 was intended to encourage the development of health maintenance organizations by providing them with some financial and other advantages if they met some standards and became 'federally qualified', and it laid down some standards for charges, service provision and access, fiscal stability, enrolment procedures and premium setting. Plans do not have to apply to be federally qualified (about 45 per cent of plans are), but CMS manages the regulatory process for qualification. The more recent Health Insurance Portability and Accountability Act 1996 (HIPAA) established federal minimum health insurance standards which apply to all insurers and plans, and which do things like limiting the use of pre-existing condition restrictions on coverage, guaranteeing availability of coverage to individuals and small employers, and requiring some specific forms of cover for maternity and mental health services. Again, CMS is the main agency responsible for regulating health plans' compliance with HIPAA (Fuchs 1997).

However, the federal Department of Labor is also an important federal regulator of health plans, through the provisions of the confusingly named Employee Retirement Income Security Act 1974 (ERISA). This legislation was brought in to provide some consistency across states in the provision of employee welfare benefits like pensions, but it also covers 'self-insured' or employer-sponsored health plans, where the employer retains some or all of the risk rather than just passing it to an insurer by buying an insurance product for its employees. The ERISA trumps state legislation, preventing states from making laws to regulate such health plans, and sets out standards for plans across a range of areas, including fiduciary and financial standards, reporting and disclosure requirements, non-discrimination, provision for independent claims review, and continuation of cover when employment changes. The differences between insured and self-insured employer health plans used to be quite clear, but the growth of managed care has narrowed the distinction and made it possible for employers to structure their plans to fit ERISA and so be exempt from state regulation – an attractive prospect, especially for employers who operate across multiple states, or in states which have tough local regulatory standards (Fuchs 1997; Copeland and Pierron 1999). About 73 per cent of people with employer-provided health cover are in health plans regulated through ERISA.

There is one more federal agency with a hand in health plan regulation, the Office for Personnel Management, which runs the widely admired Federal Employees Health Benefits Program (FEHBP) and provides health cover to federal employees, retirees and their families. The FEHBP is the nation's largest employer-sponsored health plan and the Office for Personnel Management is itself responsible for setting standards for participation and ensuring they are met (Ignagni 1999).

In practice, these federal agencies exercise their regulatory control in quite different ways. The CMS regulates health plans within Medicare and Medicaid through a process akin to that for regulating other entities within those two programmes – it produces conditions of participation and surveys health plans periodically to assess whether they meet those conditions. The CMS takes a less directive approach to its regulatory responsibilities under the Health

Maintenance Organization Act and HIPAA, relying mainly on state insurance regulators to certify that state laws or regulations are 'HIPAA equivalent', and only directly intervening where this is not the case or where there are complaints or cause for concern (GAO 2001a). Similarly, the Department of Labor traditionally relies on complaints from consumers to enforce ERISA, although in recent years it has moved towards undertaking random reviews of a proportion of employer-sponsored health plans every year. Its approach to enforcement is equally low-key. Although about a quarter of reviewed plans have some kind of violation of ERISA or HIPAA standards, they are generally resolved by raising the matter with the employer and seeking voluntary correction. Although the Department of Labor has the power to take legal action and seek the imposition of an additional tax on non-compliant employers, it has not needed to do so (GAO 2001).

State regulation of health plans in California

All states have their own laws under which they regulate health plans, although it should be noted that a substantial number of health plans escape state scrutiny through the federal provisions under the Employee Retirement Income Security Act 1974 (ERISA) outlined above. Often, the regulatory role is split between the state department of insurance, which oversees the financial solvency and stability of health plans, and the state department of health, which deals with healthcare provision, quality, access, complaints and other issues. There is some commonality across states – the National Association of Insurance Commissioners has produced model insurance laws and regulations which 29 states have taken up in whole or in part, and which cover areas such as licensure, access to services, quality assurance, financial solvency, grievance procedures and utilization review. But many states have enacted additional legislation which reflects the growing public and political dissatisfaction with some aspects of managed care. For example, 28 states have laws requiring health plans to give women direct access to obstetricians/gynaecologists; 39 states have laws prohibiting the use of 'gag clauses' which stop physicians discussing treatment options with patients; six states prohibit the use of physician financial incentive arrangements and ten require that any such arrangements be disclosed; and 36 states have laws which mandate minimum lengths of stay for specific procedures, such as childbirth or mastectomy (Fuchs 1997).

The ability of health plans to evade state regulation through the provisions of ERISA has been a continuing source of frustration for state legislators and consumer groups, who argue that a substantial proportion of people with employer-provided health insurance are thus left without proper regulatory protection and support. For example, ERISA effectively prevents those patients suing their health plan even if they suffer an obvious and grievous wrong through, for example, being denied necessary healthcare services. The regulatory limitations of ERISA were one motivation for the passing of the Health Insurance Portability and Accountability Act 1996 (HIPAA) and they continue to fuel calls for a patient bill of rights that would 'federalize' health plan regulation (Finkelstein *et al.* 1995; Pollack 1999).

The picture of overlapping, multidimensional health plan regulation which emerges at a federal level is mirrored at a state level, as the following description of state regulation in California illustrates. California is one of the states in which managed care emerged first and in which it has become most established as the dominant model for healthcare provision (Robinson 1999, 2001a,b; Rosenthal *et al.* 2001). Unsurprisingly, it was also one of the first states to enact comprehensive health plan regulation in the Knox-Keene Health Care Service Plan Act 1975. Until relatively recently, the state Department of Corporations was responsible for regulating health plans under the Knox-Keene Act, which contained a range of regulatory provisions on financial standards, contracting processes, quality assurance, grievance and appeals mechanisms, marketing activities and mandatory minimum benefits. It required health plans to file extensive documentation on their arrangements for providing care in order to get and maintain licensure, and gave plan members a range of consumer protections, including the right of appeal to the Department of Corporations. At the same time, the state Department of Insurance was responsible for regulating health insurers and preferred provider organizations and the state Department of Health Services had oversight of Medicare and Medicaid health plans.

In 2000, a review by an independent task force concluded that state regulation of health plans in California was fragmented and uneven, with some entities facing little or no regulatory oversight while others underwent much more rigorous scrutiny. It made over 100 recommendations aimed at strengthening oversight of managed care in California and, in the resulting reorganization, a new state Department of Managed Health Care was created with the intention that it should lead the regulation of health plans and related entities and provide a powerful new focus for effective state-level regulation (Little Hoover Commission 1998; Singer and Enthoven 1999).

The Department of Managed Health Care came into being in 2000, tasked with 'work[ing] towards an accountable and viable managed health care delivery system that promotes healthier Californians' (Department of Managed Health Care 2001). It took over the regulatory responsibilities for health plans from the Department of Corporations and is tasked with developing greater integration in future. However, as Table 3.10 shows, oversight of health plans in California remains fragmented, with four different state agencies playing some part in the regulatory process.

The most obvious area of overlap is in the regulation of preferred provider organizations, whereby those that are run by a managed care entity are regulated by the Department of Managed Health Care, while those that are part of an indemnity insurer are regulated by the Department of Insurance. The two regulators have different legal powers under state law and have quite different standards

Table 3.10 State governmental regulation of managed care organizations and health insurers in California

Regulator:	Department of Health Services	Department of Managed Health Care	Department of Insurance	Managed Risk Medical Insurance Board
Who it regulates:	Health plans participating in MediCal (the state's Medicaid programme). Also regulates fee-for-service MediCal and all health care facilities and providers	Licensed health care service plans (health maintenance organizations) and preferred provider organization/point-of-service products administered by licensed health care service plans	Preferred provider organizations, which are not administered by a licensed health care service plan, and indemnity insurers. Also regulates any other health insurers	Health plans participating in Healthy Families (S-CHIP) and Access for Infants and Mothers programme

in many areas, including solvency, consumer complaints, quality assurance, marketing, contracting and benefits provided. They are even charged differently for their regulatory licence and pay tax differently (ACLHIC 2001).

Non-governmental regulation of health plans: NCQA and JCAHO

Two main non-governmental organizations regulate health plans, the National Committee for Quality Assurance (NCQA) and the ubiquitous Joint Commission on the Accreditation of Health Care Organizations (JCAHO). The NCQA is the dominant force in health plan accreditation, while JCAHO's presence in this area is more limited.

The NCQA was created in the 1980s by the emerging managed care industry, in part as a response to the threat of external, federal regulation. For the first few years of its existence, NCQA made little headway either in persuading managed care organizations of the value of external review or in convincing the public that it was an effective regulator of the industry which had created it. However, in 1990, the managed care organizations which had founded NCQA took the remarkable step of making it independent. The NCQA board was reconstituted, with a much wider range of membership, including consumers, employers and other major healthcare purchasers, and other stakeholders. Managed care organizations, which had dominated the board, were now in the minority. As managed care grew during the 1990s, NCQA grew rapidly too. It was successful in building a coalition of support for its work among health plans, providers, professional groups, healthcare purchasers, consumer groups and government, and in asserting its independence from the managed care industry (Iglehart 1996).

The NCQA began by developing an accreditation process for health plans, but then moved on to create a set of standardized performance measures for health plans (the Health Plan Employer Data and Information Set, HEDIS), which it subsequently extended to include a range of measures of plan members' views of their health plans (the Consumer Assessment of Health Plans Survey, CAHPS). These two initiatives are now partially integrated, in that all plans undergoing accreditation are required to take part in the HEDIS initiative, and HEDIS data are used in the accreditation process. However, some health plans choose to take part in HEDIS without undergoing full NCQA accreditation, and the HEDIS data set is used independently by some healthcare purchasers and funders

(NCQA 2000, 2001). The NCQA accreditation process is described in Table 3.11, using the same evaluative framework as before.

The regulatory stance of NCQA is largely compliance-oriented, although it constantly stresses its independence from the managed care industry and its commitment to the consumer. It provides regulatory direction through its published accreditation manuals (NCQA 2002a,b), which contain about 60 standards in five main areas: access to care and services; provider qualifications and credentialing; health promotion; acute care management; and chronic care management. In each of these areas, several measures from the HEDIS data set are integrated into the process of accreditation alongside the assessment of the accreditation standards. Although HEDIS data are collected from accredited organizations on an ongoing basis and are published annually, the main mechanism for regulatory detection is the NCQA survey visit, which usually takes place once every 3 years.

Health plans know well in advance when their accreditation visit will take place and prepare for it carefully. The NCQA survey team usually consists of two physicians and two managers, all with recent or current experience of working in a managed care organization. About 10 per cent of surveyors work full-time for NCQA; these surveyors tend to be used in particular on training or complex surveys. The rest are part-time and will generally be working in a health plan elsewhere; they undertake about four surveys a year each and their organizations are reimbursed for releasing them to take part. For health plans, there are considerable advantages in having a member of their senior staff involved in NCQA surveying because of the detailed knowledge of the process which they can then contribute when the organization undergoes its own accreditation survey. New surveyors undertake a brief training programme and several training surveys before being allowed to work as qualified surveyors. All surveyors come together once a year for an annual meeting and training session.

The survey visit takes 4–5 days, during which the surveyors have a series of meetings with senior executives, plan staff, board members and participating provider organizations and professionals. They also undertake direct reviews of a small sample of patient records. They report back provisionally to the organization on its performance at the end of the visit, but the information they gather is then processed to provide the formal accreditation report from NCQA 2–3 months later. There are five categories of accreditation outcome, listed in Table 3.12, from excellence through to denial of

Table 3.11 A regulatory analysis of NCQA health plan accreditation

Characteristic	Analysis of NCQA accreditation of health plans
Regulating organization	The National Committee for Quality Assurance (NCQA) is an independent, private sector, not-for-profit organization, which has no formal legal powers or authority over health plans. It was established by bodies which now form the American Association of Health Plans in 1979, and became independent of them in 1990. It is governed by a board, the majority of whose members represent purchasers of healthcare, health plans or consumers. There is considerable market pressure on health plans to have NCQA accreditation, and it is increasingly deemed by states and the federal government to meet some or all of their certification and licensing requirements
Regulatory goals/objectives	NCQA sees its mission as 'to improve the quality of healthcare delivered to people everywhere' by 'becoming the most trusted source of information driving healthcare quality improvement'
Scope of regulation	NCQA accredits managed care organizations or health plans. About 460 plans (or half of the total number of plans and most of the larger ones) have accreditation. NCQA's oversight covers almost all areas of plan performance
Regulatory model	Generally mainly compliance-oriented, with little recourse to enforcement, but emphasizes independence and objectivity of scrutiny. Focus of accreditation process is on quality improvement and organizational systems and processes, but HEDIS measures provide a harder quantitative component of assessment
Direction	NCQA maintains an accreditation manual for health plans with around 60 standards in five main areas. It also maintains the HEDIS (Health Plan Employer Data and Information Set) measures, a set of quantitative measures of health plan performance
Detection	Three yearly accreditation visits to health plans, usually involving a team of four people for 4–5 days. Main focus on interviews and meetings but also review some sample records. Annual monitoring through the HEDIS measures, which can trigger an early accreditation visit if problems are detected

Table 3.11—*continued*

Characteristic	Analysis of NCQA accreditation of health plans
Enforcement	Accreditation visit results in denial of accreditation in less than 1 per cent of cases. Accreditation outcome is made public, but report is confidential to health plan. HEDIS data are published for most organizations (although this is voluntary)

Table 3.12 Outcomes of NCQA accreditation

Level of accreditation	Definition	Impact on organization and future NCQA action
Excellent	For health plans that meet or exceed NCQA's accreditation standards and achieve HEDIS measures	Organization can use results in marketing. Re-survey in 3 years
Commendable	For health plans that meet or exceed NCQA's accreditation standards	Organization can use results in marketing. Re-survey in 3 years
Accredited	For health plans that meet most of NCQA's accreditation standards	Organization can use results in marketing. Re-survey in 2–3 years
Provisional	For health plans that meet some but not all of NCQA's accreditation standards	Organization can continue to say it has NCQA accreditation but will face early review of performance to check improvements made
Denied	For health plans that do not meet NCQA's accreditation standards	For some organizations, denial will result in major efforts to change and a resubmission, or in management changes such as a takeover/change of ownership

accreditation. Few organizations score at either end of the spectrum (1 per cent or less of accreditation surveys result in a denial); the most common outcomes are commendable accreditation or simple accreditation. The accreditation results are published by NCQA, although the detail of the report remains confidential between the health plan and NCQA.

The NCQA accredits about 460 health plans from 340 different organizations across the USA. Coverage varies from region to region – about 40 per cent of plans in the southern states have accreditation, while 69 per cent of plans in the north east are accredited (NCQA 2001, 2002a). This level of coverage was achieved largely through market pressures on health plans from healthcare funders and purchasers like large employers, who often require health plans to have NCQA accreditation to compete for their business. However, just as the JCAHO hospital accreditation programme has been adopted by governmental regulators through 'deemed status', so too has NCQA's health plan accreditation programme. About 18 states accept NCQA accreditation as part of their state regulatory arrangements for health plans, and a small number actually require health plans to have NCQA accreditation. More recently, NCQA accreditation has been given 'deemed status' by the Centers for Medicare and Medicaid Services (CMS) for the federal Medicare+ Choice programme, which is the managed care component of Medicare. This means that health plans taking part in Medicare+ Choice will be largely exempted from CMS's certification process if they have NCQA accreditation, a potentially valuable benefit (NCQA 2001).

However, the changes in managed care itself, and particularly the popular backlash against managed care organizations, have affected NCQA and forced it to diversify. The NCQA has found itself cast as the defender of the quality of managed care, arguing to a sceptical public and political audience that managed care organizations do a better job of delivering healthcare than traditional, fee-for-service indemnity insurers. Although the data suggest this may well be true, the public's perception of managed care organizations as greedy, profit-seeking corporations that make their money by scrimping and saving on healthcare costs and denying patients access to necessary health services is difficult to change (Barron 1999). Increasingly, patients have turned away from traditional managed care organizations (like staff-model, integrated health maintenance organizations that aim to provide most health services through a tightly managed and integrated single organization) towards more loosely coupled models such as preferred provider organizations, in which patients can choose their own healthcare providers from a network of participating hospitals, physicians and other facilities, and can even go outside that network if they really want to. Preferred Provider Organizations make less use of the access controls and utilization management techniques that characterize managed care, and often pay providers through a combination of capitation and fee-for-service arrangements. The NCQA has responded by developing an accreditation process for preferred provider organizations, although it has been difficult to adapt standards that were designed for integrated service delivery organizations, and that presumed the existence of corporate structures and mechanisms, and get them to work with network-based organizations like Preferred Provider Organizations, in which those structures and mechanisms are absent. It has also moved to accredit other entities like medical groups, physician associations and pharmacy benefit management organizations.

The JCAHO has a broadly similar approach to health plan accreditation, which is clearly modelled on its approach to accrediting hospitals (see pp. 58–65) and nursing homes (see pp. 99–101). It has developed standards for health care networks, a term it uses to describe a range of models of health maintenance organizations and point of service systems, and it too has a separate but linked set of standards for preferred provider organizations. It publishes a comprehensive accreditation manual for each of these, and its survey, scoring and accreditation processes are essentially the same as those used in hospital accreditation. The JCAHO accreditation process for health plans does not make use of the HEDIS data set, but it does involve visits not only to the health plan itself but also to a selection of healthcare providers or facilities within the plan's network. As has already been noted, the JCAHO programme of health plan accreditation has not achieved the same market coverage and acceptance that NCQA has, and it is not used in governmental regulation through deeming to anywhere near the same extent.

Summarizing health plan regulation

If the arrangements for US hospital regulation described earlier seemed complex and prone to duplication, the regulation of health plans makes them seem simple and straightforward by comparison. For regulators, health plans, healthcare providers and especially for patients, the systems of federal, state and non-governmental health plan regulation described above add up to a confusing mess of different and conflicting regulatory requirements. For ordinary patients, simple questions like what right of appeal against a decision by my health plan do I have, or how do I make a complaint about my health plan, or what services and treatments is my health plan required to provide, are remarkably difficult to answer. It all depends on what kind of health plan it is, who regulates it and how it is regulated. For health plans themselves, the different and conflicting demands of different regulators create a considerable workload. A health plan provider will often have several different products – a health maintenance organization product, a preferred provider organization product, a Medicare+ Choice plan and so on – each of which can be regulated by a different regulator with different standards that the health plan has to follow. For healthcare providers such as hospitals or physician groups, which may be contracted to work with quite a number of health plans, each plan makes separate and different demands for information to meet its own regulatory requirements. Each plan may impose different sets of guidelines, protocols, formularies and other controls, and the provider is expected to be familiar with them all.

In the future, health plan regulation may become less important as the form and function of managed care changes. The rise of looser, network-based forms of managed care (like preferred provider organizations) means that health plans increasingly draw on a common pool of providers like hospitals and physician groups or associations. Differentiating between health plans on the basis of health care provision thus becomes less meaningful, and health plans are less likely to have the corporate structures and management mechanisms to manage provider performance. As a result, attention may shift back towards regulating providers more directly, rather than via health plans.

REGULATING NURSING HOMES

Over 1.6 million Americans live in nursing homes, most of whom are elderly and whose health problems mean they can no longer live independently or be cared for in their own home. Many are frail and vulnerable individuals who are likely to live out the remainder of their lives in a nursing home. Because of their physical or mental infirmity and their dependence on their nursing home caregivers, they are often not well placed to act as assertive, well-informed con-sumers. In 1999, the US spent about $90 billion a year on nursing home care (about $55,900 for each resident), with most of the cost

(60 per cent) being borne by states and the federal government through the Medicare and Medicaid programmes (Heffler *et al.* 2001). There are about 1.8 million nursing home places in over 17,000 nursing homes, the great majority of which (93 per cent) are operated in the private sector, most of them by for-profit organizations, including a growing number of large corporations that own or operate networks of hundreds of nursing homes with thousands of residents (AHCA 1999; Harrington *et al.* 2000).

As Table 3.3 shows, nursing homes, like hospitals and health plans, are regulated by both governmental regulators at a state and federal level, and by non-governmental regulators like the Joint Commission on the Accreditation of Healthcare Organizations (JCAHO). However, while hospital regulation is dominated by a non-governmental agency (JCAHO), nursing home regulation is primarily carried out by the state and federal government agencies. This section first describes these governmental regulatory arrangements and then examines non-governmental regulation.

State and federal regulation of nursing homes

Public concern about the quality of care in nursing homes can be traced back at least to the 1950s. Before the establishment of the Medicare and Medicaid programmes in 1965, there were essentially no federal standards regulating nursing homes, regulation was left up to the states and standards varied widely. Although federal regulations were enacted once the Medicare and Medicaid programmes began to pay for nursing home care, they were inadequate in design, poorly implemented and often unenforced by the federal Health Care Financing Administration (HCFA) and the state agencies which shared responsibility for nursing home regulation. A succession of studies in the 1970s and early 1980s (Mendelson 1974; Moss and Halamandaris 1977; Vladeck 1980) highlighted continuing serious problems with the quality of care, and were one reason why Congress asked the Institute of Medicine in 1984 to investigate and make recommendations for reform (Hawes 1996).

The Institute of Medicine's 1986 report outlined proposals for a comprehensive and radical reform of regulatory arrangements (Institute of Medicine 1986). The standards for nursing homes were to be revised, to make them more focused on the quality of care, more detailed and comprehensive in their coverage, and more explicit about the rights of residents in nursing homes. The survey or inspection process used to check compliance with the standards was also to be reformed, to make it less oriented towards paper records and structures and more focused on direct observation of care and communication with residents. A much broader range of enforcement mechanisms was to be introduced, including financial penalties, blocks on payment for new admissions or all residents, provisions to take over the management of failing homes and, ultimately, termination of participation in Medicare/Medicaid. These reforms passed Congress with broad bipartisan support and were enacted as the Nursing Homes Reform Act, part of the Omnibus Budget Reconciliation Act (OBRA) in 1987 (Jost 1990).

It took the HCFA 3 years to put into operation the regulations to implement OBRA and 7 years to implement the regulations needed to implement its regulatory enforcement mechanisms. Over that time, political support for the OBRA reforms slackened and a number of proposals were brought forward in Congress in the mid-1990s aimed at repealing or weakening nursing home regulation, but none were successful (Hawes 1997). Even once the reforms were in place, a succession of General Accounting Office reports highlighted continuing quality of care problems in nursing homes and significant flaws in the implementation of OBRA and the management of nursing home regulation by HCFA (GAO 1999a,b,c,d, 2000). In response, the Clinton administration launched a nursing homes initiative in 1998 aimed at improving the effectiveness of regulation (Walshe 2001a).

The current regulatory arrangements for nursing homes are summarized in Table 3.13 using the same analytical framework as before. The Centers for Medicare and Medicaid Services is responsible for producing and maintaining the 'conditions of participation', federal regulations with which all homes that wish to participate in Medicare and Medicaid must conform. The state survey, licensing and certification agencies are responsible for surveying or inspecting nursing homes to check their compliance with these regulations, investigating complaints, and reporting the results to CMS. When deficiencies are identified, state agencies and CMS regional offices share responsibility for taking enforcement action to make sure that nursing homes deal with the problem and come back into compliance with the regulations. The CMS funds most of the costs of Medicare/Medicaid certification and oversees the performance of state survey agencies to make sure that the federal regulatory arrangements are implemented appropriately. States also have their own licensing requirements for nursing homes, with which all homes (not just those participating in Medicare and Medicaid) must conform. State nursing home regulations may parallel or exceed the

Table 3.13 A regulatory analysis of federal and state nursing home regulation

Characteristic	Centers for Medicare and Medicaid Services (CMS) and state licensing and certification agencies (such as, in California, the Department of Health Services, Licensing and Certification Division)
Regulating organization	CMS and the state survey agencies (such as the California Department of Health Services) are jointly responsible for regulating nursing homes. The federal Nursing Homes Act 1987, state legislation, and extensive federal and state regulations provide these agencies with their formal legal powers and authority. CMS is responsible to the Department of Health and Human Services and to Congress; the state survey agencies are responsible to CMS for implementing the federal regulatory regime (which CMS funds and contracts with them to do) and are responsible to state governments and legislatures for implementing state provisions
Regulatory goals/ objectives	CMS/state agencies aim to 'promote the timely and economic delivery of appropriate quality of care [and] efficiency and quality within the total health care delivery system'
Scope of regulation	There are about 17,000 nursing homes in the USA that are licensed and certified by state agencies on behalf of CMS. The regulators have broad oversight across most areas of nursing home performance. It should be noted that state agencies also have oversight of nursing homes which do not participate in Medicare/Medicaid
Regulatory model	Generally deterrence-oriented, with a strong focus on identifying deficiencies, penalties and sanctions. The survey process is highly specified and structured. Surveyors are not allowed to offer nursing homes education, advice or developmental support
Direction	The Health Care Financing Administration's *State Operations Manual* sets out the Conditions of Participation for Medicare/Medicaid and outlines in detail the arrangements for surveys and enforcement. In addition, many states have their own, separate legislation and regulations

Characteristic	CMS/state licensing and certification agencies
Detection	Annual certification surveys of nursing homes, usually involving a 3–4 day visit to the organization by a 3–4 person surveyor team. Surveys are all unannounced, can start at any time and focus on identifying and categorizing 'deficiencies' (areas where the Conditions of Participation are not met)
Enforcement	Only 18% of nursing homes are found to have no deficiencies – on average, each home has about six identified deficiencies at survey. They are graded according to severity. Homes can be required to put the problem right and may face other sanctions, including financial penalties, denial of payment, closure to new admissions, imposition of temporary management and, ultimately, delicensing/removal from Medicare/Medicaid

federal requirements and generally have separate provisions for licensing nursing homes, undertaking surveys or inspections, investigating complaints, identifying deficiencies and taking enforcement action.

The requirements of the CMS certification process are set out in great detail in the CMS *State Operations Manual* (HCFA 2000), which attempts to specify exactly almost every aspect of the conditions of participation and the survey process. The manual is several thousand pages long; Table 3.14 provides an example of how just one of the 185 regulations is defined at some length.

Before 1987, American nursing home regulation was widely criticized for doing too little to deal with persistent poor performance and widespread and longstanding quality problems. While approaches varied from state to state, many regulators used a compliance model (Klein 1987). It was felt that some nursing homes flouted the regulations with impunity, regulators did not have sufficient powers to deal with such offenders, and so the whole process of regulation was brought into disrepute (Institute of Medicine 1986). Since the implementation of the OBRA reforms, nursing home regulation in the USA has developed most of the features of deterrence regulation – with great stress placed on developing and applying formal, written regulations, undertaking inspections or surveys, recording deficiencies and issuing citations, and enforcing regulation through the use of sanctions like civil money penalties,

Table 3.14 An example of the Medicare conditions of participation for nursing homes

Regulation:	*Privacy and confidentiality:* The resident has the right to personal privacy and confidentiality of his or her personal and clinical records
Definition	1. Personal privacy includes accommodations, medical treatment, written and telephone communications, personal care, visits, and meetings of family and resident groups but this does not require the facility to provide a private room for each resident
	2. Except as provided in paragraph (e)(3) of this section the resident may approve or refuse the release of personal and clinical records to any individual outside the facility
	3. The resident's right to refuse release of personal and clinical records does not apply when (i) the resident is transferred to another healthcare institution or (ii) record release is required by law
Guidance to surveyors	'Right to privacy' means that the resident has the right to privacy with *whomever* the resident wishes to be private and that this privacy should include full visual and, to the extent desired for visits or other activities, auditory privacy. Private space may be created flexibly and need not be dedicated solely for visitation purposes
	For example, privacy for visitation or meetings might be arranged by using a dining area between meals, a vacant chapel, office or room, or an activities area when activities are not in progress. Arrangements for private space could be accomplished through co-operation between the facility's administration and resident and family groups so that private space is provided for those requesting it without infringement on the rights of other residents

With the exception of the explicit requirement for privacy curtains in all initially certified facilities (see §483.70(d)(1)(v)) the facility is free to innovate to provide privacy for its residents, as exemplified in the preceding paragraph. This may, but need not, be through the provision of a private room

Facility staff must examine and treat residents in a manner that maintains the privacy of their bodies. A resident must be granted privacy when going to the bathroom and in other activities of personal hygiene. If an individual requires assistance, authorized staff should respect the individual's need for privacy. Only authorized staff directly involved in treatment should be present without the individual's consent while he/she is being examined or treated. Staff should pull privacy curtains, close doors or otherwise remove residents from public view and provide clothing or draping to prevent unnecessary exposure of body parts during the provision of personal care and services

Personal and clinical records include all types of records the facility might keep on a resident, whether they are medical, social, fund accounts, automated etc.

Additional guidelines on mail, visitation rights and telephone communication are addressed in §483.10(i), (j) and (k). See §483.70(d)(1)(iv) for full visual privacy around beds

Procedures   Document any instances where you observe a resident's privacy being violated. Completely document how the resident's privacy was violated (eg 'Resident #12 left without gown or bed covers and unattended') and where and when this occurred (eg '2B corridor 3.30pm February 25'). If possible, identify the responsible party

---

Source: Centers for Medicare and Medicaid Services *State Operations Manual*, Appendix PP.

denials of payment or decertification. It is therefore unsurprising that it suffers the problems of deterrence regulation, such as strained relationships between the various players in regulation, a defensive and uncooperative response to regulation from nursing home providers and high regulatory costs. Despite its overt deterrence orientation, nursing home regulation still appears to be relatively ineffective at dealing with many problems of persistent poor performance (Walshe 2001a).

Although there have been many studies of the implementation of nursing home regulation and the management of regulatory arrangements (ABT Associates 1998; OIG 1999b,c), these reports are of limited help in determining what impact regulation has had on nursing home performance and on the quality of nursing home care. The impact of nursing home regulation has received little attention (Kapp 2000), in part perhaps because it presents several methodological challenges. First, the absence of any control or comparison group (since virtually all nursing homes are regulated) means that we can only really study changes in quality over time, and attempt to determine whether those changes can be attributed to regulatory interventions. There are many potential confounders to such studies, which make determining association, let alone causation, difficult. Secondly, much of the data available on the quality of care in nursing homes is a product of the regulatory process itself, which means that changes in the regulatory process affect the data, and are difficult to distinguish from underlying changes in the quality of care. For example, changes in the deficiency rates found in nursing home surveys over time or variations in these rates across states may result from differences in the stringency, scope or implementation of the survey process, or from real differences in the quality of care, and it is not possible to disentangle the two (Harrington and Carillo 1999; Walshe and Harrington 2002). Thirdly, the reliability, validity, completeness and timeliness of much of the routinely available data (such as the MDS data collected on every nursing home resident, and the OSCAR database of survey findings) have been questioned, and caution is needed in using them (Kane 1998).

Nevertheless, there is some evidence that the quality of care in nursing homes has improved significantly in many areas over the past 10–15 years, and that at least some of that improvement has been brought about by the OBRA regulatory reforms (ABT Associates 1998; Kapp 2000; Institute of Medicine 2001). For example, the inappropriate use of physical and chemical restraints has declined, as have rates of urinary incontinence and catheterization.

Hospitalization rates for nursing home residents (which may be a good proxy for quality of nursing home care if poor care increases the risk of hospitalization) have also fallen. On the other hand, pressure sore rates have not changed, malnutrition, dehydration and other feeding problems remain relatively common, and rates of bowel incontinence have risen slightly.

Most stakeholders in nursing home regulation – such as HCFA and the state survey agencies, nursing home providers, consumer groups, researchers and independent governmental evaluators – would concur that the OBRA reforms have brought some improvements in the quality of nursing home care, but beyond that opinions fall broadly into two camps. Some think that because many quality problems still exist, regulation should be tightened with tougher standards and more aggressive enforcement, and they argue for more frequent inspections, more use of sanctions and penalties, and the more uniform and rigorous application of existing regulatory arrangements. Others believe that the current regulatory burden is already too great, and that regulation has created a punitive adversarial climate that is antipathetic to quality improvement. They argue that regulation should be simplified and reduced, focused mainly on a smaller number of 'problem' nursing homes, and re-orientated towards a model based on cooperation and partnership between regulators and regulated organizations. There is little consensus among stakeholders about whether the benefits of nursing home regulation over the last decade outweigh its considerable costs. The debate about nursing home regulation has become polarized and politicized and, in the absence of robust empirical evidence on the effectiveness of regulation, it is likely to remain so (Walshe 2001a).

The long-term care ombudsman programme

Introduced in 1972 as a pilot initiative, the long-term care ombudsman programme is a federally led programme run by the Administration on Aging, part of the Department of Health and Human Services. It supports a long-term care ombudsman's office in every state. These are generally based within state agencies concerned with ageing, but in some cases are free-standing not-for-profit entities, or part of a larger state government ombudsman function. The main functions of the ombudsman programme are: to identify, investigate and resolve complaints about long-term care made by or on behalf of residents; to provide information to residents and to educate and inform residents, families and the public about issues concerning long-term care; to represent residents' interests and to undertake advocacy in policy development and implementation; and to promote public involvement in long-term care through resident and family councils and other forms of citizen participation (Administration on Aging 1999). The programme costs about $47 million, 58 per cent of which comes from the federal government and the rest from state sources. While there are 927 paid ombudsman programme staff, much of the work is done by unpaid volunteers, of whom there are over 13,000 (Administration on Aging 1999).

Much of the work of the ombudsman programme is focused on dealing with the individual problems and concerns of residents and their families. They handle over 200,000 individual complaints a year, most commonly about unheeded requests for assistance for residents, neglected personal hygiene, poor handling or accidents, lack of respect for residents, poor staff attitudes and physical abuse. However, they also visit nursing homes regularly, take part in surveys undertaken by the state survey agencies, help to set up and run resident and family councils at nursing homes, provide training and consultation for both consumer and provider groups, and work on the development of policy in long-term care.

The long-term care ombudsman programme is widely acknowledged to have been an important force in improving the quality of long-term care. An evaluation by the Institute of Medicine found that the regular on-site presence of ombudsman programme volunteers in nursing homes had been effective in building awareness of the programme, detecting and dealing with residents' problems before they become serious, and promoting good working relationships with nursing home staff and management, but suggested that the programme was underfunded and needed more resources to do its job properly (Institute of Medicine 1995).

From a regulatory perspective, the ombudsman programme appears to represent a very different and innovative approach to governmental regulation of healthcare. First, by enlisting volunteers and working with resident and family groups, it seems to have achieved a remarkable degree of community engagement – a form of tripartism that gives it far more influence over nursing homes than it could ever have directly through programme staff. Secondly, although the programme has set no explicit standards in published regulations, it has established clear principles of good and poor performance through its work, particularly on individual complaints. By focusing its attention on resident and family complaints about nursing homes, the ombudsman programme is effectively targeting its resources and attention on homes where there appear to be quality problems. Thirdly, the ombudsman programme has no real enforcement powers over nursing homes, yet it seems to be able to get things done and sees most complaints resolved to the complainants' satisfaction. It relies much more on informal influence and dialogue than on any kind of formal sanctions. Fourthly, the ombudsman programme's wider remit to contribute to education, information and policy development in long-term care enables it to play an advocacy role that appears wholly consistent with its regulatory purpose. In some senses, the ombudsman programme can be the kind of regulator that it is because of the existence of the more deterrence-oriented regulatory regime of the Centers for Medicare and Medicaid Services and the state survey agencies, and it could be argued that the two complement each other quite neatly and fulfil quite different regulatory roles. However, their very different approaches and levels of resourcing (the ombudsman programme costs about $47 million a year; the state survey agencies cost about $382 million a year) raise important questions about their relative effectiveness in improving the quality of long-term care.

JCAHO nursing home accreditation

The Joint Commission for the Accreditation of Healthcare Organizations (JCAHO) is the main non-governmental regulator of long-term care. It runs an accreditation programme that is unsurprisingly similar in philosophy, aims, structures and methods to its much larger hospital accreditation programme (which was described earlier and summarized in Table 3.4). There is a comprehensive accreditation manual setting out over 500 standards; JCAHO surveys each nursing home once every 3 years, using a team of surveyors who visit for about a week to assess the home against the JCAHO standards; a report is produced and the home may be accredited fully (with or without some recommendations for changes), conditionally accredited, or not accredited as a result. Most homes get accreditation; only one or two fail to be accredited each year.

No non-governmental nursing home accreditation programmes have been given deemed status by CMS for Medicare or Medicaid or by states for state-level licensing, which means that a nursing home with JCAHO accreditation still has to face exactly the same scrutiny by CMS and the state survey agencies as one that is not accredited. Without this crucial lever to promote participation, the JCAHO nursing home accreditation programme has failed to achieve the kind of market coverage that JCAHO has among acute hospitals. About 1700 (10 per cent) nursing homes have JCAHO accreditation.

Although the Department of Health and Human Services, of which CMS is part, has the necessary legal powers to grant deemed status, there has been considerable longstanding political opposition from consumer groups and state survey agencies to such a move. There is a profound clash of philosophies between the deterrence-oriented, adversarial approach of state and federal regulators, and the compliance-oriented, collaborative approach of JCAHO; their perspectives are summarized in Table 3.15.

Table 3.15 Nursing home regulation: a clash of philosophies

Views of nursing home consumer groups, some trade unions and state survey agencies	*Views of nursing home administrators, provider associations, some professional associations and accrediting bodies*
• The JCAHO accreditation process is weak and ineffective at finding and dealing with quality problems	• The state/federal survey processes are bureaucratic and inflexible
• There are many nursing homes that perform poorly and existing rates of deficiencies suggest most need continuing high level of scrutiny	• Although there are a few poor performers, most nursing homes strive to provide good quality care but this is not acknowledged by the state/federal survey processes
• Most nursing homes are managed as businesses and the professional ethic that might help maintain standards is lacking	• Nursing home management is increasingly professionalized and governed by the codes of conduct and cultural norms of other healthcare organizations
• Private accrediting bodies are insufficiently accountable to the public and to government, and are too closely linked to the providers they are meant to regulate	• Good performers will respond to the educational, developmental model – rewards are needed as well as punishments
• Deeming private accreditation programmes like that of JCAHO would weaken regulation and increase costs	• Deeming private accreditation programmes like that of JCAHO would provide a better system for regulation for most nursing homes

Opponents of deeming see JCAHO as fundamentally compromised by its close relationship with the industry it regulates, and
regard its standards and survey process as insufficiently rigorous.
Supporters of deeming believe that the current CMS and state
survey agency systems of regulation are bureaucratic, costly and
ineffective, and that the accreditation model is more likely to produce
improvement. Neither group has much empirical evidence to back
up its arguments.

LESSONS FROM US HEALTHCARE REGULATION

Three decades of healthcare regulation in the USA have produced
a set of regulatory arrangements that are considerably costly
and complex, for which it is difficult to tell what works (and what
does not), let alone understand how and why different regulators
influence the performance of healthcare organizations. However,
a number of important lessons from the US experience can be
discerned.

First, the costs of regulation are considerable. Table 3.16 sets out
the annual costs of running some of the regulatory agencies that
have been described in this chapter, but it should be remembered
that this is only the tip of the iceberg. Most of the costs of regulation
fall on the regulated organizations and, although there is little
available data, it is likely that they substantially exceed the costs
of the regulatory agencies. The costs of regulation are frequently the
cause of complaint from regulated organizations, but often seem
to be ignored by regulators and researchers into regulation
(Walshe and Shortell, submitted). Yet it is difficult to see how any
meaningful assessment of the benefits or impacts of regulation
on organizational or system performance can be made, without
knowing what it all costs.

Secondly, the interaction of governmental and non-governmental
regulation in the USA offers some important advantages which
deserve further consideration. Non-governmental regulators like the
Joint Commission on the Accreditation of Healthcare Organizations
and the National Committee for Quality Assurance are often acting
on behalf of government, but without some of the corresponding
powers and responsibilities that a government regulator might have.
Freed, for example, from the due process requirements of the
Administrative Procedures Act and the budgetary scrutiny of state
and federal legislatures, non-governmental regulators can act much

Table 3.16 A comparison of the costs of selected US healthcare regulatory agencies

Regulator (and who it regulates)	Annual budget	Number of organizations regulated	Approximate cost per organization
Joint Commission for the Accreditation of Healthcare Organizations (across all its accreditation programmes for various healthcare entities)	$100 million	19,000	$5300
National Committee for Quality Assurance (health plans)	$22.5 million	325	$69,200
California Department of Health Services (30 different types of healthcare entity in the state)	$101 million	6000	$16,800
California Department of Managed Health Care (managed healthcare service plans in the state)	$40 million	123	$325,200
National network of Medicare peer review organizations (all organizations participating in Medicare)	$250 million	—	—
Federal and state agencies regulating nursing homes (all licensed nursing homes)	$382 million	17,000	$22,500
Long-term care ombudsman programme (all licensed nursing homes)	$47 million	17,000	$2800

Note: All costs are 1999 or 2000 budget figures.

more quickly to update and change their regulatory regimes, and can often resource the activity of regulation more generously. Distance from government allows them to assert their independence and frees them from direct political control. However, they lack some of the enforcement powers that a government agency would have, and it can be argued that they are insufficiently accountable and prone to capture by sectional interests. Nevertheless, in some circumstances, it is likely that this form of non-governmental regulation is more efficient and effective than direct governmental regulation.

Thirdly, it is worth considering how the amount of regulatory fragmentation to be found in the USA affects the regulatory process. On the face of it, regulatory fragmentation is a problem because it results in duplication, confusion, waste and conflicting requirements from different regulators. It may have other effects too – weakening regulation because no one regulatory agency knows the full picture of an organization's performance and none has the necessary leverage to drive change and improvement in regulated organizations. In some circumstances, it leads to 'forum shopping', in which regulated organizations arrange their affairs so that they are regulated by the least demanding regulator with the lowest standards. On the other hand, some authors see benefits in fragmentation, because it introduces an element of regulatory competition which may drive regulators to be more responsive to stakeholders' needs and expectations. It can also be argued that some degree of redundancy in the oversight of organizational performance is necessary and even useful, because problems missed by one regulatory agency may be picked up by another.

Fourthly, the growth of healthcare regulation in the USA is an example of what has been called the 'regulatory ratchet effect' (Bardach and Kagan 1982). There are often more incentives and reasons to regulate than there are to deregulate and, even at times when the political climate has been actively hostile to regulation, it has proven remarkably difficult to roll back the frontiers of regulation. In US healthcare, the scope and intensity of regulation has increased steadily over the last two decades, and some of the complexity of current regulatory arrangements results from this process of organic and incremental growth. Despite the frequent protests of regulated organizations, there seems to be little prospect of regulatory reforms that might bring greater coherence through some rationalization, let alone any changes that would bring regulatory relief.

Healthcare regulation in the USA costs billions of dollars each year, but remarkably little is known about the effectiveness of that investment in achieving the objectives of regulation and particularly in bringing about improvements in the performance of healthcare organizations. It was noted at the start of this chapter that, in the absence of much empirical evidence, there is little consensus about the impact or value of regulation. Some see it as an important force for improvement, and a key protection for healthcare consumers and the public; some argue it is often a sham, with regulators and the healthcare industry working too closely for comfort; and some believe it is costly, bureaucratic and prone to stifle improvement and innovation rather than promote it. Without more and better research, it is difficult to tell which, if any, of these perspectives is closest to the truth.

4

REGULATING HEALTHCARE IN THE UNITED KINGDOM

This chapter describes how healthcare regulation in the UK has developed, for both its National Health Service (NHS) and for the private healthcare sector. It first sets the context by providing an overview of the UK healthcare system. It then goes on to explore the current systems of regulation and the regulatory agencies involved, and examines what is known about how regulation works. Because there has been considerable regulatory change in the UK over recent years, and that change is continuing, the chapter first describes how the NHS has been regulated, then explores the recent growth of regulation in the NHS and the arrival of a number of new regulatory agencies. It goes on to examine how private healthcare has been regulated and how those arrangements for regulation have changed. Next, it analyses current developments and the future shape of healthcare regulation. It concludes by drawing out lessons for the future from the UK experience of healthcare regulation.

BRITISH HEALTHCARE AND THE RISE OF REGULATION

The healthcare system in the UK is perhaps the largest central government run, tax-funded, publicly provided health service in the world. Among the developed countries, the UK is unusual in the extent to which healthcare is funded by the state through general taxation, and in the extent of direct state ownership or control of systems of healthcare provision. Table 4.1 provides an overview of the UK healthcare system, using the same structure as Table 3.1, which analysed the US healthcare system. It is evident that it would

Table 4.1 An overview of the UK healthcare system

Expenditure	The UK spends about £78 billion per annum on healthcare for its 60 million population; it is one of the lowest spenders in the OECD in real terms ($1461 per person per annum) and as a proportion of GDP (6.7%). In broad terms, health expenditures are between a third and half of spending levels in the USA
Funding sources	Most healthcare costs are funded directly by government through general taxation – this accounts for 88% of funding. About 8% of costs are met by patients directly through out-of-pocket payments. Private health insurance accounts for the remaining 4% of overall health funding
Coverage	Everyone is covered by the National Health Service (NHS), which provides a wide range of health services and is largely free at the point of use. However, access to services is on the basis of clinical need and some scarce services are rationed through mechanisms like waiting lists or supply constraints. About 12% of the population has some form of private health insurance to supplement NHS provision, which is used mainly for such things as elective surgery
Delivery	The NHS in each of the four countries of the UK (England, Wales, Scotland and Northern Ireland) is organized on broadly similar lines, although there are some differences. In England, the government's Department of Health has overall responsibility for health care provision. It has a network of 28 strategic health authorities, each of which manages health services across a geographic area with a mean population of about 2 million. Each strategic health authority is accountable to the Department of Health and, in turn, manages a network of NHS trusts and primary care trusts – public bodies that run health services. There are around 300 NHS trusts, mostly running acute, tertiary, specialist and mental health services. There are about 300 primary care trusts, running primary care and community-based services, leading on public health and prevention/health promotion, and commissioning acute and other services from around 300 NHS trusts. The private healthcare sector is small, focused on acute care, particularly elective surgery, and contains both for-profit and not-for-profit providers

Usage	Fewest acute hospital beds per population in OECD. Low acute hospital admission rates (1.0 days per person per annum) and average lengths of stay (mean 9.8 days), but slightly higher than average costs ($320 per day). Fewest physician visits per capita per annum (5.9), fewest physicians per 1000 population (1.7) in OECD, and second lowest per capita spending on physicians in OECD ($184 per annum). Fewer coronary bypasses, hysterectomies, dialysis and other acute or high-tech interventions than most other OECD countries
Health statistics	Life expectancy at birth of 79.7 years for females and 74.9 years for males. Infant mortality rate of 5.7 per 1000 births, which is above the OECD median and average rates of mortality in non-aged population. Average or low incidence of breast and prostate cancer, but higher than average mortality

Sources: Anderson and Hussey (2000) and Wanless (2002).

be hard to find two approaches to funding and providing healthcare that were more different.

In international terms, the UK healthcare system is remarkably cheap. The UK is one of the lowest spenders in the OECD, both in absolute terms and as a proportion of gross domestic product, a position which it has maintained for 40 years. Its parsimony is probably a result of its structure, with strong central government control over levels of spending through the annual budget-setting process, over levels of provision through public ownership of healthcare providers, and over levels of supply through public funding for medical schools, research and development, and so on. Although this fiscal restraint was once seen as a virtuous trait, in recent years it has been widely acknowledged that the NHS is significantly under-funded in comparison with healthcare systems in the rest of Europe, and that this has resulted in significant constraints on its capacity to meet the need for healthcare. Long-term underinvestment has produced an impoverished, unresponsive health service that cannot cope with patients' legitimate expectations of speedy access, high quality and consistent performance. Following a government review in 2002, NHS spending is set to rise at about 5 per cent per annum in real terms over coming years, with the intention that the UK should be spending between 10 and 12 per cent of gross domestic product on healthcare in 20 years' time (Wanless 2002).

Unlike in the USA, the NHS provides universal coverage to all its citizens. There is no defined 'benefits package' – the principle is that most of what the tax-funded health service does is simply free to patients. Primary medical care, mental health care, hospital care, prescription drugs, community nursing services, all are included. There are some user charges, such as co-payments of about £6 for each prescribed medication and charges for some dental treatment and opticians' services, but many patients – including the elderly, those with chronic conditions and those on low incomes – are exempt from making these payments. However, this does not mean that patients can use whatever health services they want. The governing principle of the NHS is that services are provided according to clinical need, and several mechanisms exist to manage and control patient demand, some of which are not too dissimilar to those used in US managed care organizations (Weiner *et al.* 2001).

First, the NHS has a very well-developed system of primary care. All patients are registered with a primary care doctor, their general practitioner (GP), who acts as their first point of contact with the health service, providing continuity of care over time and across the range of services a patient might require. The GP acts as gatekeeper, referring patients onwards to specialist services when they are needed; apart from emergency hospital care, patients cannot go direct to NHS services without a referral from their GP. General practitioners are mainly paid on a capitated basis, so there is no financial incentive for them to see patients or to refer them. Secondly, the NHS manages demand for some services through a variety of rationing mechanisms, most obviously (but not only) waiting lists (Devlin *et al.* 2002). Patients may have to wait both to see a hospital specialist when they are referred by their GP, and then to be treated by that specialist if they require, for example, an operation. Waiting times for elective surgery in the UK average 2.2 months, longer than other countries (Anderson and Hussey 2000). While urgent conditions are prioritized, patients with non-urgent problems may wait many months or even years for treatment. Waiting lists are unpopular with both the public and the government, and considerable effort and resources have been invested in attempts to increase capacity and manage services better to reduce waiting times (Derrett *et al.* 2002).

Until 1997, health services in the four countries of the UK – England, Wales, Scotland and Northern Ireland – were financed and provided in a very similar fashion. The Department of Health in England took the lead in health policy development, which tended to be closely followed by the Scottish Office, Welsh Office and Northern Ireland Office, which ran the NHS in the other three countries. However, responsibility for the NHS has now been devolved to new political institutions – the Scottish Parliament and the Welsh and Northern Ireland Assemblies. As a result, health policy has begun to diverge, and the structures and systems for funding and providing healthcare are now, to some extent, different (Greer 2001). This chapter focuses primarily on describing the healthcare system and the regulation of healthcare in England, although it refers where appropriate to parallel developments in the other countries of the UK.

The NHS is a public bureaucracy, whose nearest analogue in the USA is probably the Veterans' Administration healthcare system. In England, it is run from Whitehall by central government. The Department of Health finances and manages a total of around 600 public bodies, which, in turn, provide health services. The structure is outlined in Figure 4.1.

There are 28 strategic health authorities, each of which manages health services in a defined geographic area for a population of around 2 million people. They are responsible for the overall performance management of the NHS trusts and primary care

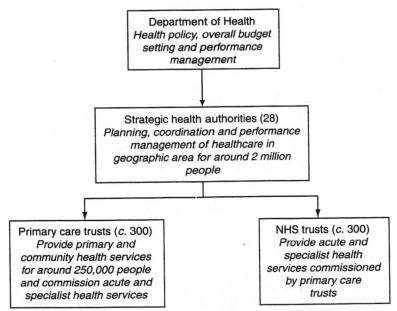

Figure 4.1 The structure of the National Health Service in England.

trusts, which provide health services. Each strategic health authority manages around 20 primary care trusts and NHS trusts, and is responsible for the overall planning, coordination, delivery and development of health services in its area. Primary care trusts provide primary and community health services to a defined geographic area, usually for a population of around 250,000 people. They also commission acute and specialist health services for their population from local NHS trusts, which run hospitals, mental health services and so on (Department of Health 2001). Money flows down this hierarchy from the Department of Health which has an annual budget set by the government and Parliament, to strategic health authorities and primary care trusts, and then via service or commissioning agreements to NHS trusts.

The NHS has changed considerably over the last two decades and some of the key changes are summarized in Table 4.2. In summary, governments of both major political parties have been engaged in a continuing search for ways to square the circle and reconcile ever rising public expectation and demand for healthcare with tight financial controls and limited increases in health spending (Klein 2001a). The result has been 20 years of almost continuous reform in the NHS, with a constant succession of policy initiatives following hard on each others' heels (Webster 1998; Harrison and Wood 1999). In the 1980s, the right-wing Conservative administration tried first to slim down the NHS bureaucracy and devolve responsibility to a local level; then it reformed the management of NHS organizations, creating 'business-like' general managers with more power over clinical issues; finally, and most radically, it attempted to introduce competition within the NHS through an 'internal market', splitting local responsibility for purchasing and providing healthcare. The 1990s brought a growing focus on primary care, with GPs leading the commissioning of all health services through GP fundholding and commissioning schemes; it also saw a series of reforms aimed at measuring and improving the quality of care and making it more clinically and cost-effective (Klein 2001b).

When a new Labour government was elected in 1997, it remoulded some of its predecessor's ideas, abolishing GP fundholding but introducing new primary care groups with a similar function; it signalled the end of the internal market but retained the split in responsibility for purchasing and providing care. It also embarked on some reforms aimed at strengthening the national direction and oversight of healthcare organization performance and the quality of health services (including the greater use of regulation). In its second term,

Table 4.2 A brief chronology of health policy changes in the UK, 1980–2002

1980–1992 Conservative Margaret Thatcher	At first the Thatcher government paid little attention to health policy, having more important economic problems to address. In 1982, it abolished one layer of the organizational hierarchy in the NHS and, in 1985, it replaced a system of consensus-based decision-making dominated by clinicians with new general management structures which gave lay managers much more power. But in 1989, provoked initially by a waiting list scandal and resource constraints, Thatcher launched a major set of reforms to the NHS. An internal market was created, with purchasers – health authorities and general practitioner (GP) fundholders – and providers – new, more autonomous NHS trusts. The reforms also introduced mandatory quality assurance systems, and separated management of the NHS from the Department of Health
1992–1997 Conservative John Major	The Major administration presided over a continuation of the 1989 reforms, with a gradual extension of GP fundholding and the increasing transfer of power and resources to primary care. It also reorganized health authorities, merging many of them to form larger health authorities, and it restructured the NHS Executive and regional health authorities
1997–2002 Labour Tony Blair	The Labour government came to power in 1997 with few health policy commitments apart from an ill-advised promise to cut waiting lists by 100,000. In its first term, it abolished GP fundholding and replaced it with new, larger primary care groups (PCGs). It also claimed to replace the internal market with 'service agreements'. It introduced new national mechanisms for setting and monitoring clinical standards and measuring performance. Its second term brought an ambitious plan for expansion in the capacity of the NHS and significant additional funding aimed at bringing the UK closer to European levels of healthcare spending. It also saw more organizational change with the replacement of PCGs by primary care trusts (PCTs) and the abolition of most health authorities and the NHS Executive regional offices

it has initiated a major structural reorganization of the NHS, changing roles and functions with the declared intention of promoting
greater decentralization and devolution of responsibility to the front-
line, and has set about a sustained attempt to increase the capacity of
the NHS through a combination of substantial new investment and
reforms to the way care is delivered (Department of Health 2001).

Surveys suggest that the NHS is still seen by the general public as
one of post-war government's great achievements, and as a manifest
expression of enduring social values in British society, such as social
solidarity, fairness and compassion towards those in need. However,
the rise of consumerism and increasing public expectations mean
that people's willingness to tolerate an NHS that offers poor
customer service, variable clinical standards, shabby physical sur-
roundings, long waiting times and restrictions on access to some
services has been much diminished. The current government's
attempts to 'modernize' the NHS represent an attempt to re-engineer
healthcare delivery to meet the demands of modern patients, while
leaving the fundamental values and funding arrangements of the
health service much as they have been for the last 50 years (Department of Health 2000b, 2001).

As a publicly funded, owned and managed health service, the
NHS made relatively little use of regulation for many years. Instead,
it relied largely upon traditional, bureaucratic central direction, with
the Department of Health issuing instructions, guidance and rules to
health authorities and NHS trusts through a blizzard of policy
papers, health circulars, executive letters and other means every year.
Conventional wisdom held that there was no need for a separate
regulatory function in such a vertically integrated, directly managed
structure, and that regulation might conflict with or constrain the
Department of Health's ability to run the NHS (Scrivens 1995).
Before 1980, the only real example of a regulator was the Health
Advisory Service, established in 1969 following a series of scandals
over poor standards in long-term care institutions for the mentally
ill and those with learning disabilities.

The 1980s saw a rapid expansion in the use of regulation in both the
private and public sectors in the UK. Despite an overt political commitment to deregulation, the Conservative administration created a
host of new regulatory agencies, many of them to oversee newly privatized industries such as telecommunications, water, gas, electricity
and railways (Hancher and Moran 1989). It also made increasing use
of regulation to manage the performance of public sector organizations, by establishing the Audit Commission and the National Audit

Office in its current form, and creating or strengthening regulatory agencies for schools, higher education, social care and many other public services (Hoods *et al.* 1998). Hood *et al.* (1999) conservatively estimated that the costs of regulating the public sector in the UK in 1995 ranged from £770 million to over £1 billion (or about 0.3 per cent of public expenditure), that there were at least 135 different bodies or authorities concerned with regulating the behaviour of public sector organizations, and that the investment in regulatory agencies had doubled or even quadrupled between 1976 and 1995. The growth of regulation across the public sector in the UK can be seen at least in part as a consequence of changes in the 1980s and 1990s to the way that public sector organizations were managed and structured. What is sometimes termed the 'new public management' (Ferlie *et al.* 1996) brought greater delegation of responsibility, a more arm's length relationship between public sector organizations and government, the separation of responsibility for funding and providing public services, and the increased use of competition within the public sector. With these new freedoms for some parts of the public sector came new accountabilities and the creation of compensating monitoring and reporting mechanisms, such as regulation.

However, the real growth in healthcare regulation in the UK has occurred since 1997. The present Labour government has moved away from relying on the market as a primary mechanism for managing and improving performance in the NHS for both ideological and pragmatic reasons, but has also been unwilling to rely on the traditional bureaucratic mechanisms for controlling the NHS through the line of accountability from the Department of Health downwards to NHS trusts and primary care trusts. Instead, it has turned increasingly to regulation. Over the past few years, several new regulatory agencies have been created, to regulate both the NHS and the private healthcare sector (Walshe 2002).

THE DEVELOPMENT OF REGULATION IN THE NHS UP TO 1997

The Health Advisory Service: the first regulator for the NHS

The Health Advisory Service (HAS) was set up in 1969 as a result of a public inquiry into major problems with the quality of care at Ely Hospital, a long-stay institution in Cardiff. The inquiry report uncovered ill treatment, abuse and neglect of patients, resulting from poor staff training, little leadership, low clinical standards and resource constraints. Among its 44 recommendations, it proposed the creation of an inspectorate to monitor the quality of care in long-stay institutions and take action to rectify their shortcomings (Department of Health and Social Security 1969). The then Secretary of State, Richard Crossman, pressed for its establishment against the wishes of his civil servants who did not want a formal inspectorate. He wrote that 'the key to it in my mind is that it should be an organisation completely separate from the policy making and administrative setup in the Ministry. It should be an independent group of people inspecting and reporting to me' (Crossman 1977).

Originally titled the Hospital Advisory Service, HAS was based from the start on the compliance model of regulation, as its name suggests. Although it formally reported direct to ministers, it saw itself as existing primarily to advise and support those in the health service, to spread good practice and to promote improvement. Table 4.3 provides an overview of HAS using the same analytical framework as that used throughout Chapter 3.

Although HAS was launched in 1969 with some enthusiasm, and continued to command considerable attention for the first 6–7 years of its life, its influence began to wane as health authorities grew accustomed to its periodic visits and learned to understand and, perhaps, to manage its interventions. As its political visibility and importance diminished, HAS became more and more reliant on the credibility of its regulatory process as its source of authority. However, that process was much criticized for features that resulted from its highly compliance-oriented, professionalized nature. It was argued that HAS reports were highly variable in quality, that different teams would produce quite different findings and recommendations, and that there was no consistency in the visit process. In part this resulted from the absence of explicit standards, which also meant that findings were difficult to justify and often appeared subjective. It was also argued that the professional domination of the HAS process produced a rather closed and introspective form of review, in which other stakeholders – particularly patients or users – played little part (Day *et al.* 1988; Henkel *et al.* 1989).

Two separate and independent evaluations, undertaken after HAS had been at work for almost two decades, reached similar and rather bleak conclusions about its impact. Henkel *et al.* (1989) observed that HAS reports and recommendations were 'percolative', with a slow and gradual impact on organizations and change only happening at the margins for the most part. Day *et al.* (1988)

Table 4.3 A regulatory analysis of the Health Advisory Service

Characteristic	Health Advisory Service (HAS)
Regulating organization	An organization set up by the Department of Health and Social Security (DHSS) and accountable to it. The Director was appointed by and reported directly to the Secretary of State, and the budget was provided and set by the DHSS. However, written guidance to the NHS emphasized that HAS was independent of the DHSS
Regulatory goals/ objectives	'Exists to maintain and improve the standards of management and organisation of patient care services, mainly those for the elderly and mentally ill'
Scope of regulation	All health authorities, with a broad remit to examine services for the mentally ill, the elderly and those with learning disabilities (though the latter responsibility was passed in the 1970s to another agency). HAS worked across England and Wales; Scotland had its own Health Advisory Service, which is still in existence
Regulatory model	Highly compliance-oriented. HAS was staffed by clinical professionals and managers from the NHS, many of them spending a short time working for HAS on secondment. Its Director was always a senior medical professional from psychiatry and care of the elderly medicine. Its whole approach was modelled on professional peer review and deliberately rejected notions of inspection
Direction	HAS did not issue formal directions about the standards to which services should be provided, but it did give implicit direction through the written guidance to survey teams which it issued (and which specified some areas to be examined and issues to consider). Implicit direction was also present in its reports and recommendations, particularly a number of national reports which it undertook on specific service areas
Detection	The only form of detection available to HAS was its programme of visits to healthcare organizations. While some visits were undertaken 'for cause', most were done on a rotational basis and, on average, a health authority could expect a HAS visit once every 10 years or so. Visits involved a multidisciplinary team of five or more people, drawn from backgrounds in professional practice in the service areas being reviewed. Visits took between 2 and 5 weeks and no predefined standards or structures were laid

Table 4.3—*continued*

Characteristic	Health Advisory Service (HAS)
	down, although most visits involved extensive interviews with a wide range of staff and users, observation, visits to sites where care was delivered, reviews of documents, etc. Teams had no predefined leader. Visits culminated in a written report which provided a narrative account of findings and recommendations
Enforcement	HAS had few enforcement powers. Health authorities were required to provide a follow-up report showing how they had responded to the HAS recommendations, but compliance with this varied widely. HAS undertook few follow-up visits and little was done to test the impact of recommendations. From the mid-1980s, HAS reports were published

described HAS reports as 'an exercise in persuasion' and pointed out that the way in which reports were followed up and implementation was monitored was very limited. In 1997, the Health Advisory Service was formally disbanded for England and Wales (although the Scottish Health Advisory Service is still in existence). It was replaced by a consortium of professional bodies that continue to provide advice and support on quality improvement issues in the care of the elderly and those with mental health problems, but without the statutory authority, funding and direct access to ministers which HAS once enjoyed. This rather inglorious end to the 27 year history of the Health Advisory Service as the first real regulator for the NHS, born out of real political concern about the quality of care and a public scandal at Ely, may hold lessons for the new regulators of the NHS discussed below, whose genesis has been remarkably similar.

The Audit Commission and the National Audit Office

The National Audit Office and the Audit Commission both have their roots in financial audit: certifying the accounts of public bodies, including NHS organizations, to be a true and accurate reflection of their financial position; undertaking inspections to check compliance with financial instructions and standards; and investigating problems of probity, regularity or even fraud and misconduct. However, they also undertake 'value-for-money' audit, in which their remit is much wider, and they scrutinize the economy, efficiency and effectiveness with which NHS organizations use public funding. The rubric of value for money allows them to examine, in effect, almost any area of NHS performance.

The National Audit Office and the Audit Commission were both created in their current form in the 1980s, and their similar sounding titles and apparently similar remits often cause some confusion within the NHS. However, they are, in reality, quite different organizations as the regulatory analysis set out in Table 4.4 demonstrates. The National Audit Office was created in its current form by the National Audit Act in 1983; before that it was a part of the Treasury, and it can trace its history as the government's auditor back for several hundred years. The National Audit Office and its chief officer, the Comptroller and Auditor General, report directly to Parliament on the use of public funds and are effectively the executive arm of the House of Commons Public Accounts Committee. Their work in healthcare is just a small part of their remit, which

Table 4.4 A regulatory analysis of the National Audit Office and the Audit Commission

Characteristic	National Audit Office	Audit Commission
Regulating organization	Part of central government, although independent of the executive and reports directly to the Parliamentary Public Accounts Committee	An extra-departmental public body, established by primary legislation and accountable through a Board of Commissioners to the Secretaries of State for Health, the Environment and Wales
Regulatory goals/ objectives	To provide assurance that public money is spent as Parliament intended, to improve financial control in government and public bodies, and to improve value obtained from public resources	Aims 'to be a driving force in the improvement of public services by promoting proper stewardship of public finances, helping local authorities and the NHS to deliver economic, efficient and effective public services'

Table 4.4—*continued*

Characteristic	National Audit Office	Audit Commission
Scope of regulation	Undertakes financial and value-for-money (VFM) audit across all government departments and agencies. Its primary relationship in healthcare is with the Department of Health	Undertakes financial and value-for-money (VFM) audit across local authorities and NHS organizations. It is the lead auditor for health authorities, NHS trusts and primary care trusts
Regulatory model	National Audit Office largely exhibits a compliance approach – VFM audit topics and methods are negotiated with Department of Health officials, reports are discussed in draft and consensus has to be reached about content before publication. However, the Public Accounts Committee can be more deterrence-oriented, especially in committee hearings	The Audit Commission is somewhat compliance-oriented in its approach – both nationally and locally – but has shown itself willing when necessary to be quite combative and critical in its public comments on both national issues and on the performance of local NHS organizations
Direction	Although there are clear accounting standards which guide the National Audit Office's financial audit, its VFM work does not rely on predefined standards or performance measures; topics are selected because of apparent problems or variation in practice or Public Accounts Committee interest	Like the National Audit Office the Audit Commission VFM work is topic-based. Each topic is selected and studied nationally and produces a study guide which is then used to review services locally

Characteristic	National Audit Office	Audit Commission
Detection	VFM audits vary but often use a combination of methods, including: national surveys of NHS organizations; case study visits to selected organizations; and interviews with a wide range of individuals and groups	VFM audits vary, but often use a combination of methods, including: national surveys of NHS organizations; case study visits to selected organizations; and interviews with a wide range of individuals and groups
Enforcement	National Audit Office reports are first agreed with the Department of Health and then published. For most reports, the Public Accounts Committee holds a hearing at which Department of Health civil servants are questioned. The Department of Health has to produce a formal response to the report. A follow-up report is produced by the National Audit Office about 18 months later, which details what progress has been made. The Public Accounts Committee sometimes chooses to return to a topic in later years if it is felt that problems remain	Audit Commission reports are not subject to clearance or agreement by the Department of Health. They are published and gain widespread media attention. No formal Department of Health response is required. The Commission then follows up national audits by doing local studies in NHS organizations, and may then aggregate these results to measure progress nationally. It can continue to pursue a topic if it feels that problems remain

runs across the whole of government. The Audit Commission, in contrast, was established in 1983 to consolidate and strengthen the auditing of local authorities, reflecting a political concern in government about their performance and accountability. In 1991, its remit was extended to include NHS organizations as well as local authorities. It is an extra departmental public body, established by primary legislation, with a board of commissioners who are appointed by the Secretaries of State for Health, the Environment and Wales.

In essence, the National Audit Office is a regulator of central government – while it undertakes fieldwork in the NHS for its value-for-money reports, those reports are addressed to the Public Accounts Committee, and it is largely Department of Health ministers and civil servants who are held accountable and required to respond to its findings. In contrast, the Audit Commission is much more focused on regulating NHS organizations directly. Although it, too, undertakes national value-for-money studies, they are then translated into an audit guide that is used locally with individual NHS organizations by their external auditors – which may be an accountancy provider or may be District Audit, which is part of the Audit Commission itself. Sometimes, the Audit Commission then aggregates the results from these local studies to produce a second, national report summarizing progress across the NHS.

Both the National Audit Office and the Audit Commission take a topic-based approach – they do not attempt to review every aspect of NHS performance, but choose a few areas on which to focus their attention. In theory, the criteria used to select topics are quite straightforward – high cost, volume or risk areas, those in which there is substantial variation in practice and where there is a prima facie opportunity for improvement, those which have not been scrutinized by other agencies and where National Audit Office or Audit Commission intervention can bring significant added value. In practice, the choice of topics can appear rather arbitrary; by way of illustration, a list of topics studied by both organizations is shown in Table 4.5, and it would be simple to think of an alternative list of topics that could fit the criteria outlined above equally well. Both organizations solicit suggestions for future study topics quite widely, but the way that the large number of rather diverse ideas they receive is reduced down to the very small number that enter the value-for-money programme is far from clear.

It has already been noted that there is some potential for confusion and overlap between the National Audit Office and the Audit Commission, despite their different origins and orientations. Their value-for-money study methodologies are fairly similar, and most value-for-money topics in the NHS could, in reality, be tackled by either body. Although they do liaise and undertake some joint

Table 4.5 An illustrative selection of value-for-money study topics, 2000–2002

National Audit Office	Audit Commission
• Management of surplus NHS property	• The quality of patient-based information
• NHS Direct	• Procurement and supply services
• Inpatient and outpatient waiting	• Medicines management
• Clinical negligence	• Day surgery
• Professional education and development	• Cancer care
• Obesity	• Ward staffing
• The National Blood Service	• Accident and emergency services
• Hip replacements	• Rehabilitation and remedial services for older people
• Hospital-acquired infection	• Diabetes services
• Inpatient admissions and bed management	

planning of their future work programmes, it could not be said that they collaborate enthusiastically. There is some caution and territoriality in attitudes on both sides because they are, effectively, in regulatory competition.

The impact of National Audit Office and Audit Commission value-for-money studies on the NHS is difficult to measure, but the evidence suggests it is decidedly mixed. While some studies, particularly those which fit in with other national and local priorities, do produce change, others do not, especially when their conclusions are not accepted by key NHS stakeholders (such as clinicians) or when the changes they seek are difficult or complex to implement. Although the National Audit Office has the power of the Public Accounts Committee behind it and can use that leverage to secure Department of Health compliance, the Audit Commission has no formal enforcement powers. Its combination of national studies with local replication and follow-up is designed to help bring about change, but ultimately it relies solely on the persuasive power of its findings and recommendations, and the pressures that can be brought to bear through putting them in the public domain (Day and Klein 1990, 2001).

Finally, it is worthwhile considering how the apparent independence of the National Audit Office and the Audit Commission affects their behaviour as regulators. The National Audit Office is wholly independent of government and gets its funding directly from a Parliamentary vote, although the Comptroller and Auditor General is always a former senior civil servant and its relationship with Whitehall tends to be more collaborative than adversarial. The Audit Commission is formally accountable, as an extra-departmental public body, jointly to three Secretaries of State, who appoint its board of Commissioners. However, it is financed directly through audit fees paid by the local authorities and NHS organizations which it regulates, and perhaps for this reason it has managed to assert and sustain its independence from government.

The Health Service Ombudsman

The Health Service Ombudsman is part of the Parliamentary Ombudsman's Office, which exists to undertake fair and independent investigations into complaints about maladministration on the part of central government, and is formally accountable to the Parliamentary Committee on Administration. Although the Parliamentary Ombudsman only takes up complaints which are referred to it by a Member of Parliament, the Health Service Ombudsman accepts and investigates complaints directly from members of the public about NHS organizations. A separate Local Government Ombudsman's Office performs the same function in respect of local authorities.

The Health Service Ombudsman only considers complaints once local arrangements for resolving them through the NHS Complaints Procedure have been exhausted, and the complainant is either not satisfied with the results or does not feel the complaint was handled properly. Until the mid-1990s, the Health Service Ombudsman confined itself to examining problems of administration, and clinical issues were regarded as outside its domain. Since that policy changed, complaints about clinical care concerns have come to represent the great majority of those it considers. In 2001–2002, the Ombudsman received 2662 complaints, 3 per cent more than in the previous year. The numbers of complaints have been rising steadily for several years and have doubled over the last decade. However, the Health Service Ombudsman only actually investigates a minority of the complaints received – around 240 of the 2662 cases received in 2001–2002 – for several reasons. First, up to 60 per cent of cases are judged to be not within the Ombudsman's jurisdiction, usually because the complainant has not yet made full use of local complaints procedures. In these cases, he or she will be advised to seek redress directly from the NHS organization concerned. Of the cases that are classified as 'investigable', only about 28 per cent result in a full investigation. Many are resolved because the Health Service Ombudsman, having reviewed the case papers, concludes that the complaint has already been dealt with fairly, or that further action would be unlikely to benefit the complainant, or that there was no evidence that the complainant has suffered unremedied injustice or hardship. Some are resolved without an investigation because the NHS organization immediately agrees to take further action locally to address the concerns. The net effect of all this is that of around 2600 complaints a year, the Ombudsman initiates a formal investigation and produces a report on less than 10 per cent, about 240 cases a year (Health Service Ombudsman 2001a,b).

Investigations by the Health Service Ombudsman can be lengthy and complex affairs; on average, they take 51 weeks to complete. The Ombudsman has statutory powers of access to NHS organizations to gather evidence and interview staff, and the investigating staff will both review the existing records and gather fresh evidence. Because around 80 per cent of complaints are to do with clinical care, the Ombudsman has a number of professional advisers who review the clinical issues concerned. Once the investigation has been completed, the Ombudsman issues a statement of findings; when a complaint is upheld, the Ombudsman seeks to agree with the NHS organization concerned the steps that it should take to remedy the situation. This may mean making an apology, changing practices or procedures to prevent any recurrence of the problem, reporting on those changes once they have been made, and making good the situation for the patient either by providing further health services or by making a payment in some cases. All investigations are summarized in a report issued three times a year by the Health Service Ombudsman, which highlights key issues and themes or trends (Health Service Ombudsman 2002). All cases are also reported upon to the Parliamentary Committee on Administration; when NHS organizations fail to respond adequately to individual complaints or are seen to have multiple investigations, they can be required to appear before the Committee in public. There is no mechanism for appeal for complainants or NHS organizations against the Ombudsman's decision, apart from seeking a judicial review.

The office of the Health Service Ombudsman is, in many ways, a powerful one. It has statutory legal powers of investigation, and the processes of reporting, publication and parliamentary scrutiny mean that NHS organizations generally take its investigations very seriously. However, while it has an important impact on individual cases, it investigates only a small number of those which come to its attention – and that in itself is just a tiny proportion of complaints about the NHS. Therefore, for the Health Service Ombudsman's work to have a wider impact on the NHS, there would need to be a mechanism for securing change not only in the NHS organizations it investigates, but in other places too. Although the Ombudsman's reports are widely circulated in the NHS, it is far from clear that they are read and acted upon locally, and no mechanisms exist to translate the individual complaints which they describe into wider or more sustained improvement.

The non-governmental regulation of the NHS

Apart from the statutory, governmental regulators outlined above, there are a host of other non-governmental agencies which regulate the NHS. Some examples are given in Table 4.6. They include: the medical Royal Colleges, which regulate medical training; the Clinical Negligence Scheme for Trusts (CNST) operated by the NHS Litigation Authority, a risk-pooling arrangement for litigation against NHS organizations that oversees their risk management arrangements; and a number of accreditation programmes for different services and organizations.

These regulators have no formal, statutory powers over NHS organizations, either to compel them to submit themselves to scrutiny or to enforce their regulatory requirements. However, some have considerable informal power. For example, if the medical Royal Colleges withdraw accreditation for medical training posts, the NHS organization concerned will not be able to recruit junior doctors and will find it very difficult to sustain clinical services without them. The NHS organizations that do well on CNST's assessment of their risk management systems have their contributions to its negligence litigation fund reduced to take account of this, which provides a significant financial incentive to comply.

Most of the regulators shown in Table 4.6 deal with a single facet of the NHS organizations they regulate, rather than with the organization as a whole, and the result is a mosaic of regulatory arrangements and some potential for duplication or conflict. There are few arrangements through which they share information and no systems to coordinate their fieldwork and the demands it places on the NHS. This has led some NHS organizations to complain of 'inspectorial overload' in the past. It may also mean that even if

Table 4.6 Some examples of non-governmental regulation in the NHS

Name	Who or what it regulates	Brief overview
Medical Royal Colleges	Education and training of junior doctors	Each Royal College has its own accreditation process for doctor training posts in NHS organizations, usually based around some standards that are checked or tested in a periodic survey visit every 5 years or so by a team of College staff and senior clinicians. Accreditation can be withdrawn if standards are not met, which may have serious implications for clinical service delivery
Clinical Negligence Scheme for Trusts (CNST)	Risk management arrangements in NHS trusts	CNST was set up in 1995 as a self-funded risk pooling arrangement through which NHS trusts shared the costs of clinical negligence litigation. It established a risk management accreditation scheme and a set of risk management standards. NHS trusts which are found through a survey visit to comply with the standards pay a discounted CNST contribution. It is operated by the NHS Litigation Authority
National External Quality Assurance Scheme (NEQAS)	Pathology services	UK NEQAS was established in the 1970s and provides an external quality assessment service for pathology laboratories in the NHS. Sets of control samples are sent to laboratories for testing and the results are compared to check laboratory performance
Clinical Pathology Accreditation (CPA) UK	Pathology services	CPA was established by the Royal College of Pathologists in the early 1990s as an accreditation programme for pathology services, based around sets of accreditation standards and a survey process using senior laboratory and clinical staff from other NHS organizations. It was wholly voluntary, but now some laboratories participating in national screening programmes (e.g. cervical cytology) are required to have CPA accreditation

Table 4.6—*continued*

Name	Who or what it regulates	Brief overview
Health Quality Service (HQS)	Health care providers in the NHS and the private sector	HQS was first established in the 1980s by the Kings Fund as an organizational audit or accreditation programme, modelled on those in the USA, Canada and Australia. It is now an independent organization, providing mainly hospital accreditation services to the NHS and the private sector. Participation is wholly voluntary and is based on the value of the process to the organization and the status associated with being accredited
The National Confidential Enquiry into Perioperative Deaths (NCEPOD) and other national confidential inquiries	NCEPOD oversees surgical and perioperative care in hospitals	NCEPOD was established in 1987, tasked with reviewing and improving surgical and perioperative care by reviewing cases of post-operative mortality. There are other standing confidential inquiries into maternal deaths, neonatal and infant deaths, and suicides and homicides in mental health patients. Anonymous, structured reviews of selected instances of post-operative mortality are used to produce general reports which highlight common problems and recommend changes

several of these agencies had serious concerns about the performance of a particular organization, it is unlikely that any one of them could see the bigger picture of organizational failure.

THE NEW NHS REGULATORS: 1997 ONWARDS

When a new Labour government was elected in 1997, it came to power determined to move away from the internal market and competition as mechanisms for driving improvement in the NHS, but it did not want a return to traditional and somewhat discredited systems of bureaucratic direction. It was also committed to reducing the variations in NHS services and performance which the market had generated, such as differences in service provision or in access to new treatments in different geographic areas, and replacing them with a more nationally directed, consistent and equitable approach. For both purposes, it turned to regulation, announcing in its first White Paper the creation of two new regulatory agencies, a National Institute of Clinical Excellence tasked with providing national guidance and direction on clinical practice and technology assessment and a Commission for Health Improvement with in essence the remit of a new NHS inspectorate (Department of Health 1997). Since then, a further three new agencies have been added to the increasingly crowded regulatory landscape. Two – the National Clinical Assessment Authority and the National Patient Safety Agency – deal with the very specific areas of poor clinical performance and adverse event reporting respectively. The third – the Modernization Agency – has a very broad remit to work with almost any NHS organization in almost any area of performance improvement. Each of these new regulators is summarized in Table 4.7.

In some respects, these new regulators are quite different from some of the existing regulatory agencies detailed in Table 4.6 and in the previous section. First, they are well-resourced organizations, for whom regulation is their primary mission rather than being one function among many which they undertake. Secondly, they generally have a broad remit to oversee NHS organizations which is not limited to particular service areas or functions as many of the existing regulators have been. Thirdly, they are all essentially agents of the government – all are accountable to the Department of Health and have their boards appointed by the Secretary of State. They have little formal independence and, taken together, they represent a significant strengthening of central government control of the NHS. Fourthly, and perhaps most importantly, these new regulators are all primarily concerned with the clinical quality of healthcare. Past regulation has often focused on more peripheral administrative and managerial matters, not on clinical practice.

The growth of regulation in the NHS since 1997 can be viewed quite straightforwardly as the pragmatic adoption by the Labour government of another mechanism for getting things done in public sector organizations, to be used alongside (not instead of) alternatives like traditional bureaucratic control and limited competition. From the perspective of government, the quasi-independent status of these new regulatory agencies may distance politicians from

Table 4.7 An overview of new regulatory agencies in the NHS

Name	Who it regulates	Date established	Annual budget for 2001– 2002	Mission/purpose	How it works	What it is
National Institute for Clinical Excellence www.nice.org.uk	NHS in England and Wales	April 1999	£10.6 million	To provide patients, health professionals and the public with authoritative, robust and reliable guidance on current 'best practice'	Uses teams of experts to review health technologies and interventions and produce guidance that is then disseminated	A special health authority, set up by Statutory Instrument (SI 1999 Nos 220 and 2219)
Commission for Health Improvement www.chi.nhs.uk	NHS in England and Wales	November 1999	£24.5 million	To help improve the quality of patient care by assisting the NHS in addressing unacceptable variations and to ensure a consistently high standard of patient care	Undertakes clinical governance reviews of all NHS organizations every 4 years; monitors implementation of guidelines from the National Institute for Clinical Excellence, national service frameworks, etc., investigates major system failures within the NHS	A non-departmental public body established by the Health Act 1999

Organisation	Location	Date	Budget	Aim	Description	Status
Modernization Agency www.modernnhs.nhs.uk	NHS in England	April 2001	£54.6 million	To help the NHS bring about improvements in services for patients and contribute to national planning and performance improvement strategies	Encompasses existing National Patient Action Team, Primary Care Development Team, Collaboratives Programme, Leadership Centre, Beacon Programme, and Clinical Governance Support Unit	Part of the Department of Health
National Patient Safety Agency www.npsa.org.uk	NHS in England (at present)	April 2001	£15 million (in 2002–2003)	To collect and analyse information on adverse events in the NHS, assimilate safety information from elsewhere, learn lessons and feed back to the NHS, produce solutions, set national goals and establish mechanisms to track progress	Will establish and operate a new, mandatory national system for reporting adverse events and 'near misses', and provide national leadership and guidance on patient safety and adverse events	A special health authority set up by Statutory Instrument (SI 2001 No. 1743)
National Clinical Assessment Authority www.ncaa.nhs.uk	NHS in England (at present)	April 2001	£10.1 million (in 2002–2003)	To provide a support service to health authorities and hospital and community trusts who are faced with concerns over the performance of an individual doctor	Deals with concerns about doctors in difficulty by providing advice, taking referrals and carrying out targeted assessments where necessary	A special health authority set up by Statutory Instrument (SI 2000 No. 2961)

difficult issues or unpleasant decisions, shifting responsibility for them to the regulator, while retaining and even increasing the reach and scope of governmental control. The rest of this section examines three of these new regulators in some detail: the National Institute for Clinical Excellence, the Commission for Health Improvement and the Modernization Agency.

The National Institute for Clinical Excellence

Before the National Institute for Clinical Excellence (NICE) was created, there was a host of organizations offering advice on clinical practice and the use or uptake of healthcare interventions to NHS organizations and to individual clinicians. Some, such as the NHS Centre for Reviews and Dissemination (Sheldon and Chalmers 1994) and the Wessex Development Evaluation Committee (Best *et al.* 1997), were created as part of a policy-maker and practitioner movement towards the ideas of evidence-based healthcare (Walshe 1998). Others, such as research and audit units at the Royal Colleges producing clinical guidelines, originated in the development of clinical audit and the quality movement of the late 1980s (Walshe 1995). But although all this advice was on offer, it was wholly up to individual clinicians and NHS organizations such as health authorities and NHS trusts whether they took it. In practice, much guidance appeared either never to reach the key decision-makers or to be ignored by them (Walshe and Ham 1997). There were few, if any, mechanisms to follow up and manage the adoption of guidance or advice, decisions taken by different healthcare organizations and clinicians often seemed conflicting and poorly reasoned, and unjustifiable variations in provision and practice – popularly dubbed 'postcode prescribing' – were commonplace (Klein *et al.* 1996).

The National Institute for Clinical Excellence was created to 'put an end to postcode prescribing' and bring both rationality and national direction to the use of new and existing health technologies and to clinical practice more broadly (Department of Health 1998). It has two main roles. First, it undertakes assessments of new or existing technologies such as pharmaceuticals, diagnostic tests and surgical procedures and offers guidance to NHS organizations, clinicians and the public on their use. Secondly, it coordinates the production of clinical guidelines for a range of major conditions, areas of care and patient groups. A regulatory analysis of NICE is shown in Table 4.8.

The National Institute for Clinical Excellence has established and progressively refined its approach to assessing technologies, with

Table 4.8 A regulatory analysis of the National Institute for Clinical Excellence

Characteristic	National Institute for Clinical Excellence (NICE)
Regulating organization	NICE is a special health authority, whose chair and non-executive directors are appointed by the NHS Appointments Commission. It is accountable to the Department of Health and the Welsh Assembly, which provide its funding
Regulatory goals/ objectives	NICE exists 'to provide patients, health professionals and the public with authoritative, robust and reliable guidance on current best practice'
Scope of regulation	The use of diagnostic and therapeutic interventions (in particular the adoption of new technologies or interventions) in NHS organizations in England and Wales
Regulatory model	Because NICE is only involved in regulatory direction, it is difficult to place it on the traditional spectrum of regulatory models from deterrence to compliance. However, the highly formalized, quasi-judicial and relatively adversarial style of its appraisal process and its often strained relationships with pharmaceutical companies and other technology producers are more characteristic of deterrence than compliance
Direction	NICE is only involved in regulatory direction – setting standards through its official guidance to the NHS on health technologies and through the clinical guidelines it develops in partnership with other organizations. NICE has a complex, highly formalized and quasi-judicial process for setting its directions through guidelines or technology appraisals issued to the Department of Health and the NHS. In short, those with an interest in a new technology (such as its producers or promoters) are invited to present a range of evidence on its costs and effectiveness. NICE undertakes a review of the evidence and its appraisals committee hears evidence and reaches a provisional judgement, which can then be commented upon or appealed before it is finalized
Detection	NICE has no role in the processes of regulatory detection, which it leaves to other agencies, such as the Department of Health and strategic health authorities, and to the Commission for Health Improvement
Enforcement	NICE has no enforcement powers but, as noted above, compliance with its guidance is compulsory for NHS trusts and primary care trusts and enforcement is handled by the Department of Health and strategic health authorities

the intention that it should be objective, fair and transparent (Department of Health 1999). Despite this, it has faced criticisms from various quarters for not paying sufficient attention to evidence submitted by some stakeholders such as patient groups, for being insufficiently transparent and unfair in the appraisal process and in handling appeals against its decisions, and for being too reluctant to say no to new technologies of dubious benefit (Cookson *et al.* 2001; Raftery 2001).

The Department of Health selects the technologies which NICE will review, using four criteria: possible health benefit, links to health policies, impact on NHS resources and the likely added value of NICE guidance. The institute is explicitly tasked with reviewing both the clinical and cost-effectiveness of technologies, but also takes into account a number of other considerations, including: the broad clinical priorities of the NHS; the extent of clinical need of patients with the condition under consideration; the broad balance of benefits and costs; any guidance from the Secretary of State on the resources likely to be available to the NHS or on other matters; the effective use of available resources; and the encouragement of innovation (Dent and Sadler 2002).

The sponsors of a technology and other stakeholders (such as patient groups or professional organizations) are invited to submit evidence to the NICE appraisals committee, which also commissions an independent assessment of the evidence from an academic team of health economists and health services researchers. Although the sponsors and other stakeholders are invited to the relevant meetings of the appraisals committee and have the opportunity to put their case, the final decision is reached in a closed session. The committee produces a provisional appraisal, which, after consultation, is finalized and forms the basis of guidance to the NHS, which NICE issues on behalf of the Secretary of State (Raftery 2001).

Officially, NICE simply offers guidance to NHS organizations, but that guidance is, in practical terms, binding upon them – it is advice they cannot really refuse or ignore. When some organizations have disagreed with the results of NICE's appraisal process and have not followed the NICE guidance, they have generally been forced back into line by the Department of Health through the NHS performance management hierarchy. Indeed, it has been made an explicit requirement that primary care trusts and NHS trusts implement NICE guidance once it has been issued within a fixed time-scale (Dent and Sadler 2002). However, while the Department of Health can and does require NHS organizations to follow NICE guidance, rather paradoxically it does not have any statutory legal powers to require individual clinicians to do the same, and doctors are at least in theory still free to prescribe and treat as they like (Newdick 2001).

Between January 2000 and September 2002, NICE issued around 15 appraisals a year, most of which concerned therapeutic pharmaceuticals, as Table 4.9 shows. Of the 22 technologies assessed

Table 4.9 Health technologies reviewed by NICE, 2000–2002

Year	Disease areas and technologies/interventions appraised
2000	Hips – prostheses for primary total hip replacement Wisdom teeth – removal Heart disease (ischaemic) – coronary artery stents Ovarian cancer – taxanes Breast cancer – taxanes Cervical smear tests – liquid-based cytology Dyspepsia – proton pump inhibitors Hearing disability – new advances in hearing aid technology Asthma – inhalers for children under 5 years Diabetes (type 2) – rosiglitazone Arrhythmias – implantable cardioverter defibrillators Glycoprotein IIb/IIIa inhibitor guidance for acute coronary syndromes Attention deficit hyperactivity disorder (ADHD) – methylphenidate Hepatitis C – alpha interferon and ribavarin Flu – zanamivir (Relenza) Colorectal cancer – laparoscopic surgery Knee joints (defective) – autologous cartilage transplantation
2001	Alzheimer's disease – donepezil, rivastigmine and galantamine Hernia (inguinal) – laparoscopic surgery Motor neurone disease – riluzole Diabetes (type 2) – pioglitazone Obesity – orlistat Brain cancer – temozolomide Wound care – debriding agents Pancreatic cancer – gemcitabine Lung cancer – docetaxel, paclitaxel, gemcitabine and vinorelbine Osteoarthritis and rheumatoid arthritis – Cox II inhibitors Ovarian cancer – topotecan Leukaemia (lymphocytic) – fludarabine Breast cancer – taxanes – review Obesity – sibutramine Multiple sclerosis – beta interferon and glatiramer acetate

Table 4.9—*continued*

Year	Disease areas and technologies/interventions appraised
2002	Advanced colorectal cancer – irinotecan, oxaliplatin and raltitrexed Breast cancer – trastuzumab Crohn's disease Juvenile idiopathic arthritis – etanercept Rheumatoid arthritis – etanercept and Infliximab Schizophrenia – atypical anti-psychotics Smoking cessation – bupropion and nicotine replacement therapy Lymphoma (follicular non-Hodgkin's) – rituximab Asthma – inhaler devices for older children Pregnancy – routine anti-D prophylaxis for rhesus negative women Human growth hormone in children Hip resurfacing – metal on metal Obesity (morbid) – surgery Ovarian cancer (advanced) – PLDH (caelyx) Glycoprotein IIb/IIIa inhibitor guidance for acute coronary syndromes – review Haemodialysis – home versus hospital Ultrasound locating devices for placing central venous catheters

by NICE over its first 18 months of operation up to March 2001, 18 were recommended for adoption (though often with some caveats about the patient groups or indications for which they should be used) and only three were rejected (Raftery 2001). It has been suggested that NICE has been too reluctant to reject any technologies and has erred on the side of adoption even when there has been poor evidence of clinical and cost-effectiveness. The net cost of implementing these decisions was calculated to be about £200 million per annum, or about 0.5 per cent of NHS spending. Because the NICE decision-making process is closed, it is not possible to determine conclusively how the evidence on the costs and benefits of interventions was used by the NICE appraisals committee, although it appears that an informal cost ceiling of £30,000 per quality adjusted life year (QALY) has been applied (Raftery 2001).

Because NHS organizations are effectively instructed to fund new treatments which NICE recommends, such interventions now have the first call on any new development moneys that those organizations have, and take priority over any local initiatives or any new interventions that have not been reviewed by NICE. Since

NICE only reviews a small proportion of interventions, this means that NICE guidance skews new investment towards those interventions which it has reviewed and recommended and may actually leave more worthwhile and cost-effective interventions unfunded (Cookson *et al.* 2001; Sculpher *et al.* 2001).

As the regulatory analysis in Table 4.8 shows, NICE does not monitor the uptake of its guidance in the NHS, nor does it have any responsibility for following up or enforcing its guidance. Those tasks are left to other agencies, while NICE concentrates almost wholly on the task of regulatory direction or standard-setting. To some extent, NICE's guidance is published so widely and so well known that its implementation locally may be watched very closely by stakeholders, such as patient groups or professional organizations, who will follow up any failure to comply. However, the Department of Health through strategic health authorities also monitors compliance through both routine and special information gathering. Formally, the Commission for Health Improvement is tasked with monitoring and following up compliance with NICE guidance through its programme of clinical governance reviews of NHS trusts and its focused reviews of specific service areas. However, because the Commission for Health Improvement visits NHS organizations to review them once every 4 years or so, its ability to provide timely and effective detection or enforcement of NICE guidance is limited.

The Commission for Health Improvement

The Commission for Health Improvement (CHI) was established in 1999, just after the statutory demise of the Health Advisory Service, the first NHS regulator (Walshe 1999). There are some similarities in the genesis of the two organizations, in that both were created in response to a perceived crisis in the quality of NHS services; both were established by ministers who wanted them to be tough hospital inspectorates while civil servants and professionals wanted a more consensual and collaborative approach; and both began life with considerable political support and a high public profile. But there the similarities seem to end. The Health Advisory Service was set up at a time when inspection and regulation in public services were the exception rather than the rule, and public trust in the quality of services provided by the NHS was generally high. In contrast, the Commission for Health Improvement was created after regulation had already been extended to almost all areas of the public sector, and the largely unregulated NHS was starting to look like the exception. It came into being at a time when public faith in the NHS had been shaken by a series of very public failures in the quality of care. Perhaps most importantly, the remit of the Health Advisory Service was always restricted to areas such as long-term care for the elderly and mentally ill, in which public and political interest was relatively low and the professions involved were fairly weak, while the Commission for Health Improvement was tasked with overseeing all NHS organizations, including the much more politically powerful and visible acute sector.

The Commission for Health Improvement is an extra-departmental public body, like the Audit Commission, but it is solely responsible to the Secretary of State at the Department of Health, who exercises considerable power and influence over the agency's work. The CHI's board of Commissioners are appointed by the Secretary of State, who also sets the Commission's annual budget and can direct it on what areas or issues it examines, and to whom its reports and recommendations are addressed. The Commission was created with few powers of its own and is arguably less able to be independent than the Audit Commission.

The Commission for Health Improvement had four main statutory functions, which were laid down in the legislation that created it:

- To undertake a rolling programme of four yearly clinical governance reviews of NHS organizations.
- To investigate serious service failures in the NHS when requested to do so by the Secretary of State or when asked to do so by others.
- To conduct national service reviews, which should monitor progress in the implementation of standards set by the National Institute of Clinical Excellence, national service frameworks and, where required, other priorities.
- To provide advice and guidance to the NHS on clinical governance.

In addition, it was given a further responsibility in the NHS Plan (Department of Health 2000b) for leading the collation and publication of performance assessment data on the NHS, in collaboration with the Department of Health and the Audit Commission. Table 4.10 presents a regulatory analysis of the Commission for Health Improvement, using the same framework as before.

Two of the Commission's five functions have already come to dominate its work – the programme of clinical governance reviews of NHS organizations, and its investigations of service failures or problems. Each of these is now described in more detail.

Table 4.10 A regulatory analysis of the Commission for Health Improvement

Characteristic	Commission for Health Improvement (CHI)
Regulating organization	CHI is an extra-departmental public body created by the Health Act 1999. It is accountable to the Secretary of State for Health (in England) and the National Assembly (in Wales), who appoint its Commissioners, set its annual budget, and can direct what areas or issues it examines and to whom its reports and recommendations are generally addressed
Regulatory goals/ objectives	'To help bring about demonstrable improvement in the quality of NHS patient care throughout England and Wales'. CHI has four main statutory functions – undertaking clinical governance reviews, investigating serious service failures, conducting national service reviews and providing advice and guidance on clinical governance
Scope of regulation	All NHS organizations in England and Wales – NHS trusts, primary care trusts and health authorities
Regulatory model	Generally compliance-oriented, with a strong philosophical commitment to quality improvement and to working with the NHS organizations which it regulates. However, some of its clinical governance reviews and investigations have resulted in strong public criticisms of NHS organizations and have forced significant changes in their leadership or management, so CHI has seemed prepared in some cases to take a less compliance-oriented approach
Direction	CHI does not set explicit standards or criteria for its clinical governance reviews, although it does define in some detail the areas to be examined and the way that its review teams reach their judgements
Detection	CHI is mandated to undertake a clinical governance review of each NHS organization every 4 years. Because it is still in its first cycle of reviews, it is not yet possible to ascertain whether that target will be met
Enforcement	CHI has few enforcement powers of its own. It can and does publish the reports of its clinical governance reviews and can continue to pursue problems it has identified through action planning and follow-up visits. However, primary responsibility for enforcement rests with the NHS organization that has been reviewed, its strategic health authority and the Department of Health

Clinical governance has been defined as 'a framework through which NHS organizations are accountable for continuously improving the quality of their services and safeguarding high standards of care by creating an environment in which excellence in clinical care will flourish' (Department of Health 1998). More concisely, it has been described as 'corporate accountability for clinical performance', emphasizing that NHS organizations and those who lead them are statutorily accountable for the quality of care they provide (Walshe 2000b). The Commission for Health Improvement was in part created to provide a mechanism for monitoring the progress of clinical governance in the NHS through a rolling programme of reviews of clinical governance at individual NHS organizations. These reviews are intended to provide an objective and fair assessment of each organization's position, to promote improvement and reduce unacceptable variation, to identify and disseminate good practice, and to increase understanding of clinical governance and the factors that determine its effectiveness.

The Commission's approach to establishing its expectations of clinical governance in NHS trusts has not been to define a set of requirements in explicit standards and criteria, as many regulatory agencies do. Although it has set out quite clearly how the process of a clinical governance review is intended to work and the components of clinical governance which those reviews will examine (see Table 4.11), it has not defined how each component is to be measured or how the judgements reached by its review teams relate to the evidence collected by the clinical governance review (CHI 2001a). While the increasing number of clinical governance reviews undertaken by the Commission provide a clear track record of past assessments from which it is possible to glean considerable understanding of how such assessments have been made, the review process is still less transparent and explicit than might be expected.

Reviews by the Commission for Health Improvement are undertaken by a review team made up of around five reviewers plus a CHI review manager. The team is multidisciplinary – usually including a doctor, a nurse, a manager and another clinical professional – and always has one lay member. The CHI review manager coordinates the review, acts as the main liaison point between the Commission and the NHS organization, leads and supports the review team during the visit itself, ensures that all the relevant evidence has been collected and documented, and writes the report. All the other members of the team (apart from the lay member) are senior members of staff currently working in other NHS organizations.

Table 4.11 The components of clinical governance examined by the
Commission for Health Improvement review process

Strategic capacity	Leadership; accountabilities and structures; direction and planning; health economy partnerships; patient and public partnerships; performance review. These dimensions are indicative – work is ongoing to establish an assessment process in this area
Resources and processes	Patient and public involvement; clinical audit; risk management; clinical effectiveness programmes; staffing and staff management; education, training and continuing professional development. In each of these six areas, an assessment is made across five main headings (accountabilities and structures; strategies and plans; application of policies, strategies and plans; quality improvements and learning; resources and training) under each of which there are further detailed criteria
Use of information	Use of information to support health care delivery looking in particular at information management and technology issues; the use of information in monitoring and reporting on performance and outcomes; health records systems and management; and issues of privacy and confidentiality

They undertake a two and a half day training course before they do their first review and work on short-term secondment to the Commission, committing about 10 days to each review and usually doing one or two reviews a year. For the NHS organization for which they work, there is a clear benefit from their involvement in understanding the Commission's review process better and being able to prepare for its own review when it is scheduled, but some inconvenience in losing up to a month a year of a senior member of staff's time (even though the organization is reimbursed). In practice, it has been difficult recruiting the most senior staff, such as chief executives, to undertake CHI reviews (Randall 2002).

The Commission is required by the legislation which created it to undertake a rolling programme of four yearly clinical governance reviews of NHS organizations; subsequently, the Department of Health has indicated that poorly performing organizations will receive more frequent oversight (Department of Health 2000b). The Commission selects organizations for review using a random sampling methodology that is intended to spread reviews geographically and across different types of organization. It can choose either to delay a review or to 'fast-track' it if circumstances make this necessary. Reviews can be postponed if local circumstances – such as a recent or imminent organizational change or merger, a major change in leadership or other event – mean that a review would impose an unfair burden and would not provide a fair assessment of performance. Reviews can be accelerated or fast-tracked when there are concerns about the performance of an organization on behalf of other stakeholders, which might have been raised through a CHI investigation or where a request for an investigation has been made but a review is thought to be more appropriate.

Once an organization has been selected for clinical governance review, the process takes 24 weeks in total, of which 15 weeks are allowed for preparation; the review visit itself takes 1 week and the subsequent production of the report takes 8 weeks. Each of these three phases is described below.

When an organization is selected to be reviewed, it is asked to nominate a person to coordinate the process, who works with the CHI review manager. The first step is to gather data from a range of sources; the Commission uses national performance indicators and data sets but also asks the organization to provide a wide range of information, including a profile, its business plans and annual reports, information about areas such as clinical audit, risk management and patient surveys, and reports from other external review processes (such as those of the medical Royal Colleges and the Clinical Negligence Scheme for Trusts). The aim is to use existing documents as much as possible, but the organization is asked to complete a detailed self-assessment of its progress in clinical governance. The second step is to consult other stakeholders – the Commission meets with local statutory and non-statutory organizations to seek their views and conducts a patient diary survey of a random sample of 200 patients.

The Commission uses the data it has collected to choose three clinical areas or teams on which it will focus during its review visit, as examples of progress in clinical governance. The mechanism for making that choice is not explicit, but presumably the intent is to examine areas where either particularly good or poor progress is being made. It also uses the data to brief the review team, with the intention that they should begin the review visit itself with a detailed understanding of the organization and some early indications of the areas which the visit might need to examine more closely.

The review visit itself involves a team of around five reviewers and the CHI review manager who leads the process. It takes about

5 days and begins with meetings and presentations with the NHS organization's board and senior leaders. Most of the time is spent in interviews with selected staff, visits to a wide range of service areas and observation of the work of the organization. The review team meet up on a daily basis for a debriefing and information-sharing session through which they start to establish their view of the organization's performance. At the end of the week – which is highly intensive and exhausting both for the CHI review team and the NHS organization concerned – the reviewers provide some limited feedback on their initial impressions. However, most analysis and reporting takes place after the visit has concluded.

The CHI review manager and the reviewers meet a couple of weeks after the review visit to discuss and agree their key findings. They try to assess how confident the Commission can be in the conclusions they reach and how well they are supported by the evidence. Soon after this meeting, the CHI review manager provides a verbal feedback to the NHS organization. The report itself is drafted, checked by the reviewers and the NHS organization for factual accuracy and is then published. The NHS organizations are required to produce an action plan showing how it will respond to the CHI review findings; responsibility for taking this forward then rests with the organization itself and the Department of Health.

The Commission's report combines a narrative assessment of the NHS organization's performance across the three main areas listed in Table 4.11, with quantitative scoring in two areas – resources and processes, and the use of information. In each of the dimensions in these areas, the organization is scored on a scale from 1 to 4, as follows:

1 Little or no progress at strategic and planning level, or at operational level, which means that systems and processes do not exist, although there may be isolated examples of progress made through an individual's enthusiasm or initiative.
2 Worthwhile progress and development at strategic and planning levels, or at operational level, but not both, which means that systems are being developed but are incomplete, do not cover the whole organization or all key areas.
3 Good strategic grasp and substantial implementation, with alignment across the strategic, planning and operational levels, which means that systems for improvement are implemented across all or most of the organization.
4 Excellence – coordinated activity and development across the

organization and with partner organizations in the local health economy, which is demonstrably leading to improvement.

The Commission for Health Improvement is a relatively new organization and so far little is known about the impact of its clinical governance reviews on the NHS organizations involved, even though about 110 reviews had been completed by April 2002. However, early studies have highlighted three key issues for consideration (Day and Klein 2002; NHS Confederation 2002). First, while the absence of explicit standards and criteria for assessment allows the Commission to be flexible in its reviews, adjusting the process to fit the local context and making the most of the expertise of its reviewers, it may do so at the cost of some inconsistency and subjectivity in the process and its results. Report findings can appear to represent a rather haphazard set of concerns or the particular interests of individual reviewers, and may lack much empirical foundation beyond the opinions of the reviewers and the people whom they interviewed. Secondly, the heterogeneity of NHS organizations and their sheer scale and complexity makes it difficult for the CHI review to be anything more than a superficial assessment of organizational systems and processes. But whether that assessment is valid and meaningful, in the sense that it correlates with clinical performance and the quality of care delivered, can be questioned. Moreover, since the Commission examines progress at a largely strategic level and looks in detail at just three clinical service areas, it is likely that performance within the NHS organizations reviewed varies widely from service to service, but the Commission is not well placed to identify such variations. Thirdly, the impact of CHI reviews depends not just on their quality, but on the process for following up and pursuing the issues raised until changes are implemented. At present, this responsibility does not rest with the Commission, but with the Department of Health and strategic health authorities. Anecdotally, it seems that NHS organizations accord a much greater priority to preparing for a CHI review beforehand than they do to action planning and implementation afterwards.

The Commission also has powers to undertake investigations into service problems or failures in NHS organizations, either when asked to do so by the Department of Health or when issues come to its attention through other stakeholders or through its clinical governance reviews process. These investigations are not meant to substitute for local, internal inquiries into individual complaints or problems. Rather, they are meant to provide a mechanism for investigating, dealing with and learning from substantial and significant service failures that merit some kind of independent and external review. In the past, such investigations were largely undertaken on an *ad hoc* basis by health authorities or the Department of Health, who would appoint an independent chair and small panel to undertake a private inquiry and report their findings either privately or through a published report. In giving this responsibility to the Commission for Health Improvement, the aim is to make such investigations more clearly external and independent of the NHS organizations being investigated, and to develop greater continuity in investigatory expertise. In its first 2 years, the Commission completed seven such investigations, into problems in clinical services such as breast screening, heart and lung transplantation, and surgery, and management issues like the use of locum medical staff, the handling of serious allegations about the conduct of a GP, and the leadership and management arrangements of an NHS trust. Each report has been published, although the process of the investigation itself and the evidence or data gathered has remained confidential.

The Modernization Agency

Modernization has been a key theme in many areas of government policy including healthcare since 1997 when the Labour government's first White Paper on the NHS, titled 'The new NHS: modern, dependable' – set out a 10 year programme for 'the modernisation of the NHS' (Department of Health 1997). However, the term is rarely defined (Maddock 2002) and it has become a catch-all phrase for almost any innovation – NHS organizations undertake local modernization reviews, development moneys are called modernization funds, new posts as director of modernization are created and so on. In essence, the central ideas of modernization seem to be a willingness to embrace innovation and reform in the public sector, a desire to put the interests of service users above those of service providers, and a determination that good performance should be recognized and rewarded and poor performance should be addressed and dealt with.

The Modernization Agency was established in April 2001 as a part of the Department of Health; it is not a separate, freestanding authority or body like the National Institute for Clinical Excellence and the Commission for Health Improvement. It contains a diverse and somewhat disconnected range of activities, including:

the national patients' access team, which works on reducing waiting lists and times; the service redesign and collaboratives programme, which supports team-based service improvement initiatives; the national leadership centre, which focuses on leadership and management development; the primary care development team; the clinical governance support team, which works on training and development in clinical governance; and the changing workforce programme, which is directed at human resources development and new working practices (Modernization Agency 2001). In broad terms, the Modernization Agency's main function is to support NHS organizations in delivering the ambitious targets for service improvement that were set out in the NHS Plan (Department of Health 2000b). Its rather diverse portfolio of activities in part reflects the way it has been used as a convenient location to house a range of national initiatives which do not fit easily within the Department of Health or other organizations. It is not a conventional regulatory agency, although much of what it does – in areas like waiting list reduction, service redesign and clinical governance – fits the definition of regulation outlined in Chapter 2 and is similar in form and function to the activities of other regulators in the USA and the UK. Teams from the Modernization Agency oversee the progress of NHS organizations in these areas and may be sent into the organization to intervene when problems are identified. However, the Modernization Agency has no independence and little 'third-party' status, and could legitimately be argued simply to be part of the Department of Health's performance management function.

THE REGULATION OF PRIVATE HEALTHCARE: PAST AND PRESENT

Although most healthcare in the UK is provided by the National Health Service, there is a significant component both of private funding and private provision, especially in some sectors such as long-term care. The total value of health services provided by the private and independent sector was estimated at £14.5 billion per year in 1997–98. As Figure 4.2 shows, nearly half of that related to the provision of long-term care for the elderly and physically disabled in nursing or residential homes, or through home care. In 1997, there were around 5559 nursing homes in England, with around 186,000 beds. The acute sector makes up the second largest area of private healthcare provision, about 230 private or independent

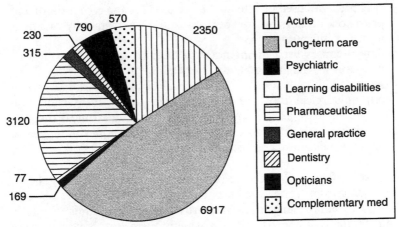

Figure 4.2 The value of the independent sector's supply of health services in the UK, 1997–98 (£ million).
Source: Health Select Committee (1999).

hospitals with about 9700 beds. There is often no clear dividing line between the NHS and the private sector. For example, much privately funded acute healthcare takes place in NHS hospitals, many of which have private beds in dedicated private patient units or wings (there are around 3000 private beds in the NHS). At the same time, it is estimated that 20 per cent of elective surgery funded by the NHS is undertaken in private hospitals, which do a third of all hip replacements and half of all abortions. There are some other sectors where private healthcare provision is especially significant, like palliative care (the NHS manages less than 18 per cent of specialist palliative care beds in England; most are in independent hospices) and non-acute psychiatric care (the independent sector provides 67 per cent of all beds) (Health Select Committee 1999).

Regulation by health authorities

Until relatively recently, the regulation of the private healthcare sector was, rather paradoxically, undertaken by the NHS. Health authorities (on behalf of the Secretary of State) had statutory responsibilities under the Registered Homes Act 1984 and other legislation for regulating a wide range of healthcare providers. The title of the Act is somewhat misleading, since it defines the organizations which come within its scope as:

- Any premises used or intended to be used for the reception of and provision of nursing for persons suffering from any sickness, injury or infirmity.
- Any premises used or intended to be used for the reception of pregnant women immediately after childbirth.
- Any other premises used for any or all of the following: carrying out of surgical procedures under anaesthesia; the termination of pregnancies; endoscopy; haemodialysis or peritoneal dialysis; or treatment by any 'specially controlled techniques' (a cover-all for things like laser cosmetic surgery, etc.).

This still left many healthcare providers almost wholly unregulated, from diagnostic services like pathology or MRI/CAT scans and health screening clinics to private drug and substance misuse clinics and domiciliary and day care providers. Even for those that were regulated, the regulatory arrangements were widely regarded as somewhat unsatisfactory, for several reasons. First, the legislation was often criticized for giving health authorities little power to set standards of practice and placing upon them the responsibility for proving that the healthcare provided was not adequate, rather than expecting the provider to show it was meeting the standards. While in theory health authorities had the power to sanction and ultimately delicense healthcare providers, in practice such sanctions were rarely used even in the face of continuing poor performance. Secondly, the process was very fragmented, with over 100 health authorities each running its own registration and inspection unit and often interpreting the standards very differently. For healthcare provider organizations which had multiple nursing homes or hospitals, there were considerable costs and problems associated with having to deal with multiple, different regulatory regimes. Although some health authorities – particularly those with a substantial local private sector to regulate – did a good job, many gave their regulatory responsibilities a low priority, and evaluations suggested that most had serious flaws (Social Services Inspectorate 2001). Thirdly, the process was largely focused on premises and facilities and did little to assure the quality and expertise of staff, or of processes of clinical care. Health authorities had few powers, for example, to concern themselves with the quality of clinical practice in private hospitals, and it was not unknown for clinicians removed from NHS organizations because of performance problems to resurface and continue to work unchecked in the private sector. Fourthly, and perhaps most importantly, the regulations had been drawn up at a time when the private healthcare sector was much smaller and largely confined to non-acute services such as nursing home care, as the title of the legislation suggests. Overall, the growth of private healthcare in the UK over the 1980s and 1990s and the fragmented, outdated and incomplete systems of regulation meant that there was an overwhelming case for regulatory reform (Nazarko 1997).

The National Care Standards Commission

The regulation of private health and social care was reformed in 2000 following a number of critical reports which highlighted the deficiencies and problems that have been outlined above (Burgner 1996; Health Select Committee 1999). A new national regulatory agency, the National Care Standards Commission (NCSC), was established by the Care Standards Act 2000, and it formally assumed responsibility for regulating a wide range of health and social care providers in England from April 2002. It took over the work undertaken by 95 health authority registration and inspection units (which regulated nursing homes, independent hospitals and other healthcare providers) and 150 local authority inspection units (which regulated care homes and some other social care providers). A list of the types of organizations now regulated by the Commission is shown in Table 4.12. Although it may appear comprehensive, many healthcare providers – especially complementary or alternative

Table 4.12 Health and social care providers regulated by the National Care Standards Commission

- Care homes
- Nursing homes
- Children's homes
- Residential family centres
- Domiciliary care agencies
- Nurses agencies
- Independent fostering agencies
- Voluntary adoption agencies
- Independent acute hospitals
- Independent mental health hospitals
- Hospices
- Maternity hospitals or clinics
- Abortion clinics
- Private (non-NHS) doctors
- Other healthcare providers

therapies and non-invasive interventions like counselling and slimming advice – remain unregulated (Mills 2001).

The Commission is a non-departmental public body, accountable to the Secretary of State for Health to whom the Care Standards Act gives considerable power to direct the Commission's work programme. It is funded in part by registration fees charged to the organizations it regulates and in part by the Department of Health. Although it is a very new organization, it is already facing major changes, which are described in the following section. However, it can still be analysed using the same evaluative framework as before (Table 4.13).

The National Care Standards Commission has four main functions: inspecting and regulating the health and social care providers who fall within its remit; improving the quality of services; supporting consumers by providing information and investigating complaints; and advising government on the quality of health and social care services. Its creation was intended to promote greater consistency and fairness through the application of one regulatory system across England, to bring greater independence and transparency to the regulatory process, to integrate health and social care regulation, and to extend regulatory protection to some that were not previously regulated (Hume 2001).

The early life of the Commission has been dominated by the challenges of creating such a large new agency, while maintaining the normal business of regulation. With an annual budget of around £70 million and about 2500 staff, the Commission is a very substantial undertaking. It has had to manage the transfer of staff, information and resources from existing health and local authority inspection units, establish its own infrastructure of regions, areas and offices, and design almost from new its regulatory mechanisms – standards, registration and inspection processes, enforcement procedures and so on. Tasked with regulating such a broad and diverse range of care providers, it is not surprising that the Commission has struggled to fulfil its complete mandate from the start. In effect, most of its attention has been focused on securing its regulatory infrastructure and ensuring all care providers are registered, rather than on the actual business of regulation.

However, the Commission has published the standards it plans to use to regulate care homes, healthcare providers and most of the other entities listed in Table 4.12. For example, the regulations for care homes list 38 separate standards, which are grouped together under seven main headings, as Table 4.14 illustrates (NCSC

Table 4.13 A regulatory analysis of the National Care Standards Commission

Characteristic	National Care Standards Commission (NCSC)
Regulating organization	NCSC is an extra-departmental public body created by the Care Standards Act 2000. It is led by a board of Commissioners appointed by the Secretary of State for Health. It is responsible to the Secretary of State, who sets its budget and can direct its programme of work
Regulatory goals/ objectives	NCSC 'aims to be a champion for safe, high quality services, instilling public confidence in social care and independent healthcare service'
Scope of regulation	All organizations providing social care for adults and children and organizations providing independent healthcare services in England. NCSC regulates at least 15 different sectors or areas, from care homes to nurses agencies, from hospices to abortion clinics
Regulatory model	It is still rather early to predict what model of regulation NCSC will display in the longer term. In most of the areas in which it works (e.g. care and nursing homes), the previous tradition inherited by NCSC has been one of compliance regulation. However, there is some early evidence from the way that regulations and standards have been set that NCSC is likely to be less compliance-oriented and more willing to tackle performance issues, using deterrence methods if need be
Direction	For each of the areas listed in Table 4.12, NCSC produces and publishes a set of regulatory standards which set out its requirements across several areas of practice. Within each area, a number of standards are defined, each of which is specified in some detail
Detection	In its first year of operation, NCSC concentrated on getting all organizations registered rather than on mounting inspections of all organizations, but this is likely to change. In theory, NCSC should be visiting each nursing or care home at least once or twice a year, but this is unlikely to be achieved at present
Enforcement	NCSC has some significant enforcement powers. In addition to being able to publish its findings and take follow-up actions, such as further inspections of poorly performing organizations, it can also levy fines of up to £5000 on organizations or on individuals through the courts. Most significantly, it will be able to delicense organizations and so effectively close them down.

Table 4.14 National Care Standards Commission minimum standards for care homes

Choice of home	Information, contract, needs assessment, meeting needs, trial visits, intermediate care
Health and personal care	Service user plan, health care, medication, privacy and dignity, dying and death
Daily life and social activities	Social contact and activities, community contact, autonomy and choice, meals and mealtimes
Complaints and protection	Complaints, rights, protection
Environment	Premises, shared facilities, lavatories and washing facilities, adaptations and equipment, individual accommodation space requirements, individual accommodation furniture and fittings, heating and lighting, hygiene and control of infection
Staffing	Staff complement, qualifications, recruitment, staff training
Management and administration	Day-to-day operations, ethos, quality assurance, financial procedures, service users' money, staff supervision, record-keeping, safe working practices

Standard 10: Privacy and dignity: service users feel they are treated with respect and their right to privacy is upheld

10.1   The arrangements for health and personal care ensure that service users' privacy and dignity are respected at all times, with particular regard to:

- personal care-giving, including nursing, bathing, washing, using the toilet or commode
- consultation with, and examination by, health and social care professionals
- consultation with legal and financial advisers
- maintaining social contacts with relative and friends
- entering bedrooms, toilets and bathrooms
- following death

10.2   Service users have easy access to a telephone for use in private and receive their mail unopened

10.3   Service users wear their own clothes at all times

10.4   All staff use the term of address preferred by the service user

10.5   All staff are instructed during induction on how to treat service users with respect at all times

10.6   Medical examination and treatment are provided in the service user's own room

10.7   Where service users have chosen to share a room, screening is provided to ensure their privacy is not compromised when personal care is being given or at any other time

2002a). For each of the 38 standards there is a brief statement of the intended outcome or purpose of the standard, followed by a detailed breakdown of its components. To comply, a home must meet all parts of the standard. Table 4.14 contains one standard as an example, which covers the right to privacy and dignity. It can be compared with the standard for privacy and confidentiality in US nursing homes (see Table 3.14).

The aim of the NCSC care home standards has been to focus on 'achievable outcomes for service users – that is, the impact on the individual of the facilities and services of the home' (NCSC 2002a). Most of the standards concern processes and activities, yet it is the standards for premises and physical facilities that have been most controversial and problematic for current providers. The standards required homes: to provide 4.1 square metres of communal space per service user; to have at least one assisted bath per eight service users; to provide en-suite toilet and handbasin facilities; to have 800 mm wide doorways; to provide single rooms for service users with at least 12 square metres of space; not to require any service user to share a room if they do not want to; and to meet a host of other standards for furnishing, lighting and heating. Some existing homes had exemptions from some of these requirements and were not required to comply with others until 2007, but the potential capital cost of upgrading some smaller care homes in non-purpose-built accommodation means they may not be economically viable. These regulations were met with considerable hostility from providers, who felt that they favoured larger, purpose-built care homes and disfavoured smaller, traditional care homes in converted residential properties. When the regulations were introduced, there was much anecdotal evidence that some homes were being closed and converted to other purposes because they would not be able to comply. Eventually, under considerable pressure, the Commission and the Secretary of State suspended this part of the new regulations.

The 81 page manual of care home standards is relatively straightforward compared with the 221 page manual outlining the regulations for independent healthcare providers – acute hospitals, maternity services, psychiatric clinics, day surgery units and so on (NCSC 2002b). This contains 32 core standards, which apply to any organization, and then further service-specific standards for different entities: 44 standards for acute hospitals, 47 for mental health establishments, 15 for hospices, 8 for maternity hospitals and so on. The core standards deal mainly with process-oriented generic issues, such as the provision of information to patients and systems for quality management, human resources, complaints, risk management and health records. The service-specific standards are more clinically oriented; for example, the acute hospital standards include sections on children's services, surgery, critical care, radiology, pharmacy, pathology and cancer services.

The Commission has several enforcement powers. First, it will publish the reports of its inspections and could use this mechanism to put non-compliance in the public domain and to pressure regulated organizations to comply. Secondly, it will be able to take legal proceedings against regulated organizations that fail to comply with the regulations, which could result in a fine of up to £5000 either against the organization or against individuals such as a nursing home manager or proprietor. Thirdly, it will be able to delicense both organizations and individuals, taking away an organization's ability to provide regulated services and preventing an individual from working in a management capacity in regulated organizations in the future. It has been argued that the Commission's powers to fine and delicense providers are high-level sanctions which are likely to be used rarely, and that the Commission lacks lower-level or intermediate sanctions which it is more likely to need to use (Kerrison and Pollock 2001). For example, it does not have powers to make a provider stop taking new admissions, to withhold payments to the provider pending compliance, or to require changes in management or to install new management.

Overall, it seems certain that the National Care Standards Commission will bring a welcome improvement to the rigour, consistency and comprehensiveness of private or independent healthcare regulation in England, although it is still too soon to say how effective the regulatory approach it has adopted will prove to be. Indeed, we may never know because just a few weeks after the Commission formally assumed its regulatory responsibilities in April 2002, the government announced plans to reform the regulation of both health and social care in England, which are discussed in the next section.

THE FUTURE FOR HEALTH AND SOCIAL CARE REGULATION IN ENGLAND

National Health Service organizations have long complained about the problems of regulatory or inspectorial overload and fragmentation (Day and Klein 1990; Scrivens 1995) – too many regulatory agencies or oversight mechanisms, each making considerable demands for information, and sometimes conflicting with each other over the data they seek or the requirements they impose. At best, this might represent unnecessary duplication and a waste of resources. More seriously, it could have high opportunity costs for NHS organizations, impair their capacity to manage effectively, and create a culture of defensive compliance rather than one of creativity and innovation. As Figure 4.3 shows, NHS organizations interact with at least 16 different agencies which regulate or oversee them, in addition to being performance-managed by strategic health authorities and the Department of Health. However, factories, banks, retailers, insurance companies and many other entities also face multiple, overlapping forms of regulation, and it is hard to see why healthcare organizations should be an exception.

Nevertheless, almost as soon as the government created the National Institute for Clinical Excellence, the Commission for Health Improvement and the other new regulators for the NHS

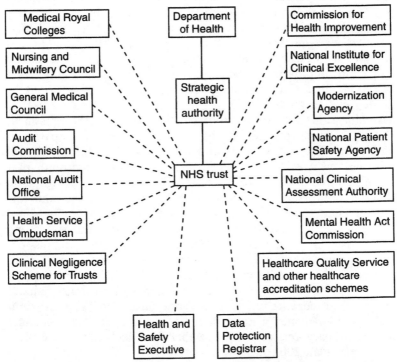

Figure 4.3 The regulatory landscape from the perspective of a NHS trust.

listed in Table 4.7, plus the National Care Standards Commission for the private sector, a number of commentators began to suggest that there were now too many separate regulatory agencies with overlapping and duplicative remits. From quite early in its existence, the Commission for Health Improvement was tasked with leading attempts to coordinate the work of different regulators, by creating bilateral memoranda of agreement (CHI 2001b) and by bringing regulators together to share data and coordinate their activities.

In April 2002, the Department of Health announced a wholesale reform of the systems for regulating health and social care in both the public and private sector in England (Department of Health 2002). Just 2 years after the creation of the Commission for Health Improvement, and only 2 weeks after the National Care Standards Commission had taken over responsibility for regulating private health and social care, the Department published proposals to rationalize health and social care regulation by creating two new 'super-regulators' – a Commission for Healthcare Audit and Inspection, to regulate all healthcare provision, and a Commission for Social Care Inspection, to regulate all social care. The primary responsibilities of these two new agencies are set out in Table 4.15.

It can be seen that the Commission for Healthcare Audit and Inspection will take over all the responsibilities of the Commission for Health Improvement, the private healthcare regulation function of the National Care Standards Commission, the value-for-money audit function for the NHS of the Audit Commission, as well as assuming some functions (like producing performance assessment statistics and star ratings) previously performed by the Department of Health. The new Commission for Social Care Inspection will take over the role of the Social Services Inspectorate (currently part of the Department of Health), the private social care regulation function of the National Care Standards Commission, the value-for-money audit function for social care of the Audit Commission, and some of the performance assessment statistic and star rating functions of the Department of Health and the Audit Commission. The Commission for Health Improvement, the National Care Standards Commission, and the Social Services Inspectorate will all cease to exist, and the Audit Commission will be much reduced in scale and scope, returning to its core business of financial audit and value-for-money work with local government. These changes require primary legislation and are, therefore, likely to take full effect sometime in late 2003 or 2004.

It is still too early to tell what effects these major regulatory

Table 4.15 The reform of health and social care regulation in England, 2002–2003

Regulatory agency	Commission for Healthcare Audit and Inspection	Commission for Social Care Inspection
Key functions	• Inspects all NHS hospitals • Licenses private healthcare provision • Conducts NHS value-for-money audits on a national basis • Validates published performance assessment statistics on the NHS, including waiting lists • Publishes star ratings for all NHS organizations with the ability to recommend special measures where there are persistent problems • Publishes reports on the performance of NHS organizations both individually and collectively • Independent scrutinization of patient complaints • Publishes an annual report to Parliament on national progress in healthcare and how resources have been used	• Carries out local inspections of all social care organizations – public private and voluntary – including care homes and publishes reports of these inspections • Registers services that meet national standards • Carries out inspections of local authority social services departments • Validates all published performance assessment statistics on social care • Publishes the star ratings for social service authorities, with the ability to recommend special measures where there are persistent problems • Publishes an annual report to Parliament on national progress on social care and an analysis of where resources have been used
Replaces regulation by:	Commission for Health Improvement, Audit Commission, National Care Standards Commission and Department of Health	Social Services Inspectorate, Audit Commission, National Care Standards Commission and Department of Health

reforms will have on health and social care regulation and on the performance of health and social care providers. However, a number of important themes and issues can be identified. First, these two new regulators may be more independent of government than their predecessors have been, and the reforms seem to signal a transfer of power from the Department of Health to these independent regulatory agencies. Both will be extra-departmental public bodies accountable to the Department of Health, but the Department plans to hand over responsibility for appointing the board and chief executive of the Commission for Health Audit and Inspection to the NHS Appointments Commission. Key functions which used to be part of the Department (including the Social Services Inspectorate) are to be transferred to the new regulators, and they will have expanded enforcement powers which they can exercise for themselves rather than being reliant on the Department of Health to take up their recommendations. It is not yet clear how they will be funded or to what extent their budgets will be set and controlled by the Department, but it is likely that a growing proportion of their income will come from fees paid by the organizations they regulate, meaning they may be financially less dependent on central government. Most importantly, both the new regulators will report annually directly to Parliament on their work, a very significant change in practice which further lessens Department of Health control.

Secondly, particularly in the healthcare arena, the reforms appear to represent a move away from compliance regulation towards a more deterrence-oriented approach. In its short existence, the Commission for Health Improvement has consistently adopted a collaborative, consensual approach in which it focuses on improvement through learning and sharing good practice (CHI 2002). Despite some political pressure to deliver tough and adversarial inspection reports in the style of the Office for Standards in Education (OFSTED), the Commission for Health Improvement has stood its ground and stuck to its continuous improvement principles, but this seems unlikely to continue. The name of the new healthcare regulator – the Commission for Healthcare Audit and Inspection – seems to signal an underlying change in philosophy, as does the language of the policy paper announcing the changes, which speaks of the Commission as 'a single rigorous inspectorate armed with the ability to expose poor practice and highlight good practice' (Department of Health 2002). It remains to be seen whether the new regulators are able to behave responsively, using both compliance and deterrence approaches when appropriate, or whether circumstances result in them adopting a less flexible and deterrence-oriented style of regulation.

Thirdly, the Commission for Healthcare Audit and Inspection, which takes over NHS healthcare regulation from the Commission for Health Improvement (CHI) and private and independent healthcare regulation from the National Care Standards Commission (NCSC), will have to reconcile two very different styles of regulation. As was noted earlier, CHI has avoided setting explicit clinical standards, has focused on systems and processes for clinical governance, and has adopted a relatively implicit approach to review that relies heavily on the expertise and professional skills of their review teams. In contrast, NCSC has defined explicit standards which tend to be more functionally or departmentally focused, covering issues like health records, radiology services, surgery and anaesthesia, and so on. There are many other differences: CHI is scheduled to review NHS organizations once every 4 years, while NCSC visits private healthcare providers twice every year; CHI uses teams of reviewers drawn from other regulated organizations, while NCSC uses full-time inspectors. Perhaps most importantly, CHI has few formal powers of enforcement – it can publish its reports, make recommendations to the Department of Health and make further follow-up visits. In contrast, NCSC can take providers to court and see them fined, and can take away the licence to operate of either an individual or an organization. The boundaries between the private and NHS healthcare sectors have never been especially clear, and the current trend towards the greater use of the private sector in healthcare delivery seems likely to make any distinctions between the two increasingly artificial. This means there will be a strong rationale and considerable pressure for a 'level playing field' – the same systems for direction, detection and enforcement at the Commission for Healthcare Audit and Inspection for NHS and independent healthcare providers alike.

Finally, the new structure splits regulation of health and social care between two agencies, when the direction of public policy is, and has been for some time, towards integration, with efforts to get local authorities and NHS organizations to pool resources, share staff and work more cooperatively. The most recent embodiment of this policy is the care trust – an NHS trust providing both health and social care services within a single organization – which might end up being regulated by both the two new regulators. The government considered creating a single agency to regulate both health and social care, but decided that the risks and problems associated with managing such a large regulatory body were too great, at least in the first instance. It remains to be seen whether, once they are established, the two new regulators manage to work collaboratively.

The creation of the Commission for Healthcare Audit and Inspection and the Commission for Social Care Inspection appears to represent a significant step away from national, centrally directed bureaucratic structures and systems in health and social care, and a genuine transfer of power and responsibility from central government to these new regulatory agencies. If the politicians can be persuaded to let go, these new regulators could represent a genuinely new approach to performance management and improvement. The longstanding tradition of direct ministerial accountability for everything that happens in the NHS could be replaced by a more indirect and distanced relationship in which managed regulation by intermediate and quasi-independent organizations plays a growing role. In that environment, the new regulatory agencies may be more able to develop a responsive approach to regulation, learning from the experience of regulation in other settings, and focusing regulation on delivering real improvement for patients.

5

ANALYSING HEALTHCARE REGULATION

Chapters 3 and 4 provide a rich and detailed account of the development and use of healthcare regulation in two very different healthcare systems, those of the USA and the UK. However, the great diversity in regulatory agencies, regimes and methods that they describe raises many questions. What causes these variations? Do they represent legitimate and necessary adaptations of regulatory approach to the specific regulatory task and context, or are they an unproductive and unnecessary result of poor regulatory design and a lack of understanding of the determinants of effective regulation? For the researcher, this variation provides an opportunity to study and attempt to understand the causes of variation in regulatory design, the dynamics of the regulatory process and its impact on organizational performance. Regulatory agencies are often rather risk-averse and cautious about regulatory experimentation, so this kind of inter-agency, inter-sectoral or international comparison of regulation may be the best way to improve our understanding of how regulation works.

This chapter first examines the impact of regulation on organizational performance. It then uses the evaluative framework first introduced in Chapter 2 and then used throughout Chapters 3 and 4 to describe the use of healthcare regulation in the USA and the UK, to examine the similarities and differences in systems of healthcare regulation and to draw out from the available evidence some lessons about what may constitute effective regulation.

DOES REGULATION WORK?

Perhaps the most important question to pose (and the most difficult to answer) is whether regulation 'works', which might be rephrased as two linked concerns: What impact does regulation have on the performance of healthcare organizations and to what extent does regulation achieve its objectives?

Although healthcare regulation is widespread in both the USA and the UK, there is surprisingly little research evidence to help us to answer either of these two questions. Evaluating the impact of healthcare regulation is methodologically challenging. One obvious strategy is to compare the performance of regulated and unregulated organizations but this is often not possible because all healthcare organizations fall within the regulatory process. Even when there are some unregulated organizations to serve as a control group, if organizations can decide for themselves whether to participate in regulation, the resulting groups are unlikely to be comparable. A second strategy is to examine changes in the performance of regulated organizations over time, perhaps before and after a specific regulatory intervention. This may be more feasible, but there will always be many potential sources of bias and confounding that make it difficult to interpret any changes over time. When the data about the impact of regulation are a product of the regulatory process, as they often are, then comparisons become even more difficult to make, as any observed changes could result either from real changes in performance or simply from changes in how regulatory data are collected.

However, a brief review of the findings of evaluative research – some of which have already been detailed in relation to specific areas of regulation in Chapters 3 and 4 – provides some immediate insights into the impact of regulation. For example, in relation to US managed care regulation, the National Committee for Quality Assurance (NCQA 2000, 2001) has used the Health Plan Employer Data and Information Set (HEDIS) to show some improving quality trends in managed care over time, and has demonstrated that health plans which undergo NCQA accreditation and those which allow their HEDIS scores to be published do better than those who do not, although some caution is needed in attributing these differences to the effects of regulation. Among US hospitals, despite years of regulation, there is still relatively little data available on the effects of regulation on their performance or on the quality of care. For example, studies examining the relationship between JCAHO (Joint Commission on the Accreditation of Healthcare Organizations) accreditation results and other measures of hospital performance (Hadley and McGurrin 1988; Jessee and Schranz 1990; HCIA/ JCAHO 1993) have struggled to find any meaningful association. A recent Office of the Inspector General investigation of hospital regulation concluded that the JCAHO accreditation process mattered greatly to hospitals and was effective in prompting some improvement, but was insufficiently searching to identify or deal with many quality problems (OIG 1999a). A parallel examination of state agencies' Medicare certification of hospitals concluded that the process for undertaking regular surveys of hospitals was seriously deficient but had little to say about its actual impact (OIG 1999b). Rather better data exist for the impact of regulation on US nursing homes. Since regulatory reform in the 1980s, there are indications that the quality of care has improved to some extent (Hawes 1996; Kapp 2000). For example, the inappropriate use of physical and chemical restraints has declined, as have rates of urinary incontinence and catheterization. Hospitalization rates for nursing home residents (which may be a good proxy for quality of nursing home care if poor care increases the risk of hospitalization) have also fallen. On the other hand, pressure sore rates have not changed, malnutrition, dehydration and other feeding problems remain relatively common, and rates of bowel incontinence have risen slightly (Harrington *et al.* 2000). Interestingly, the numbers of deficiencies found by regulators in their nursing home inspections at first fell but have risen again; however, this probably reflects changes in the regulatory process rather than underlying changes in the quality or performance of nursing homes. A series of General Accounting Office investigations have been critical of nursing home regulation and its enforcement by the Health Care Financing Administration and state agencies (GAO 1999a,b,c, 2000). Overall, a decade of quite aggressive and forceful nursing home regulation appears to have yielded only modest improvements in performance and quality (Institute of Medicine 2001).

In the UK, studies of the impact of regulation are somewhat rarer, but their results are broadly similar. For example, evaluations of the Health Advisory Service suggested that its impact was fairly limited (Day *et al.* 1988; Henkel *et al.* 1989); other studies of the Audit Commission and the Social Services Inspectorate were rather more positive about their ability to influence performance, although they noted that change was often still slow to happen (Day and Klein 1990). Evaluations of accreditation programmes in the UK and elsewhere have suggested that while they are often valued by various stakeholders, it is difficult to point to specific improvements that have resulted (Scrivens 1995; Walshe *et al.* 1999). Even more recent evaluations of new developments in healthcare regulation in the UK provide a similarly mixed message about their value (Walshe *et al.* 2001; Day and Klein 2002; NHS Confederation 2002).

There is little doubt that regulation does impact on the performance of healthcare organizations, but overwhelmingly the research suggests that it has both positive (or desirable) and negative (or undesirable) effects; and that those effects are not highly predictable or deterministic, in that they vary not only from regulatory programme to programme, but also within any one programme between organizations and over time. A summary of the commonly reported positive and negative effects of regulatory intervention is presented in Table 5.1. For policy-makers, regulators, regulated organizations, and other stakeholders in healthcare regulation, including patients and the public, the important question is whether regulation can be designed to deliver the positive effects listed on the left in Table 5.1, while minimizing or even avoiding the negative effects listed on the right. Any assessment of the effectiveness of regulation needs to take into account both the benefits and the harms it may cause, as the table demonstrates.

Of course, this discussion of the impact of regulation should not be simply focused on its impact on performance improvement, ignoring the wider political and social context in which regulation exists and the wide range of reasons for its development, which are set out in Chapter 2. Performance improvement is one of the objectives of regulation, perhaps even its primary objective, but regulation also serves other social and political purposes. If many of the systems of healthcare regulation in the USA and the UK, described in Chapters 3 and 4, are assessed solely in terms of their contribution to improving the performance of regulated organizations, the inevitable conclusion would be that they don't work very well, but that conclusion might miss the point if they were created for other reasons and to serve other purposes. The objectives of regulation are discussed later in this chapter, which now uses the evaluative framework introduced in Chapter 2 and used throughout Chapters 3 and 4 to present its analysis of healthcare regulation.

Table 5.1 The impact of healthcare regulation on organizational performance: a summary of reported positive and negative effects

Positive effects	Negative effects
• Specific changes and improvements in patient care resulting from regulatory attention, such as improved pain management in hospitals, reduced use of physical restraints in nursing homes, better arrangements for dealing with patients' complaints	• Temporary rather than sustained performance improvement, in which organizations 'ramp up' in preparation for regulatory scrutiny or inspection, but then drop back to their usual performance immediately afterwards
• Causing organizational reflection and comparison, as organizations both examine their own performance in preparation for inspection and compare themselves with regulatory standards and with the performance of others – this may help to avoid organizational isolation or introspection	• Pointless conformance behaviours in which things are done solely to satisfy regulators which have little or no value for patients or the organization – such as the production of policy and procedure manuals which are not used, or the setting up of committees and structures mandated by the regulator, although the organization may not need or want them; ultimately this results in a decoupling of regulatory compliance and internal performance improvement efforts
• Giving important or longer-term issues greater organizational priority than they would otherwise receive, such as the production of proper policies and procedures, the updating of guidelines, etc.; or prioritizing quality of care in an environment that would otherwise be wholly cost-driven or led by shorter-term, more urgent needs	• Defensive or minimal compliance, in which standards that set a basic minimum or floor for performance are treated as a target instead, performance improvement beyond the standards is discouraged, and they effectively act as a limit on rather than a stimulus for improvement
• Providing leverage for change – in professionally dominated organizations in which quality improvement staff and managers may have limited powers to drive change, external regulation is used to give them leverage and to sanction or validate changes that would be difficult to enact without an external force	• Creative compliance, in which organizations appear to comply with regulatory requirements, but do so not by changing underlying behaviours or practices but by

Table 5.1—*continued*

Positive effects	Negative effects
• Driving continuing improvement – as regulatory standards are continually updated and improved, each regulatory cycle demands greater performance than the last, this has been termed the 'ratchet effect'	making superficial changes such as relabelling activities using the regulator's terminology • Prevention of innovation or improvement, in which regulatory standards discourage or prevent changes that would improve patient care because they embed existing practices or are insufficiently flexible to permit change – for example, preventing nursing homes having animals as pets, or preventing patients taking care of and controlling their own medication • Distortion of organizational priorities, as organizations respond to issues raised by regulators instead of dealing with more important problems which are identified internally – the focus is not on problem-solving but on regulatory compliance • Opportunity costs, as organizations invest considerable resources, particularly clinical and managerial time, in preparing for and undergoing regulatory scrutiny, which could be used in other more productive ways

REGULATORY AGENCIES: STRUCTURE, POWERS AND GOVERNANCE

Regulatory agencies come in all shapes and sizes and the diversity of form illustrated in Chapters 3 and 4 provides an opportunity to compare and contrast their structures, powers and governance arrangements and to draw some tentative conclusions about the impact of these characteristics on regulatory behaviour. This section raises four main issues: the different characteristics of governmental versus non-governmental regulation; regulatory accountability and governance; regulatory agency size; and the relationship between regulatory and non-regulatory responsibilities.

In defining regulation in Chapter 2, it was noted that it is undertaken 'in the public interest', although not necessarily directly by government. We have seen a range of examples of regulation, from those in which the regulator is a government agency to those in which regulatory agencies are created and organized by other stakeholders, such as industry associations, professional groups and healthcare funders like large employers. It is clear that each has different advantages and disadvantages. Government regulatory agencies often have more authority and greater legal powers – regulation can be made mandatory and sanctions can have the force of law – but their proximity to government, to legislators and to the electoral process can present problems. Government regulators are often slow-moving and bureaucratic entities. They have to follow government rules about how regulations and standards are made, like the US Administrative Procedures Act (Rosenbloom 1994), which slow them down and make them appear rule-bound and inflexible; they often have ambitious mandates but strictly limited resources; and they are always accountable to government and to legislators, who tend to give them as little freedom of action and space to exercise discretion as they can. These problems of government regulation reach their apotheosis in regulators like the Centers for Medicare and Medicaid Services (CMS), the huge federal agency that is, in effect, the government regulator for hospitals and nursing homes in the USA, and whose regulatory efforts for hospitals and nursing homes are widely criticized, as Chapter 3 detailed.

However, much regulation – perhaps even most regulation – is undertaken by non-governmental regulators, often created by industry and professional organizations for a variety of motives, including a genuine desire to drive up service standards, a search for competitive advantage over other providers, an anti-competitive attempt to drive or keep others out of the marketplace, or a way to forestall more rigorous, external regulation by government. Non-governmental regulators are often smaller, more flexible and faster to respond when changes in regulatory standards or methods are needed. Without the pressures of political scrutiny, they may be more able to innovate and have more scope for discretion and freedom of action in their approach to regulation. However, with no formal legal powers or authority over the organizations they regulate, non-governmental regulators often struggle to get organizations to participate or to comply with regulatory requirements. And without the checks and balances of democratic accountability, they may be more prone to being captured or influenced by sectional interests, most obviously the regulated organizations that often played some part in setting them up in the first place.

In both the USA and the UK, hybrid models of regulation have emerged which attempt to combine the advantages of both governmental and non-governmental regulation. In the USA, by 'deeming' private regulatory processes to meet the certification needs of publicly funded healthcare programmes like Medicare and Medicaid, government has effectively endorsed the accreditation programmes of agencies like the Joint Commission on the Accreditation of Healthcare Organizations (JCAHO) and the National Committee for Quality Assurance (NCQA) and given them much of the authority and leverage which goes with government backing, while keeping them at arm's length from the bureaucratic controls, administrative limits and political interference that beset government regulation. In the UK, government has sought to strengthen the independence of public regulators like the Commission for Health Improvement (CHI), the Audit Commission, the National Care Standards Commission (NCSC) and the new Commission for Healthcare Audit and Inspection (CHAI), by putting them at arm's length from government, handing over responsibility for appointing their boards to an independent commission, giving them powers of enforcement which they can exercise for themselves without reference to government, and providing them with some independence from government funding through fees raised from regulated organizations. This kind of private–public hybrid model of regulation appears to allow an approach to regulation that is more responsive, flexible and effective than either straightforward governmental or non-governmental regulation can be.

Regardless of whether a regulator is part of government, its arrangements for governance and accountability are important determinants of its regulatory behaviour. Regulators clearly need to be held to account for their performance, but by whom? It is unhealthy for the regulator to be governed too directly by any of the main stakeholders in the process of regulation. In the USA, JCAHO is often accused of being too closely identified with the industry groupings (like the American Medical Association and the American Hospitals Association) which dominate its board and seem to have a great deal of influence on what it does. In contrast, US nursing home regulation is led by the Centers for Medicare and Medicaid Services (CMS), which is also the main governmental funder of nursing home care. The CMS thus faces a conflict of interest when making decisions as a regulator, which might raise the costs of nursing home care and which it might then have to fund. For example, the introduction of minimum staffing level regulations for nursing homes has widespread industry and public support, but it would impose considerable additional costs which nursing homes would then look to CMS to bear. In the UK, the predominance of government in healthcare funding, provision and regulation creates a similar problem of conflicting interests and priorities for regulators. For example, when the National Institute for Clinical Excellence (NICE) makes its recommendations about the uptake of new drugs and other healthcare interventions, its ability to exercise independence and objectivity in reaching its decisions is often questioned, because it is funded by and accountable to the Department of Health, which has to pay for the treatments which the Institute endorses. Together with CHI and the other healthcare regulators described in Chapter 4, NICE is essentially an instrument of government; their boards are appointed by the Secretary of State at the Department of Health, who also sets their work programmes, determines their funding, and controls most of their powers.

In general terms, if the governance and accountability of the regulator is dominated by any one stakeholder – funders, providers, patients, professionals, government or whatever – it seems to create at the very least an appearance of regulatory capture by that sectional interest, which compromises and undermines the regulator's independence and its ability to act as an honest broker, and may, fairly or unfairly, bring the whole process of regulation into disrepute. A balanced stakeholder model of regulatory governance, in which all the major stakeholders in regulation play some part, through the regulating body's board or in other ways, appears to have much to recommend it. It helps to prevent any one sectional interest group capturing the process of regulation or wielding undue influence, gives the regulator a greater legitimacy for its actions, and is likely to give it greater freedom of action and scope for regulatory discretion. In the USA, the National Committee for Quality Assurance (NCQA), which regulates health plans, provides a useful example of this kind of model of regulatory governance.

The regulatory agencies described in Chapters 3 and 4 varied widely in their size and in the extent to which they were solely a

regulator or had other non-regulatory responsibilities as well. There
is a good case for the existence of some regulatory economies and
efficiencies of scale – that larger regulators are more able to meet and
spread the costs of regulatory standard-setting, are better equipped
to enforce regulatory requirements and are more likely to hold their
own in negotiations with regulated organizations and other stakeholders in regulation. However, it is also evident that large regulatory
agencies can be bureaucratic and inflexible organizations, making it
difficult to be responsive and adaptable in their approach to regulation. In US healthcare, the very different regulatory styles adopted
by NCQA (which regulates around 325 health plans), JCAHO
(which regulates about 4500 hospitals) and CMS (which regulates
around 17,000 nursing homes) in part result from their scale, and
serve to illustrate that larger regulators are not necessarily more
effective or efficient in what they do. Smaller regulators, interacting
with a limited number of regulated organizations, may be more able
to build up good working relationships with those organizations, to
establish a deep understanding of their strengths and weaknesses,
and to tailor or adapt their regulatory interventions to take account
of this information. Larger regulators, in contrast, dealing with
many regulated organizations, are more prone to treat them all the
same way, using 'one size fits all' regulatory approaches that prioritize consistency over regulatory efficiency and effectiveness.

Finally, although some regulatory agencies have a single mission
and purpose – regulation – others combine their regulatory
responsibilities with other non-regulatory activities, and for others
regulation is only a subsidiary part of their primary role. For
example, in the UK the medical Royal Colleges accredit training for
doctors, but as part of a wider, largely non-regulatory responsibility
for professional development in the specialties. The NHS Litigation
Authority inspects NHS trusts to accredit their risk management
arrangements, but its primary, non-regulatory role is to manage
claims for clinical negligence against NHS organizations. In the
USA, JCAHO is primarily a regulator, but it also runs a thriving
consultancy, education and development business aimed at the
healthcare organizations which it regulates. The CMS and the state
survey agencies regulate nursing homes, but they have many other
non-regulatory responsibilities as well.

There might be some advantages in combining regulatory and non-
regulatory roles, if a synergy between the two can be identified – for
example, if non-regulatory activities provide a source of information
about performance which can then be used in the process of regula-

tion, or if they provide the regulator with additional leverage over regulated organizations which can be used to promote compliance with regulatory requirements. However, it is equally easy to imagine situations in which the combined responsibilities could conflict. For example, when a regulator like JCAHO is also a supplier of services like consultancy or education to the organizations it regulates, there is an obvious commercial conflict of interest, however ethically the regulator attempts to manage it. When regulation is just one of many responsibilities for an agency, there is clearly a risk that it will not be a high organizational priority, or that regulatory and non-regulatory objectives will conflict, or even that progress in non-regulatory areas will be traded off with regulated organizations in exchange for concessions in regulation. For example, it has been argued that one reason for the ineffective regulation of nursing homes in the USA by CMS and state governments is that they have many other jobs to do, and that nursing home regulation is a relatively unglamorous and low-profile task which is easily deprioritized (Walshe 2001a). On the whole, unless there is a strong case for synergy, it appears that giving a regulatory agency non-regulatory tasks to manage risks compromising the clarity and priority of the regulatory mission.

REGULATORY GOALS OR OBJECTIVES

In Chapter 1, it was shown that the primary purpose of regulation is, or should be, performance improvement. As Chapters 3 and 4 showed, most regulatory agencies define their overall aims or mission largely in these terms – for example, the Joint Commission on the Accreditation of Healthcare Organizations aims 'to continuously improve the safety and quality of care provided to the public through the provision of health care accreditation'; the Centers for Medicare and Medicaid Services regulates hospitals and nursing homes 'to improve quality and protect the health and safety of beneficiaries'; the California State Licensing and Certification Agency aims 'to improve access to care and assure quality of care'; and the National Committee for Quality Assurance defines its mission ambitiously as 'to improve the quality of healthcare delivered to people everywhere'. In the UK, the Audit Commission 'aims to be a driving force in the improvement of public services' and the Commission for Health Improvement exists 'to help improve the quality of patient care by assisting the NHS in addressing unacceptable variations and to ensure a consistently high standard of patient care.'

However, a more careful examination of regulatory theory and practice suggests that there are essentially three main objectives pursued by regulators – improvement, assurance and accountability (Klein and Scrivens 1993; Walsh and Walshe 1998). It is worth exploring each of these briefly to examine how these aims and objectives are reflected in the methods and processes of regulation. It should be noted that they are not necessarily congruent aims and it is not difficult to identify circumstances in which they can and do conflict. The first and most often stated aim of regulation is improvement, and the effectiveness of regulation in achieving this aim might be measured straightforwardly by assessing whether it brings about changes in practice that result in better quality of care for patients. As noted above, evidence to show that regulation produces performance improvement is not always easy to come by. The second aim of regulation is assurance. This aim is rather different, not to drive improvement but to assure stakeholders like healthcare funders, purchasers and users that health services meet certain standards of quality, safety and effectiveness. Here, the focus is on maintaining rather than improving performance, in particular on preventing or dealing with poor performance. The third aim, accountability, is to make healthcare organizations and the powerful healthcare professions which work within them more directly accountable to patients and the general public for their performance. Here, the focus is on empowering patients, users and the public in their interactions with healthcare organizations and with health professionals.

As Table 5.2 below illustrates, these different aims can require quite different regulatory approaches and methods. For example, a regulator aiming to achieve improvement will set demanding regulatory requirements (which most organizations cannot achieve), but will then work with all organizations to support them in moving towards those ambitious goals. In contrast, a regulator aiming for assurance will set baseline regulatory requirements, defining a safe level of performance below which no organization should fall. Its attention will be focused on the small number of organizations that fail to achieve these standards, not on the many who achieve them relatively easily. To take another example, a regulator aiming for accountability will probably seek to make the regulatory process as open and transparent as possible, and may choose to publish data on organizations and their performance. In contrast, a regulator aiming for improvement may feel that it is easier to get organizations to change when the process affords them some privacy and sensitive

Table 5.2 The aims of regulation and their relationship with regulatory methods

Regulatory method	Regulatory aim		
	Improvement	Assurance	Accountability
Direction	Sets challenging, maximal standards which few if any organizations can meet in full, so that all are encouraged to improve and have the opportunity to do so	Sets basic, minimal standards which all competent organizations should be able to meet in full – a 'safety net' performance level	Sets standards aimed at allowing users to differentiate between organizations and at embedding user perspective and user influences in organizations
Detection	Works with all organizations constructively and participatively to help them move towards the regulatory requirements	Focuses detection activities on 'low outlier' organizations with performance problems. Pays little or no attention to most organizations who are 'above the line'	Measures organizations carefully against standards and reports results publicly so that all can see how they perform
Enforcement	Makes great use of relationships, persuasion and incentives in promoting change; sanctions are a last resort	Deals with performance problems robustly – either seeks improvement or removal of organization	Uses public disclosure as an enforcement strategy, but may also use other sanctions – does so through public hearings

negotiations are not undertaken in public. For that reason, they may be reluctant to make regulatory processes fully open and transparent, and see less value in publishing data on organizational performance.

Some of the characteristics of healthcare regulators' behaviour outlined in Chapters 3 and 4 makes more sense when seen in the context of these different and sometimes conflicting regulatory aims. For example, the Centers for Medicare and Medicaid Services and the state agencies which regulate nursing homes have an overt improvement mission; however, most of their activity is focused on assurance and accountability. The adversarial, deterrence-focused style of regulation that they adopt makes little sense in improvement terms, but it can be seen that it satisfies an important political need for mechanisms of accountability and responds to some very widely publicized failures of care in nursing homes by aiming to provide assurance.

Whatever the aim of healthcare regulation, there is one further characteristic of regulatory objective setting which deserves discussion. It seems that all too often the regulatory process becomes a purpose in itself. In other words, regulatory systems and structures that are created simply as a means to an end (improvement, assurance or accountability) become an end in themselves. The metrics of regulatory performance become the numbers of standards issued, inspections undertaken, sanctions taken, organizations certified and so on. Because these aspects of the regulatory process are readily measurable, and data about them are often easily available as a by-product of regulatory activity, it is tempting to treat them as proxies for the real objectives of regulation. However, to do so carries two risks. First, it assumes that they are, indeed, useful proxies for the real objectives of regulation, but there is rarely much evidence to suggest that this is the case. Secondly, it risks creating perverse incentives for the regulator and for regulated organizations which distort the process of regulation. For example, a regulator whose performance is assessed on the numbers of inspections it performs may inflate the numbers of inspections by doing more than are needed, may opt for shorter, more superficial inspections in order to be able to do more, and may avoid more difficult and challenging inspections because they would be time-consuming. If the regulator is judged on how often it issues sanctions, then it is more likely to make routine use of sanctions and more likely to issue formal sanctions even for minor or trivial infractions, regardless of what effect these actions have on the larger aims of regulation.

Ultimately, the purpose of regulation is not regulation itself, and the performance of regulators should not be judged in terms of how well they regulate, but by assessing how well they achieve the objectives of regulation.

REGULATORY SCOPE

The scope of regulation refers to what types or forms of organizations are subject to regulation (which can be termed horizontal scope) and what activities or functions which they undertake are regulated (what can be called vertical scope). For each of the healthcare regulators described in Chapters 3 and 4, it is possible to map out and compare their scope of regulation. Some examples are shown in Figure 5.1, which compares the regulatory scope of a number of US and UK healthcare regulators.

It is immediately apparent that some regulators have a tightly bounded scope of regulation – for example, the Clinical Negligence Scheme for Trusts deals with clinical risk management in NHS

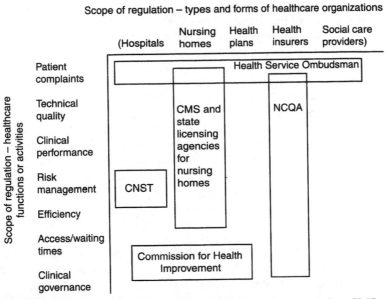

Figure 5.1 Mapping the scope of different regulatory agencies. CMS = Centers for Medicare and Medicaid Services, NCQA = National Committee for Quality Assurance, CNST = Clinical Negligence Scheme for Trusts.

trusts – while others have a very broad and less clearly bounded scope – for example, the Medicare peer review organizations in the USA have an oversight remit for any services provided within Medicare, which covers a wide range of activities and services and most healthcare organizations and providers. There are clearly some advantages for the regulatory agency to having a narrow, well-defined scope of regulation, in that it probably makes the process of regulation more straightforward. It is easier to set standards, plan and undertake inspections and take action to encourage regulated organizations to change their behaviour. The regulator is more able to become expert in the issues being regulated, and to focus its attention on a small number of relatively specific and achievable objectives or tasks. However, it is far from clear that this makes for effective regulation in the wider context. Most obviously, when the task of regulation is split up across several regulatory agencies each with a specific, bounded scope, regulated organizations end up dealing with multiple regulators, none of whom see the whole picture of organizational performance. There is a risk that some important areas of activity are left wholly unregulated and that others are subject to the attention of more than one regulator.

The problems of regulatory fragmentation – divided and over-lapping scopes of regulation – are endemic in both the USA and the UK and deserve some further discussion. Overlapping scopes of regulation lead at best to some duplication of effort, wasted resource and a sense of regulatory overload in regulated organizations. More seriously, regulatory agency directions can conflict, leaving regulated organizations to look for ways to reconcile different standards. For example, hospitals in California have to comply with the state's own Title 22 requirements, the Health Care Financing Administration's conditions of participation for Medicare and JCAHO's accreditation standards, each of which contains similar but not identical provisions on a wide range of issues, from medical record-keeping to the use of restraints. Managed care organizations in the USA, when dealing with consumer complaints, have to follow different procedures, with different time limits and other provisions, depending on which state or federal agency regulates the product in question. In the UK, NHS trusts have found themselves asked to comply with risk management standards set by the Clinical Negligence Scheme for Trusts and with standards set by the Department of Health's own controls assurance unit; they have also been asked to provide information on risk management to the National Audit Office and to subject their risk management arrangements to inspection as part of the Commission for Health Improvement's reviews of clinical governance. In each of these cases, the overlapping scopes of regulation result in little additional value and could be rationalized.

Divided scopes of regulation produce a different but equally important problem – without a single agency leading regulation, no-one has a comprehensive view of performance and problems can result, especially if regulatory agencies do not communicate and share their findings. Enforcement action to deal with performance problems can be slowed down by the interactions between different regulatory agencies, especially if their approaches to enforcement differ. When the scope of regulation is divided and different regulatory agencies take different approaches to regulation, regulated organizations may use this as an opportunity to select the least stringent and most accommodating regulatory regime, tailoring their activities if need be to fit the remit of their preferred regulatory agency. This phenomenon has been called 'forum shopping', perhaps the best example of which is found in the way that health plans and large employers in the USA have collaborated to construct health insurance products which, because they count as self-insured schemes, are free from all state regulation and are only subject to the much more lenient federal regulatory requirements of the Employee Retirement Income Security Act 1974 (Brennan and Berwick 1996).

On the other hand, it could be argued that some regulatory fragmentation, in particular overlap between the work of different regulators, is helpful. It may provide an element of necessary redundancy in what is, after all, a fairly inexact process of assessment. For example, a problem might be missed by one regulatory agency, but picked up and dealt with by another. The views of different regulatory agencies which interact with the same healthcare organization may also offer an opportunity to triangulate findings – if multiple regulators in different spheres of performance report on an organization in similar terms, their common view is likely to be seen as more robust and objective than any one regulator's findings would be.

The large amount of regulatory fragmentation found in both the USA and the UK suggests that those responsible for establishing and maintaining systems of regulation have not placed a high priority on preventing or reducing fragmentation or on controlling the resulting costs of regulation. In both countries, the overall burden of regulation could be reduced and the effectiveness of regulation could be improved in several ways: by coordinating regulations, regulatory methods and data requirements to minimize conflicting demands on regulated organizations; by setting up reciprocal recognition or deeming arrangements between regulators; and, ultimately, by merging some regulatory agencies. There appear to be considerable opportunities for rationalization, economies of scale and scope, and improved regulatory effectiveness. The proposed reorganization of healthcare regulation in the UK, which is described on pp. 152–8, represents a laudable attempt at such a rationalization.

Few of the costs or problems of regulatory fragmentation fall upon the regulators – they mainly affect regulated organizations. It follows that few of the benefits of reducing regulatory fragmentation accrue to regulatory agencies either. For this reason, it is rarely in the self-interest of regulatory agencies to cooperate to rationalize regulation in this way, as it generally means they risk ceding regulatory territory or responsibility to others and could even face major downsizing or abolition. Their self-interest is best served by expanding their own scope of regulation. The result is often covert or even overt regulatory competition – for example, between the Commission for Health Improvement and the Audit Commission in the UK, or between the Joint Commission on the Accreditation of Healthcare Organizations and the National Committee for Quality Assurance in the USA – in which regulatory agencies contest the regulatory domain.

REGULATORY MODELS: DETERRENCE, COMPLIANCE AND RESPONSIVE REGULATION

Chapter 2 introduced the concept of regulatory models or paradigms and described the two approaches commonly termed deterrence and compliance regulation, which represent the two ends of the spectrum of regulatory philosophy. Deterrence regulators see the organizations they regulate as 'amoral calculators', out to get what they can and only likely to comply with regulations if they are forced to do so. They tend to adopt a punitive, adversarial approach to the regulatory task, and to make routine use of sanctions and penalties. Their relationships with the organizations they regulate are usually poor. Compliance regulators see the organizations they regulate as 'good-hearted compliers', good and well-intentioned organizations who will generally try to do the right thing. They have a more developmental, supportive approach to the regulatory task, use formal sanctions or penalties as a last resort, and usually get on quite well with the organizations they regulate. The healthcare regulators in the USA and the UK described in Chapters 3 and 4 display a range of different regulatory models and no one paradigm predominates. On the one hand, there are deterrence regulators like the state and federal agencies which regulate nursing homes and hospitals in the USA; on the other hand, there are compliance regulators like the Health Advisory Service in the UK or the Joint Commission on the Accreditation of Healthcare Organizations (JCAHO) in the USA. Quite a number of the regulatory agencies reviewed sit somewhere between the two models of regulation, as Figure 5.2 illustrates by placing several regulatory agencies on this continuum. Although some demonstrate a fairly narrow or fixed regulatory model, which can be easily located on the spectrum from deterrence to compliance, others exhibit a rather broader or more dynamic model, which is not so easy to pin down. This difference is represented in Figure 5.2 by the width of the box for each regulator.

It is immediately apparent that healthcare regulation in the USA tends, at least in comparison with the UK, more towards the

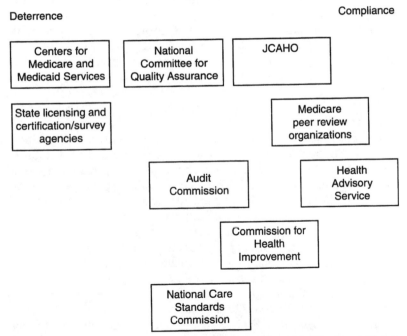

Figure 5.2 The regulatory models adopted by some healthcare regulators in the USA and UK. JCAHO = Joint Commission on the Accreditation of Healthcare Organizations.

deterrence model. This is not an unusual finding – in fields as diverse as environmental regulation, financial regulation and occupational health and safety regulation, the same contrast is found, between a European model of regulation which tends to be compliance-oriented, negotiated, consensus-based, relatively informal and reliant on cooperation, and an American model of regulation which tends to be more deterrence-oriented, adversarial, formalized, rules-based and imposed (Kagan and Axelrad 2000). It would appear that regulation is very much a creature of the social, political and economic context in which it takes place. Although in both countries a spectrum of regulatory models and behaviour can be identified, the range and extremes of those spectrums are rather different.

The experience of healthcare regulation in both the USA and the UK seems to support the general regulatory theory on regulatory models, which was discussed in some detail in Chapter 2 (see pp. 38–9). For example, theory suggests that deterrence regulation is more common in heterogeneous sectors, where regulators oversee a large number of regulated organizations and where there is a strong business culture. Nursing home regulation in the USA and private healthcare regulation in the UK both seem to fit this model. In contrast, theory suggests that compliance regulation is more likely in more homogeneous sectors, where the regulator oversees fewer organizations and where there is a strong professional ethic – and this can be seen to be the case in JCAHO's hospital accreditation activities in the USA and in the work of the Health Advisory Service in the UK.

Perhaps more importantly, the evidence in healthcare regulation seems to support general regulatory theories about the advantages and disadvantages of deterrence and compliance regulation that were summarized in Table 2.4. On the one hand, deterrence regulators like the federal and state regulators of nursing homes in the USA make regulated organizations take notice of regulatory requirements and can drive the pace of change, but at considerable cost, not just in terms of the resources required but also in terms of their long-term relationships with regulated organizations. American nursing home regulation seems beset by all the problems of creative compliance, regulatory subversion and failed enforcement that theory would predict (Walshe 2001a). On the other hand, the experience of the Health Advisory Service in the UK, perhaps the most compliance-oriented regulator of all those reviewed, seems to confirm that while this approach secures much more cooperation and support from regulated organizations, the strong professional domination of the regulatory process makes it excessively normative, and the absence of real enforcement and follow-up means that the regulator's requirements are easily ignored or deprioritized.

In Chapter 2, the ideas of 'responsive' or 'smart' regulation were explored at some length (see pp. 41–8). It was argued that regulators needed to escape the dichotomy of deterrence versus compliance and to develop a more flexible, situationally specific and adaptable style of regulation. Six key characteristics of responsive regulation were outlined: contingency, hierarchy, flexibility, tripartism, parsimony and empowerment. In the review of healthcare regulation in the USA and the UK, it is difficult to point to any one regulatory agency that might be seen as a model of responsive regulation, but it is possible to discern, especially in some more recent developments, a movement towards the responsive model or paradigm. Some regulators are certainly already more responsive than others, which was reflected in Figure 5.2 by their span on the spectrum from deterrence to compliance. For example, the Commission for Health Improvement in the UK and National Committee for Quality Assurance (NCQA) in the USA both seem to be examples of regulators that exhibit a broader range of behaviours, are less easily placed at one position on the spectrum from deterrence to compliance, and might be seen as more responsive than, for example, the Audit Commission in the UK or JCAHO in the USA.

Table 5.3 sets out the six characteristics of responsive regulation described in Chapter 2 and offers several examples drawn from Chapters 3 and 4 of regulatory behaviours and actions which suggest that a more responsive model of regulation is emerging, at least in some domains. The empirical evidence suggests that however attractive the ideal of responsive regulation is in theory, it may be difficult to realize in practice, since none of the many regulatory agencies reviewed in Chapters 3 and 4 can really seem to claim to be responsive regulators. In the USA, the NCQA seems to come closest to the responsive model, while in the UK the Commission for Health Improvement probably gets nearest to the ideal.

There could be several reasons for the failure of healthcare regulators to adopt and implement the principles of responsive regulation. First, regulators (and the organizations they regulate) may be constrained by the past and trapped by the *status quo* – the history of regulation and its development. Once a particular regulatory style or approach has developed over time, changing it radically may be perceived as a rejection of what has gone before, or an admission that past regulatory efforts have not worked. It is

Table 5.3 Examples of responsive regulation in healthcare

Contingency	Making the nature of the regulatory regime highly contingent on the behaviour of individual regulated organizations, and avoiding 'one size fits all' regulatory methods and approaches	The National Committee for Quality Assurance gives a longer period of accreditation to health plans that do well, and a shorter period to those whose performance is less good. It also uses ongoing HEDIS data to monitor performance between accreditation visits. The Commission for Health Improvement 'fast tracks' reviews in NHS trusts where it thinks there may be cause for concern
Hierarchy	Providing the regulator with a full range of regulatory interventions and enabling them to use them appropriately	US nursing home regulators have been given a wide range of 'intermediate sanctions' short of closure or delicensing. For example, they can deny payment or prevent a home taking new admissions until a problem is fixed. However, because enforcement procedures are slow and highly bureaucratic, the impact of these intermediate sanctions has been rather limited
Flexibility	Giving regulators space to exercise discretion and professional judgement in the regulatory process, rather than trying to codify and prescribe what they should do in great detail	The Commission for Health Improvement has deliberately eschewed written standards in its review process and instead gives review teams considerable latitude and freedom of action within an evaluative framework, while using reviewer training and review managers to try to ensure consistency

Tripartism	Co-opting other stakeholders to the purposes of regulation so as to extend or amplify regulatory oversight, and aligning regulatory requirements with other influences on regulated organizations	The Long Term Care Ombudsman programme in the USA has achieved a high degree of community engagement in the regulatory process, with many volunteers working with nursing home residents and their families to improve care. The Commission for Health Improvement undertakes an extensive consultation with stakeholders like local authorities, other NHS organizations, voluntary groups and the general public before and during its clinical governance reviews of NHS trusts
Parsimony	Using the lowest cost, least intrusive and simplest regulatory interventions which will achieve a given objective, seeking to minimize costs, and paying attention to the unintended consequences of regulatory intervention	Since its creation in 2000 as the state regulatory agency for managed care plans, the California Department of Managed Health Care has emphasized its desire to minimize the administrative burden imposed by regulation and to focus its resources in areas where it can make a real difference to patients' experiences of healthcare
Empowerment	Designing regulation to promote wider performance improvement, rather than simply to achieve compliance with minimum expectations or requirements	The Joint Commission's redesign of its accreditation process for hospitals in the mid-1990s moved away from the direct assessment of quality against standards and towards seeking to embed systems for continuous improvement in hospitals. This is reflected in the focus on areas like leadership, management, and performance improvement and governance. However, this transformation has been somewhat constrained by the need to sustain some compatibility with the Medicare conditions of participation

notable that the two agencies identified as closest to the responsive ideal – the Commission for Health Improvement and NCQA – are both relatively new regulators, which may have had greater freedom to design their approach to regulation on a blank canvas. Secondly, the political and social context for regulation may make it difficult to secure support for responsive regulatory approaches, even when it is evident that they would lead to more effective regulation. For example, nursing home regulation in the USA appears trapped in a deterrence model because certain stakeholders, such as politicians and consumers, would see anything else as 'going soft' on providers (Walshe 2001a). In these circumstances, political effectiveness trumps regulatory effectiveness. Thirdly, there is a notable lack of a 'regulatory community' – a willingness among regulators to share ideas and experiences and to learn from regulatory developments in other sectors (Hood *et al.* 1999). Regulators tend to emphasize the distinctiveness or exceptionalist nature of the activities they regulate and to seek home-grown solutions to problems. This may make any kind of regulatory innovation, such as responsive regulation, slow to spread. Fourthly, regulatory agencies appear to be generally cautious and risk-averse, with regulatory experimentation and innovation the exception rather than the rule. The risks of doing something new and different, especially when regulation is politically sensitive and highly visible, may outweigh any potential benefits – and the risks may all fall on the regulator while the benefits may accrue to other stake-holders in regulation. Finally, and perhaps most importantly, responsive regulation may be good for regulated organizations and for consumers and the general public interest, but very demanding of regulatory agencies. It is probably simpler and more straight-forward to design and implement a narrow, relatively prescriptive conventional regulatory regime than it is to create a much broader, more contingent and responsive approach to regulation.

DIRECTION: SETTING STANDARDS AND EXPECTATIONS

Almost all regulators use standards to communicate their expecta-tions or requirements to other stakeholders in regulation, most obviously the organizations they regulate. Those standards are gen-erally written, explicit statements, which are used to operationalize the objectives of regulation. Whether they are called standards, rules or regulations, these statements constitute a key instrument of regulation, and their development and application deserve some further exploration. This section first considers why regulators make such extensive use of standards and then examines the nature of standards and how they are constructed. It then turns to examine processes for setting standards and how they work, and concludes by exploring some of the problems involved in setting regulatory standards.

Of course, not all regulators use standards and some use them more than others. In the USA, the Long Term Care Ombudsman programme is a notable example of a regulator which does not set standards, but instead communicates its expectations more implicitly through its regulatory actions and decisions. In the UK, the Health Service Ombudsman takes a similar approach. The Health Advisory Service always resisted calls for it to set standards, relying instead on the professional judgement of its review staff. The Commission for Health Improvement, though it specifies how its clinical governance reviews will be done and what data they will draw on in some detail, has deliberately chosen not to set explicit standards for clinical governance.

However, there are often strong pressures on regulatory agencies to set standards and to make them as exact, prescriptive and detailed as they can be. It is argued that if the regulatory process is to be fair and transparent, regulated organizations (and everyone else) need to know what the criteria are on which their performance will be assessed, and the only way to do that is to set standards. Without standards, some would assert, regulatory assessment is likely to be inconsistent and subjective, driven by individual inspectors' biases and interests, open to manipulation and deal-making, and lacking in due process. These arguments are not only used to make the case for standards, but also to press for standards to be specified as exactly and completely as they can be, eliminating scope for regulatory discretion and leaving as little as possible to the judgement of regulatory staff. A second argument for standards is that they are efficient, because once the regulator has encapsulated expert knowledge and evidence in its standards, those standards can then be used to make faster assessments of regulated organizations, can be applied by less experienced and qualified regulatory staff, and can make enforcement action more straightforward and less contestable. In other words, the regulatory investment made in developing and defining standards is recouped through savings in regulatory detection and enforcement. A third reason for using standards is that only by making regulatory expectations explicit through standards can a regulator really have a significant and widespread influence on the performance of regulated organizations. It is suggested that without standards, the regulator's impact comes largely from individual interactions with regulated organizations, in detection and enforcement. But since the regulator has only got the resources to interact with a small proportion of regulated organizations, and to do so relatively infrequently, its impact is bound to be limited. By setting standards, it is argued, the regulator can influence regulated organizations much more extensively, because many or even most regulated organizations will make some effort to comply with those standards even without the immediate prospect of detection and enforcement. A fourth argument for regulatory standards is that they provide a framework which other stakeholders then use to pursue the objectives of regulation. This can happen because patients, professionals, funders and others exert pressure for regulatory compliance, or because the regulatory standards empower those groups by, for example, requiring regulated organizations to consult them or secure their support for service changes.

The nature of standards

Rules, regulations and standards vary enormously in their intent, construction and intended application, as some of the examples of regulatory standards cited in Chapters 3 and 4 illustrate clearly. It is very difficult to separate regulatory standards and the way they are set from the wider regulatory context, since they are very much a part of the overall regulatory model and design. For example, deterrence regulators are much more likely to use prescriptive, highly specified regulations oriented towards measurement, while compliance regulators are more likely to use descriptive, aspirational standards more directed at development. For this reason, it is probably unhelpful to attempt to articulate any 'standards for standards' which might attempt to define the characteristics of good regulatory standards. However, we can identify several characteristics of regulatory standards which are of importance to both their design and their use; these are set out in Table 5.4.

Perhaps the first and foremost concern is the *validity* of regulatory standards – whether or not the issues they address are important to the intended regulatory objectives. For example, if a nursing home regulator requires nursing homes to have non-slip floor coverings in bathrooms for residents, there is presumably a logic behind the regulation that it is intended to improve resident safety, that residents are prone to slip and fall on wet floors in bathrooms and injure

Table 5.4 Some characteristics of regulatory standards

Characteristic	Description
Validity	What evidence is there that the attributes or behaviours which are the subject of the standard contribute towards the intended objective of improved performance?
Measurability	To what extent can the attributes or behaviours which are the subject of the standard be measured or assessed, by collecting or using qualitative or quantitative data?
Reliability	If these attributes or behaviours are measured, how consistent is the measurement process and to what extent will differences in ratings be a function of the regulated organization or of the measurement process?
Generalizability	How far can the attributes or behaviours which are the subject of the standard be said to be universally applicable, or will there be differences in organizational or environmental context which mean that the standard is not applicable in some settings?
Specificity	In how much detail are the attributes or behaviours which are the subject of the standard specified? Is the standard a broad statement of overall principles or aims, or a detailed and prescriptive statement of required systems, processes and structures?
Subject	What is the subject of the standards? Do they focus on structure – organizational arrangements, facilities or the environment; or on process – the systems of care delivery themselves; or on outcomes – the results of healthcare services and their impact on patients or users?
Stringency	How hard is it for organizations to comply with the standard? Is it set at a minimal or safety-net level, at which all but a few organizations would comply; a normative level, at which the average organization would be in compliance; or at a maximal or aspirational level, at which few if any organizations are currently able to comply?

themselves, and that non-slip flooring will reduce the occurrence of such falls and injuries. However, when this logic is unpicked, several problems can be identified. How often do residents actually harm themselves in accidents in bathrooms? Does non-slip flooring reduce the number of falls and resulting injuries? How many accidents are prevented by non-slip flooring, and how does the benefit of reduction in harm measure up against the costs of investing in non-slip flooring? Are there other ways to prevent slips and falls in bathrooms, like providing better handrails or mechanical aids, or assisting residents who need help and might be likely to fall?

Most regulatory standards are based on a limited foundation of empirical evidence. They often represent some kind of professional or organizational consensus or compromise about what constitutes good practice, and they may have high face validity as a result. However, two problems are common – assumed causality and pre-supposition. Assumed causality refers to the tendency to assume that a regulatory standard contributes to the wider regulatory objective without ever demonstrating this empirically or even making the case explicitly. In our example above, the link between bathroom accidents, slippery floors and flooring materials is almost wholly assumed. Presupposition refers to the way that regulatory standards assume or prescribe a particular solution that precludes other potential approaches. In our example, the focus is placed wholly on non-slip flooring, without any thought being given to other, perhaps more effective, ways to prevent accidents.

Pragmatically, it may be quite acceptable for regulatory standards to be based largely on professional opinions with little empirical evidence behind them. It may not be feasible to collect and review all the empirical evidence, or there may not be much evidence to go on. However, it is desirable that the intended logic of any regulatory standard – how it connects to the wider regulatory objectives, and what assumptions or presuppositions have been made in creating the standard – should be made explicit. The issue of validity becomes particularly important when the consensus among regulators, regulated organizations and other groups breaks down, and agreement about the standards cannot be negotiated. For example, attempts to set standards for minimum staffing ratios in US nursing homes have met with opposition from funders and providers, and have led to a careful examination of the empirical evidence on the relationship between staffing levels and the quality of care (AHCA 2001).

The second issue highlighted in Table 5.4 is the *measurability* of a standard – whether or not the behaviours to which it relates can be measured or assessed. It might be assumed that a standard which cannot be easily measured has little value, but some regulators use standards to set out and communicate their vision of how regulated organizations should aim to perform. In other words, they set some regulatory standards which are not necessarily intended for use in regulatory detection and enforcement. For other regulators, especially those who have a deterrence-oriented approach, the measurability of standards is paramount, and they make great efforts to define their standards in the clearest possible terms and to provide robust guidance and systems for measurement. However, it may be true that the attributes of performance which are most important are also among the hardest to measure (and, conversely, that those things which are easy to measure are not very important). For example, it is clear that the leadership of healthcare organizations is a crucial determinant of their performance, but designing standards which encapsulate the traits of effective leadership is very difficult. In this kind of case, the regulator is faced with a difficult trade-off between validity and measurability.

The next attribute of standards, *reliability*, is related to measurability. The reliability of a standard refers to how consistently performance against the standard can be measured. In other words, if different regulatory staff using the same standard assess the same regulated organization, do they produce the same results? There will inevitably be some variation between different applications of the measurement, but some assessment is needed of how much of the difference in assessments of regulated organizations comes from real differences in their performance, and how much comes from differences in the process of measurement. Reliability can be assessed statistically, but very few regulators have either tested the reliability of their standards or made efforts to maximize reliability. Limited evidence from, for example, accreditation programmes in primary care suggests that reliability is often poor (Walsh and Walshe 1998). It is often assumed that reliability can be improved by defining standards much more exactly (the specificity of standards is discussed below), but some research suggests that this is not the case and that it is easier to secure good reliability with a small number of broadly based standards than it is with a larger number of very detailed standards (Braithwaite and Braithwaite 1995). In general terms, the level of reliability needed depends upon the use to which regulatory standards will be put. If their primary aim is to convey an overall vision of how regulated organizations should perform, then poor reliability can probably be tolerated. However, if standards are to be used in enforcement to allocate sanctions or rewards, and the performance of individual organizations against those standards is to be published, then their reliability becomes paramount.

The *generalizability* of standards is a universal challenge for regulators – to what extent can they design a single set of standards which cope with the heterogeneity of regulated organizations and their contexts or environments? For example, setting equipment or facilities standards for acute hospitals that are appropriate both for a small, 30 bed rural hospital and for a large, 1000 bed, tertiary teaching hospital is clearly difficult. Creating standards for user or patient involvement which work properly within different service areas (chronic or acute care, children and adults) and with different populations (disadvantaged groups, non-white ethnic minorities, non-English speaking groups) is similarly challenging.

Some regulators cope with the problem of generalizability by allowing the use of discretion and judgement in regulatory detection and enforcement. This is sometimes called 'over-prescription', the setting of standards which are known to be inappropriate for some regulated organizations and then relaxing those standards selectively to take account of the context of individual organizations. Another way to deal with the problem is to narrow the scope of some or all regulatory standards – that is, restricting them so that they only apply to certain kinds of regulated organizations. However, doing this can result in much more complex sets of standards. In general, the greater the heterogeneity in regulated organizations and their contexts, the more generalizability will become a problem, until the point is reached at which it makes sense to split or divide the regulatory domain in some way to produce two or more groups of regulated organizations that can be regulated separately. The evolution of managed care organizations in the USA, and the response of the National Committee for Quality Assurance and the Joint Commission on the Accreditation of Healthcare Organizations in setting up separate accreditation programmes for managed care organizations and preferred provider organizations (see Chapter 4), is a good example of this kind of response to the issues of generalizability.

The *specificity* of standards refers to how explicitly and comprehensively they are defined. At one extreme, a standard might simply state the regulatory objective – control of infection, the prevention of drug errors – and leave its operationalization and the mechanisms for achieving those objectives to the regulated organization. At the other extreme, a standard might list in lengthy and comprehensive detail the structures, systems, processes and results that regulated organizations should have in place. A control of infection standard might specify committee arrangements, infectious disease precautions, hygiene procedures, training required for staff, infection monitoring systems and so on. For an example of the differences in specificity between different regulators, compare the standards for privacy and confidentiality used by UK and US nursing home regulators (see Tables 3.14 and 4.14). Although the objectives of the standards are clearly very similar, the American regulator has chosen to make its standard much more specific about the exact processes and systems which assure residents' privacy and confidentiality, while the British regulator focuses much more on defining the intended objective in more detail rather than specifying exactly what should or should not be done.

Specificity is clearly related to the characteristics of measurability, reliability and generalizability, which have already been discussed. To make standards measurable and reliable, regulators often make them more specific. However, increasing specificity may reduce generalizability.

The *subject* or focus of standards can be categorized in several ways, but is perhaps most commonly classified using the three headings of structure, process and outcome. The point here is that the subject of standards concerned with the same regulatory objective can and does vary. Some may focus on structural issues – management arrangements, written policies, committees, training programmes, equipment and so on. Others may focus on process issues – systems of care, communication with patients, the way that care is provided and so on. Some may focus on outcome issues – the results of healthcare provision, changes in patients' health, rates of morbidity and mortality, and so on. To use the example of control of infection once again, regulatory standards could address the existence of a control of infection committee and hygiene training for clinical staff; processes like handwashing and cleaning aimed at reducing cross-infection rates; and outcomes like rates of hospital-acquired infections. Regulatory standards tend to be most concerned with issues of structure, perhaps because they are often among the most readily measurable aspects of an organization, but the validity of structural measures is often questioned. It may be useful to recognize that each of these three domains is important in its own right, which would suggest that regulatory standards should aim to cover them all to some extent, and that an undue focus on one area at the cost of others may be unhelpful (Berwick 1988).

The final characteristic of standards set out in Table 5.4 is their *stringency*. This refers to the level at which a standard is set and the likelihood that regulated organizations will be able to achieve it. Standards can be set minimally, so that all but the poorest performers can achieve them, in which case the standards represent a kind of 'safety net' level of performance. Most organizations will not be affected by such standards, but the small number of poor performers may be driven to improve. Standards may also be set normatively, around whatever represents average performance or usual practice in regulated organizations. In this case, statistically about half of all organizations will be below the standard and half above it. Those who do not meet the standard may be influenced to improve, whereas those who exceed it by some margin may be inclined to relax. A third approach is to set maximal standards, which are challenging for all regulated organizations and which most will not be able to achieve, at least at present. Such standards are aspirational, in that they express a vision of future performance rather than a reflection of current performance. Different levels of stringency suit different regulatory aims and objectives. For example, if standards are to be used strictly in detection and enforcement, and form the basis of routine sanctioning and penalties, they have to be set minimally or else detection and enforcement procedures will collapse under the sheer volume of work. However, if the main purpose of standards is to encourage development and improvement, it makes more sense to have maximal standards because almost all regulated organizations will see some scope for improvement, however good their performance already is.

If there is one conclusion to be taken from this review of the nature of regulatory standards, it is that every standard represents a series of trade-offs between the characteristics discussed above. It is simply not possible to maximize both specificity and generalizability, or both validity and reliability, and so regulatory agencies and others involved in setting standards need to have a clear idea of the purposes to which standards will be put, and the ways in which they will be used, in order to prioritize those characteristics of standards which matter most.

Approaches to standard-setting

Several approaches to standard-setting by regulatory agencies were reviewed in Chapters 3 and 4. In the USA, the bureaucratic and slow-moving approach taken by the Centers for Medicare and Medicaid Services (and mandated by the Administrative Procedures Act) and the professionally dominated system of advisory committees used by the Joint Commission on the Accreditation of Healthcare Organizations (JCAHO) to develop and maintain its accreditation standards are both examples of standard-setting processes; in the UK, the appraisals process established by the National Institute for Clinical Excellence for assessing new therapies and producing its guidance to the NHS and the promulgation by the National Care Standards Commission of new regulatory standards for nursing homes are also examples of standard-setting in action.

The setting of regulatory standards is more than simply a technical exercise. It is a political task, involving careful negotiation and eventual compromise among stakeholders as they agree not simply what the standard ought to be, but what represents a practically achievable and sensible target level of performance for regulated organizations. Standard-setting should not only produce standards, it should also produce sufficient consensus among stakeholders, and particularly among regulated organizations, in support of those standards. This does not mean that standards cannot be set without the consent of regulated organizations or in the face of some opposition, but the scale of opposition needs to be carefully gauged. Otherwise, there is a risk that wholesale non-compliance will result, the regulator will not be able to enforce the standards, and the whole process of regulation will be damaged by such a failure of enforcement. In some ways, the process of standard-setting is as important in this regard as its actual outcome. Regulators are much more likely to secure support, grudging acceptance or at least passive acquiescence with standards if they have gone through what looks and feels like 'due process' to regulated organizations, consulting widely, showing themselves willing to modify the standards if need be, engaging in dialogue with all stakeholders and especially with those who voice concerns, and demonstrating that they understand the subject matter of the standards just as well as the regulated organizations. For these reasons, it is important that regulators adopt a standard-setting process that is, and appears to be, fair, open, transparent, genuinely consultative and formative by design.

The standard-setting process also provides an important opportunity to field-test new regulatory standards before they come into operation, using the expertise of all stakeholders to test their validity, assess their measurability and generalizability, and to flush out any flaws or problems. Some regulators, like JCAHO, build a period of field testing with several pilot organizations into their approach when developing new standards.

Problems in setting standards

It is evident that setting good regulatory standards can be very difficult, and doing so in the politicized and contested environment in which many regulators operate can be especially hard. Several common problems can be identified.

First, much of the expertise needed to set regulatory standards is in the hands of regulated organizations, and some regulators struggle to gain sufficient knowledge of the organizations they regulate to set good standards. There is often a tension between the regulator's desire to bring expert knowledge and skills from regulated organizations into the process of standard-setting and its concern that doing so will result in regulatory capture and a weakening of the regulatory process. It is, in any case, usually an unequal relationship because although the regulatory agency may seem well resourced, it is almost always dwarfed by the collective size and resources of the organizations it regulates. Regulated organizations, especially large corporations like pharmaceutical companies or nursing home chains, can often bring huge resources to bear to argue their case when regulatory standards are being set.

Secondly, regulators tend to set over-inclusive, over-stringent regulations and then to relax them to some extent during detection and enforcement. By doing so they provide themselves with reserve powers and some discretion, and they allow themselves to cover every regulatory eventuality and to cope with heterogeneity in the organizations which they regulate. However, over-inclusive, over-stringent regulations look less attractive from the perspective of regulated organizations, which may find it difficult to work out what is expected of them and may feel that there is too much scope for regulatory bias. In effect, they can put regulated organizations almost inevitably into a position of non-compliance and leave them vulnerable to sanction if and when the regulator sees fit. This kind of excessive regulation has benefits for a cautious, risk-averse regulator, and its costs fall largely on regulated organizations.

Thirdly, regulatory standard-setting is generally slow and expensive, often for good reasons – setting standards is complex, and the need for due process, negotiation and compromise often lengthens the time taken to develop and implement new standards. However, in fast changing areas of practice, this means that regulatory standards often lag behind the real world and can even inhibit innovation in some leading-edge organizations. The costs of regulatory standard-setting generally fall on the regulatory agency and while investment in good regulations should be seen as an important and worthwhile use of resources, it can be seen as taking away time and money from the processes of detection and enforcement.

Fourthly, regulations tend to proliferate and to stagnate. There are often more reasons to set new regulatory standards than there are either to update existing standards or to discard outdated ones. New regulations are often developed in response to public or political interest in an issue, they may focus on new and interesting areas of practice, and they represent an opportunity for the regulator to expand its domain. In contrast, updating existing regulations is a slow and painstaking process, often rather bureaucratic and tiresome. And removing old or outdated regulations may be even less attractive, and carries with it some risk because it may be seen as a weakening or lifting of regulatory control. As a result, regulatory agencies tend to prioritize the creation of new regulations and to neglect the tasks of updating, revising and where appropriate discarding old regulations. This is especially true when the regulatory agency has limited resources, because it always has to respond to the demand for new regulatory standards, but can usually postpone or defer attention to updating and removing old regulations. The result is an accretion of regulatory standards, which at best results in some confusion about regulatory expectations and requirements, but more seriously may weaken the whole process of regulation.

But the biggest problems faced by regulators in setting standards concern their validity and generalizability. Designing standards which really contribute to regulatory objectives like improving performance and which work well across a wide range of heterogeneous regulated organizations is very difficult. Again and again, regulatory standards set with the best of intentions turn out either to be tangential to the intended objective, or to have unintended and unanticipated adverse consequences or side-effects which detract from that objective. To take one recent example, the National Care Standards Commission, which regulates nursing homes in the UK, set standards for premises and the physical environment that were clearly intended to improve the life of nursing home residents. However, although the standards were quite appropriate for new or purpose-built homes, it was simply not possible for many homes in older premises like converted houses or hotels to meet them – they demanded larger bedrooms, more bathrooms, lifts and other facilities that could not be incorporated without massive rebuilding expense. When these regulations were first introduced, they were met with opposition from the nursing home industry, which forecast that many good and valued smaller nursing homes (in which the quality of care may actually be better than in larger, less personal homes) would probably be forced to close. In due course, nursing homes began to close as they recognized that they had no long-term future in the industry under the new regulations and, at a time when there was a shortage of nursing home capacity, the overall number of nursing home beds started to fall. Eventually, and rather belatedly, the National Care Standards Commission withdrew almost all of the controversial premises and environmental regulatory standards, though by that time considerable damage had already been done. A standard which was meant to improve the quality of care for vulnerable nursing home residents ended up doing quite the reverse.

DETECTION: MEASURING AND MONITORING PERFORMANCE

Regulators need to be able to assess the performance of regulated organizations so that they know whether they are meeting regulatory requirements. This is a challenging task, since even the largest regulatory agency has a very limited amount of resources to invest in detection, and most have many organizations to regulate whose performance they need to assess. Moreover, these are complex organizations, whose performance is not straightforward to measure, and the regulatory standards that often form the foundation of assessment may be hard to use in measurement. If regulatory resources are spread evenly, it usually means that the regulator can only interact with each regulated organization once every few years at most, and may then only have the equivalent of a few person-days of regulatory staff time in which to assess performance. In effect, this means that in most regulatory regimes, self-regulation predominates, because only a small fraction of the activities of regulated organizations is subject to any form of regulatory scrutiny. Regulators rely on the premise that by publishing and communicating their expectations through regulatory directions or standards, most regulated organizations will move towards compliance of their own accord, partly because they are signed up to the purposes or objectives of regulation and partly because they anticipate that they will, at some point in the future, need to account for their performance to the regulator. Approaches to regulatory detection tend to presume compliance until the contrary is shown or suspected.

There are three main approaches to regulatory detection:

performance monitoring; surveys or inspections; and investigations or inquiries. These are described and compared in Table 5.5, Chapters 3 and 4 present several examples of each approach. The rest of this section examines each approach in turn, analysing how it has been used in healthcare regulation and what, from that experience, appear to be its main advantages and disadvantages. As in the exploration of regulatory standard-setting above, the approach that regulators take to regulatory detection is shaped by their regulatory objectives and model, and it is probably not helpful to attempt to identify one particular approach as being better or more effective than others. However, the section concludes by discussing what seem to be common problems and difficulties encountered in regulatory detection and how they might be addressed.

Monitoring performance

The most straightforward way for a regulatory agency to assess the performance of regulated organizations is to collect, aggregate, analyse and compare performance data. These data might come from a wide range of sources, including regulated organizations themselves or other agencies. They could be based on routine data collections undertaken for other administrative, financial or clinical reasons or they could have been collected especially for the purpose of performance monitoring. After some kind of validation or data quality testing, and any statistical adjustment needed to take account of differences in setting, the data can then be used to compare the performance of regulated organizations with each other, and to track and trend changes in performance over time.

Perhaps the best established example of this kind of regulatory performance monitoring in the USA is the HEDIS data set and indicators, developed and collected from managed care plans by the National Committee for Quality Assurance (NCQA). The Health Plan Employer Data and Information Set (HEDIS) is described in outline in Chapter 3, and Table 5.6 sets out a summary of the measures it contains. The NCQA collects and publishes HEDIS data from managed care plans annually; participating in HEDIS is a condition of NCQA accreditation and the HEDIS data form a proportion of an organization's accreditation score. In fact, many health plans that do not seek accreditation still participate in HEDIS, because they see some value for themselves and their clients in being able to compare their own performance with others.

Table 5.5 A comparison of approaches to regulatory detection

	Performance monitoring	Surveys, visits or inspections	Investigations or inquiries
Definition	The ongoing monitoring of regulated organizations' performance through routine data collection, aggregation, comparison and analysis of performance data	The periodic analysis of regulated organizations' performance through a special data collection exercise, usually centred on a period of on-site fieldwork at the organization	A specially initiated analysis of a regulated organization's performance, usually focused on a particular issue or cause for concern, and undertaken through a variety of fieldwork and data collection
Healthcare examples	NCQA HEDIS data set and reporting; JCAHO ORYX indicator initiative; CHI Office for Healthcare Peformance and star rating system	JCAHO survey visits; CMS/state agency nursing home inspections; CHI clinical governance reviews	LTCO complaint investigations; CHI investigations; CHI 'fast track' clinical governance reviews
How it is initiated	Process is usually an ongoing one, with no fixed start or end-point	Process is usually a periodic one, with a survey/inspection scheduled every 12 months, 2–3 years or other period	Process is usually initiated in response to information from other sources – such as complaints, concerns raised by the media or other stakeholders, or data from other regulatory detection processes

Usual methods	Data are collected from regulated organizations, either drawing on available routine data sets (e.g. on workload and activity) or on special data collections. Data are then quality checked, aggregated and processed to look at trends across organizations and over time	There is often a long period of preparation in which data are collected by the regulated organization and provided to the regulator; then a shorter and very intensive period of onsite fieldwork when regulatory staff visit and collect data directly themselves, often through interviews, meetings, etc.	Process is heterogeneous and tends to be tailored to the specific issues or cause for concern, but generally involves some fieldwork by regulatory staff with or at the regulated organization
Potential advantages	Allows regulator to keep track of performance across many organizations at relatively low cost to the regulator	Provides a detailed and in-depth analysis of organizational performance, and stimulates improvement in performance through process of survey	Provides a highly focused and targeted review of performance in one area of organization, often with very specific recommendations for change/improvement
Potential problems	Validity and reliability of indicators open to question; mechanisms for using them to influence performance often unclear; can impose high cost of data collection on regulated organizations	Validity and reliability dubious and usually untested; highly dependent on regulatory staff skills; high costs especially for regulated organization; long periodicity may mean little happens between surveys	Mechanism for initiating investigation often rather ad hoc and inconsistent; inquiry process often expensive; results may be hard to generalize from or to link to wider organizational performance

Abbreviations: NCQA = National Committee for Quality Assurance, HEDIS = Health Plan Employer Data and Information Set, JCAHO = Joint Commission on the Accreditation of Healthcare Organizations, CHI = Commission for Health Improvement, CMS = Centers for Medicare and Medicaid Services, LTCO = Long Term Care Ombudsman.

Table 5.6 A summary of the National Committee for Quality Assurance
HEDIS indicators of health plan performance

Effectiveness of care	Childhood immunization status
	Adolescent immunization status
	Breast cancer screening
	Cervical cancer screening
	Chlamydia screening in women
	Controlling high blood pressure
	Beta-blocker treatment after a heart attack
	Cholesterol management after acute cardiovascular events
	Comprehensive diabetes care
	Use of appropriate medications for people with asthma
	Follow-up after hospitalization for mental illness
	Anti-depressant medication management
	Advising smokers to quit
	Flu immunization for older adults
	Pneumonia vaccination status for older adults
	Medicare health outcomes survey
Access/ availability of care	Access to preventive/ambulatory health services for adults
	Access to primary care practitioners for children
	Prenatal and postpartum care
	Annual dental visit
	Availability of language interpretation services
Satisfaction with the experience of care	Measures from the CAHPS (Consumer Assessment of Health Plans Survey) data set
Health plan stability	Practitioner turnover
	Years in business and total membership
Use of services	Frequency of ongoing prenatal care
	Well child visits in the first 15 months of life
	Well child visits for children aged 3–6 years
	Adolescent well-care visits
	Frequency of selected procedures
	Inpatient utilization – general acute care
	Ambulatory care
	Inpatient utilization – non-acute care
	Discharge and average length of stay – maternity care
	Caesarean section rate
	Vaginal birth after caesarean section rate
	Births and average length of stay for newborns

Mental health utilization – discharges and average length of stay
Mental health utilization – use of inpatient/ambulatory care
Chemical dependency utilization
Outpatient drug utilization

Informed health choices

Management of menopause

Plan descriptive information

Board certification/residency completion
Practitioner compensation
Arrangements with public health, education and social care organizations
Total enrolment and enrolment statistics

As Table 5.6 shows, HEDIS is a large and complex data set. Behind each item in the table there is often a series of individual indicators, each of which is defined in great detail to try to make data collection as consistent and comparable as possible. Healthcare purchasers and users in the USA can access health plans' HEDIS data via the Internet and compare plan performance across all the indicators. HEDIS results form a formal part of the NCQA accreditation process and, in between accreditation visits, poor HEDIS performance can trigger NCQA to revisit an organization's accreditation status.

In the UK, the Commission for Health Improvement (CHI) has taken over responsibility for the NHS performance ratings – known as 'star ratings' – and the performance indicators which lie behind them. It will develop, collate and publish these indicators, which will be increasingly used in the Commission's inspection processes. Table 5.7 provides a summary of the current set of 32 indicators for acute NHS trusts (different indicator sets are used for primary care trusts, ambulance trusts, mental health care trusts and other specialist organizations). The process by which these indicators are aggregated to form a single star rating from zero stars (the worst) to three stars (the best) is complex, but essentially a significant failure to deliver on any of the key targets results in a rating of zero or one star. To get two stars, trusts have to do fairly well across all the other indicators; and to get three stars, they must be above average across virtually all indicators. The results of their most recent CHI review

Table 5.7 NHS performance ratings indicators for acute NHS trusts in 2001–2002

Key targets	No patients waiting more than 18 months for inpatient treatment
	Fewer patients waiting more than 15 months for inpatient treatment
	No patients waiting more than 26 weeks for outpatient treatment
	Fewer patients waiting on trolleys for more than 12 hours
	Less than 1% of operations cancelled on the day
	No patients with suspected cancer waiting more than 2 weeks to be seen in hospital
	Improvement to the working lives of staff
	Hospital cleanliness
	A satisfactory financial position
Clinical focus	Risk of clinical negligence
	Deaths within 30 days of surgery for patients admitted on an unplanned basis
	Deaths within 30 days of a heart bypass operation
	Emergency re-admissions to hospital following discharge
	Emergency re-admissions to hospital following discharge for children
	Emergency re-admissions to hospital following treatment for a fractured hip
	Emergency re-admissions to hospital following treatment for a stroke
	Returning home from hospital following treatment for a fractured hip
	Returning home from hospital following treatment for a stroke
Patient focus	Inpatients waiting less than 6 months for treatment
	Total inpatient waits
	Outpatients seen within 13 weeks
	Total time in A&E
	Cancelled operations not admitted within a month
	Heart operation
	Breast cancer
	Delayed discharges
	Inpatient survey of patients – coordination of care
	Inpatient survey of patients – environment and facilities
	Inpatient survey of patients – information and education
	Inpatient survey of patients – physical and emotional needs
	Inpatient survey of patients – prompt access
	Inpatient survey of patients – respect and dignity

Capacity and capability	Data quality as measured by hospital inpatient activity data
	Staff satisfaction as measured by the staff opinion survey
	Compliance with the new deal on junior doctors' hours (working a maximum 56 hours a week)
	Compliance with targets on confidentiality and information governance
	The sickness/absence rate for staff employed directly by the NHS

are also taken into account. Organizations with a three-star rating get additional freedoms and access to more resources, while those with zero stars face intervention from the NHS Modernization Agency and the replacement of their board level management team.

In designing sets of performance measures like these, regulators face the problems that traditionally bedevil attempts to quantify and compare the performance of healthcare organizations (Nutley and Smith 1998; Smith 2002): designing valid indicators and reliable indicators; using available data or minimizing additional data collection demands; adjusting for differences in organizational setting, case mix and so on; integrating multiple indicators into single performance scores; finding the right level of aggregation; interpreting and understanding differences in indicators; using the data to promote beneficial changes and avoiding gaming and perverse effects on organizational behaviour.

However, there are also three problems for regulators, which spring in particular from the regulatory use of performance data. First, it is clearly desirable that there should be some connection between regulatory direction (set out in standards or regulations) and the process of performance measurement and monitoring. Ideally, the performance indicators would allow direct assessment of compliance with regulatory standards, so that for each regulatory standard there would be a matching indicator (or set of indicators). However, the reality is that there are usually so many regulatory standards that it would not be feasible to monitor an indicator for every one, and many would require expensive special data collection exercises. In any case, performance indicators are often structured, pragmatically, to make best use of available routinely collected data sets at little or no additional cost, which may mean that they are at best rather indirect proxies for regulatory compliance.

Secondly, the collation of performance data from regulated organizations by a regulatory agency can create very powerful incentives for regulated organizations to manipulate and distort the data if they are in a position to do so. Where the indicators draw upon routinely collected data, there may be less scope for such behaviour, although it may still be possible to influence the ratings by changing the way that activities are coded or recorded. Where indicators rely on special data collections, there is more scope for manipulation, even though the regulator may audit the data collection process and try to check the validity of the returns. For example, NHS trusts have shown considerable creativity in coming up with ways to 'fix' the waiting time and access targets in the NHS performance ratings (see Table 5.7). In the USA, the Joint Commission on the Accreditation of Healthcare Organizations (JCAHO) requires hospitals to collect information on serious adverse events and to report them to the Commission, but because such reports may then trigger a JCAHO investigation or early accreditation survey, hospitals have been very reluctant to expose themselves by reporting significant problems. On the whole, the more deterrence-oriented the regulatory regime, the more likely it is that regulated organizations will find ways, legitimate or not, to manipulate the performance indicators.

Thirdly, regulatory agencies have to decide what to do with the performance indicator data they have collected – this may be their greatest challenge. They are likely to be faced with a large and heterogeneous set of performance indicators, of varying validity and reliability, based on data of varying quality, mapping imperfectly to the dimensions of regulatory direction, and with a high level of 'noise' from which real differences or changes in performance need to be separated. Apart from simply publishing the indicators, they need to find a way to use them in regulatory detection and enforcement. The most common approach is to use performance monitoring data to inform or trigger other detection activities, such as surveys, inspections or investigations (see below). However, the linkage is often rather weak. Regulatory staff undertaking surveys or inspections are often given a large volume of background performance monitoring information, but lack the skills and the time to interpret and use it properly. Only when an organization is an extreme outlier on some dimensions of performance is it likely that it will trigger a survey or inspection, or that the data will start to be used more fully to raise questions and set the agenda for a subsequent survey or inspection. The NCQA is the only regulator that goes one step further towards integrating its approach to regulatory detection and enforcement by making a proportion (25 per cent) of the organization's NCQA accreditation score dependent on performance monitoring data from HEDIS.

Surveys and inspections

Surveys, visits, reviews or inspections (the terms tend be used somewhat interchangeably) are the mainstay of regulatory detection. Although there are some differences in approach, the broad principles are remarkably common. The regulator sends a team of surveyors or inspectors to visit the regulated organization. In advance of the visit, they may gather background or advance information, and the organization may prepare itself for the visit. The visit itself takes place over a few days, during which the surveyors or inspectors gather data, often through interviews, meetings, direct observation, and reviewing documents and papers. At the end of the visit, the surveyors often communicate their provisional findings to the organization, but afterwards they produce a report that may describe and rate the organization and its compliance with regulatory requirements and identify any recommendations or areas for improvement. Depending on those findings, there may then be further follow-up visits to check on progress. These surveys or inspections usually take place periodically, anywhere between once or twice a year and once every 6–7 years.

Despite their widespread use, surveys and inspections are problematic tools, difficult to use well and prone to several unintended consequences and effects. First, and most obviously, the validity and reliability of survey and inspection methods and results are often questioned. Do survey findings provide an accurate assessment of an organization's performance? If two survey teams were to survey the same organization, would their findings concur? These are systems of measurement and it is reasonable to expect that conventional standards for statistical validity and reliability should be met, and that those who develop and use surveys and inspections should test the measures they produce before putting them into general use. In practice, this almost never happens, although when it does the results raise serious concerns, particularly about reliability (Walsh and Walshe 1998). Some regulators attempt to increase the consistency of their survey process by defining it in great detail, describing every standard comprehensively and specifying exactly what survey teams are meant to do. However, by doing so they probably compromise the validity of measurement and produce survey systems that just can't be done in the time available. For example, the Joint Commission on the Accreditation of Healthcare Organizations (JCAHO) has over 500 standards in its hospital accreditation programme, each of which is defined in some detail, and for each of which surveyors are expected to check compliance during a 4–5 day visit to a hospital. In practice, there just isn't time to do this, and so surveyors don't go through every standard; instead, they assume compliance by default and, when during their visit they find a problem or issue of concern in the hospital, they look for a standard under which to categorize it. The difficulties of ensuring that surveys and inspections produce reliable measurements are probably inherent in what is a highly heterogeneous process attempting to measure some hard-to-define aspects of organizational behaviour and performance. Regulators should take this into account when using the results from surveys and inspections, treating them with rather more caution and not rushing to make a judgement on the basis of one survey or inspection finding.

A second, related set of issues concern the characteristics and performance of the regulator's own staff – the surveyors or inspectors. It quickly becomes apparent that the quality of surveys or inspections seems to depend largely on the quality of the people who undertake them. Those regulators who invest heavily in recruiting, training and developing their surveyors are likely to get better survey results and a more acceptable survey process than those who do not. Table 5.8 sets out some of the commonly expressed characteristics of 'good' and 'bad' surveyors or inspectors. It can be seen that the role of the surveyor or inspector is a very demanding one, requiring a combination of three key characteristics: extensive experience in the field itself; expertise in the regulatory process and regulatory requirements; and excellent interpersonal, facilitation and communication skills. To do it well, a healthcare regulator needs to recruit some of the very best current senior managers and clinicians, allow them to continue to practice while working as surveyors or inspectors, and invest significantly in their development. But this makes surveys and inspections an expensive business, especially if the regulator has to reimburse those people's employing organizations for releasing them, and by definition these are people in high demand whose time is limited and whose organizations may not feel able to spare them. The result is that surveyors and inspectors are all too often drawn from the ranks of the semi-retired, redundant or otherwise displaced, lack the skills and abilities outlined above, and have little credibility with the organizations they survey or inspect.

Table 5.8 Some characteristics of regulatory surveyors and inspectors

Characteristic	Positive	Negative
Regulatory knowledge	Knows the regulatory requirements inside out, understands them in detail, and is able to apply them intelligently and explain them to others cogently	May know the letter of the requirements but is unable to apply them to the real world, explain their rationale, or interpret them in the context of individual organizations
Practical experience	Works or has worked very recently in a regulated organization and has real, practical experience and understanding of the realities of the business	Has never worked in practice or has not done so for some time through retirement or a change of career, and does not really comprehend what it is like
Decision-making	Makes clear, well-thought through decisions which he or she is willing to justify and discuss, and to change if need be	Makes snap decisions without sufficient thought, or is indecisive and easily swung or influenced; does not want to discuss decisions or to change them, and sees such approaches as a threat
Adaptability	Highly adaptable, able to adjust approach and style of working to fit the organization	Rigid and routinized approach in which same style and methods of working are used everywhere regardless of appropriateness
Personality	Personable, approachable, calm, friendly, compassionate and humorous	Unfriendly, distant, aggressive, cold, unhelpful and humourless
Interpersonal skills	Good with a wide range of people, sets people at their ease, able to work well in a team	Over-formal, prickly, difficult to work with

A third issue to consider concerns the scheduling or pre-notification of surveys and inspections. Some regulators give regulated organizations ample warning of a forthcoming inspection. They argue that the organizations need time to prepare for what is a significant burden of work, that the logistics of a visit are complicated and have to be planned in advance, and that much of the performance improvement stimulated by a survey or inspection occurs during the period of preparation, when organizations often undertake a self-assessment and work on problems or concerns long before the surveyors or inspectors even arrive. However, it can also be asserted that scheduled inspections or surveys are easy to fix – staff can be schooled in what to say (and what not to say), facilities can be tidied up and superficially improved, awkward individuals can be got out of the way, and plans can be made to steer the surveyors away from any problems and to shower them with good news from those parts of the organization that are doing well. This school of thought would assert that unscheduled surveys, which can take place at any time of the day or night with as little as a few hours notice, provide a much more realistic picture of organizational performance and cannot be easily distorted. Others would argue that much of the potential performance improvement benefit from such a survey is lost.

Both are valid viewpoints and the approach taken depends on the regulator's objectives, since scheduled surveys appear to maximize opportunities for improvement while unscheduled surveys may be more effective mechanisms for assurance and accountability. At their worst, scheduled surveys become a ritualized performance, a scripted and controlled encounter from which a highly sanitized and partial picture of organizational performance emerges. However, if scheduled surveys are used more flexibly, and surveyors have the time and freedom to undertake *ad hoc* data collection and reshape the survey programme as it progresses, much can be done to reduce this problem. Some regulators like JCAHO make use of a combination of scheduled and unscheduled surveys or inspections with the intention of securing the advantages of both.

A fourth set of problems concerns the costs of surveys and inspections. They are expensive interventions, both for the regulator and the regulated organization, especially when they are done properly. For small organizations like nursing homes, a survey or inspection can seem a disproportionately intensive and costly way to assess their performance. For large organizations such as a major acute teaching hospital, survey and inspection processes have to be scaled up considerably if the regulator is to get a meaningful view of performance across the organization. In both cases, the costs to the regulator may be high but they are generally dwarfed by the costs to the regulated organization of preparing for and undergoing the inspection. Much of the cost is not immediately apparent – staff time is probably the largest single item, but it is rarely accounted for and charged to a budget heading for regulation.

A fifth and final problem, linked to that of survey and inspection costs, is that of periodicity. Because surveys and inspections are expensive and intensive interventions, regulators and regulated organizations can only afford to use them relatively infrequently. Few regulators undertake surveys or inspections more than once a year, many allow 2–3 years to pass between inspections, and it is not uncommon to see inter-survey periods of 5 years or more. This gap between regulatory assessments of performance, and the predictability of the survey cycle, produce some unhelpful behaviours in regulated organizations, especially when the regulator does little or nothing to monitor performance between surveys. For much of the time, they are effectively unregulated and there are few incentives to comply with regulatory directions. In the months running up to a survey or inspection, the organization commonly 'ramps up', preparing to be scrutinized and undertaking a self-assessment against regulatory standards. The inspection happens when the organization is at a peak of performance and preparedness, but unless the regulatory agency finds problems it wants to follow up, the organization knows it is then free again from regulatory attention until the next scheduled survey. Understandably, performance is likely to slacken and regulatory compliance will probably decline. Things go back to the way they were before, until the next time. This problem of periodicity may be reduced when surveys or inspections are more frequent, because the organization spends more of its time anticipating and preparing for the next inspection. However, even with annual surveys or inspections, the regulatory cycle is very long and it can take several cycles (or several years) to find problems, identify and recommend improvements, and see those improvements implemented.

Investigations and inquiries

An investigation or inquiry can be defined as a retrospective examination of events or circumstances surrounding a service failure or problem, specially established to find out what happened and why and to learn from the experiences of all those involved (Walshe and Higgins 2002). It has two particular characteristics. First, it is a reactive approach to regulatory detection. Rather than trying to find out whether regulated organizations are complying with regulatory requirements, the regulator responds or reacts when it is presented with information that suggests that it is not, or that some problem with performance exists. That may take the form of a complaint from a patient or his or her family, a healthcare professional or another organization. It could also be a referral from another agency, such as a healthcare purchaser or funder, another regulator or a local authority, or it might simply be reports about the organization in the media. Whatever the source, the regulatory agency reacts by assessing the prima facie evidence and deciding whether it merits further investigation. The second characteristic of investigations and inquiries is that they are generally focused on service failures, quality problems and apparent poor performance. They are effectively a targeted approach to regulatory detection, which focuses regulatory resources and attention on examining the performance of organizations which are or may be at the lower end of the distribution of performance.

Some investigations and inquiries may be highly focused on the subject at hand – for example, on investigating the exact circumstances and events in a patient's complaint and adjudicating, allocating blame or requiring the organization to make amends. Other investigations and inquiries have a broader remit, in which the problem that initiated the investigation or inquiry is seen as a potential symptom of underlying organizational pathology (Walshe and Offen 2001). For this reason, the investigation may look more widely at the management and leadership of the organization, or its structures, systems and processes for assuring the quality of care, and not simply focus on the problem itself. Ultimately, as the focus moves away from the problem and towards the organization, investigations and inquiries become difficult to distinguish from routine surveys and inspections, and some regulators in the USA and the UK do undertake 'for cause' or 'fast-track' surveys and inspections that are triggered by a problem or complaint but use very similar methods to their normal survey processes.

Many regulators use investigations or inquiries alongside other methods of regulatory detection (such as surveys and inspections), but some, such as the Health Service Ombudsman in the UK and the Long Term Care Ombudsman programme in the USA, use investigations and inquiries as their primary approach to regulatory detection. But an over-reliance on investigations has some potential problems. It means the regulator may never have any contact with some organizations if there is never a complaint or referral about them. It could be argued that this is perfectly appropriate, since their performance must be good, but that presupposes that all problems and failures to comply with regulatory direction will result in complaints or referrals (which is, of course, not the case, as many may be relatively invisible to patients and others). It also assumes that complaints and referrals are always or largely justified, and this too is not necessarily so – they are a complex product of patients' experiences and expectations, influenced by many factors outside the regulated organization itself. A further problem of relying on investigations for regulatory detection is that they do not easily fit with a system of regulatory standards. Regulators who use investigations extensively tend not to produce regulatory standards to convey their expectations or directions. Instead, they often rely on the 'case law' built up from successive investigations to establish a broad regulatory direction. However, as was discussed earlier, regulatory standards play an important role in amplifying the regulator's influence, beyond the organization which they are currently scrutinizing. Without standards, there is a risk that the regulator only really influences the organizations it investigates. Although regulators who use investigations often publish their results or findings, either individually or in aggregate form, it is unclear whether such publications do much to influence how regulated organizations behave.

Conclusions

This analysis of approaches to regulatory detection, and the descriptions in Chapters 3 and 4 of how healthcare regulators in the USA and UK assess the performance of health plans, nursing homes, hospitals and the like, suggest that using a single approach to regulatory detection across all organizations and all circumstances is likely to be wasteful and unproductive. Whether it is inspecting every hospital once every 3–4 years (as the Joint Commission on the Accreditation of Healthcare Organizations and the Commission for Health Improvement both do), or investigating complaints (as the Health Service Ombudsman and the Long Term Care Ombudsman programme do), a single, uniform method cannot be well-suited to every regulated organization's needs, circumstances, history and performance profile.

Instead, it may be helpful to think of the available approaches to regulatory detection in a hierarchy of assessment, which fits well with the principles of responsive regulation outlined in Chapter 2. At the bottom of the hierarchy would be the least intrusive, lowest cost, light touch forms of assessment. They might include limited performance monitoring through indicators and data, or some form of self-assessment of regulatory compliance. At the top of the hierarchy would be the most intensive, expensive and comprehensive forms of assessment, such as full-scale inspections and large investigations or inquiries. The regulator needs to be able to use the full range of methods, rather than relying on a single one, and to move up and down this hierarchy quite freely in response to the behaviour of individual regulated organizations. So, for example, if routine performance monitoring indicates that an organization's performance may be declining, that might trigger some face-to-face contact with the organization and its leadership, which might then lead if necessary to some form of survey or inspection. In some ways, the existence of connections or links between different methods of regulatory detection, and an ability to move between them, are just as important as the methods themselves.

One other finding is evident from this analysis. Regulatory detection is at best an inexact and imperfect process. Measuring organizational performance and regulatory compliance is complex and somewhat subjective. Although regulators could do more to assure the validity, reliability and consistency of their approaches to regulatory detection, they should also do more to take into account the fallibility of their results. It is unwise to rush into regulatory enforcement action on the basis of one set of findings from a survey, inspection or other method of detection, given what we know about the inherent variability and subjectivity of those methods. Regulators might do well to seek triangulation – confirmation of their findings from a number of different sources, or congruence in results from different approaches to regulatory detection – before they initiate major regulatory enforcement measures.

ENFORCEMENT: MAKING CHANGE HAPPEN

Regulatory enforcement is the term commonly used to describe the things that regulatory agencies do to influence, persuade, support, encourage or force regulated organizations to change. It covers everything from having a friendly word informally with a senior manager about a problem to fining, 'naming and shaming' or even delicensing the organization. What connects this diverse collection of regulatory tools or approaches is that they are all intended to make change happen.

Although change and improvement are seen as the primary mission of many healthcare regulators, they commonly put less time and effort into regulatory enforcement than they invest in regulatory direction and detection. The frequent absence of a sustained and comprehensive approach to enforcement may reflect the fact that regulatory enforcement is perhaps the most difficult and sometimes unpleasant part of the regulatory process. It may also spring from the fact that some methods of regulatory enforcement can be extremely expensive, and any regulator which uses them more than very rarely can end up spending a lot of regulatory resources on enforcement action against a few organizations (Netten *et al.* 1999). However, weak or poorly planned and resourced enforcement strategies are likely to erode or negate the potential benefits of good systems for regulatory direction and detection (Hawkins and Thomas 1984).

Regulators also have varying sets of enforcement powers, something which shapes the approaches that they take. Some have no formal powers and rely wholly or largely on their ability to persuade, cajole and use informal pressures on regulated organizations to secure change. The Long Term Care Ombudsman programme in the USA is one example, and the Health Advisory Service in the UK was another. Other regulators have a more limited or indirect set of powers – for example, the Joint Commission on the Accreditation of Healthcare Organizations can refuse accreditation to a hospital, which may cause it to lose Medicare and Medicaid patients, and the Commission for Health Improvement can publish its report on an NHS trust and make recommendations for action to the Department of Health. Some, such as nursing home regulators in the USA, have a large set of direct enforcement powers available to them, ranging from the ability to bar new admissions and withhold payments, through civil money penalties or fines, up to the ability to take over the management of a nursing home or to withdraw its licence and close it down. To some extent, regulators have to work with the powers they have been given and fit their enforcement strategies to the available methods and resources. However, there is considerable scope for regulators to be creative in the way they use their powers to bring about change.

Of course, there is an important difference between having an enforcement power and using it. Regulators who have strong enforcement powers, such as the ability to take over an organization or to close it down, tend to use those 'nuclear' sanctions very rarely indeed, for two reasons. First, their severity has to be a proportionate response to the breach of regulatory requirements, and few such breaches are usually deemed to merit such draconian action. Secondly, these sanctions usually have significant adverse effects for other stakeholders as well, whose interests have to be considered. For example, closing a nursing home for persistent and serious breaches of regulatory standards means that its residents – frail, elderly and vulnerable for the most part – are made homeless, have to be moved elsewhere and are likely to be dispersed. When there is a shortage of nursing home capacity, it may make it harder for local care agencies to find places for people who need them; this results in patients staying longer in hospital while waiting for a nursing home bed to be found. In other words, the closure may have disbenefits for residents, social care agencies and hospitals that outweigh its benefits from the regulator's perspective.

It is important to recognize, before discussing and analysing the formal approaches to regulatory enforcement, the place of informal tools and techniques. In many settings, much or even most regulatory enforcement takes this form. It is often somewhat hidden from view, an implicit component of regulatory detection activities such as surveys and inspections. Regulatory staff may offer advice on how to comply with regulatory standards, or may have informal and off-the-record discussions with senior managers in which they use a combination of their expertise and knowledge and their authority as the regulator to provide leverage for change. Often, regulators may be providing an external impetus for changes, which some parts of the organization support and others do not – and the regulator's intervention shifts the balance of power in favour of change. Regulators with a more deterrence-oriented model of regulation (such as nursing home regulators in the USA) tend to discourage such informal enforcement activities, seeing them as a potential breach of probity and due process. They may instruct surveyors not to offer advice to regulated organizations (as the Centers for Medicare and Medicaid Services does to nursing home inspectors in state survey agencies) or require them to issue a formal citation whenever a breach of regulatory requirements is found to stop them dealing with anything informally.

Enforcement actions generally have two purposes – getting the regulated organization which is the subject of the action to comply or change, and communicating the importance of compliance to other regulated organizations and encouraging them to comply too. These two aims can sometimes conflict, in that it might be more productive in some circumstances to conduct enforcement actions fairly discretely to sustain good working relationships with the regulated organization. However, if the benefits of 'demonstrative enforcement' (Kagan 1984) are to be secured, it has to be done publicly and with sufficient coverage to make sure that other regulated organizations know about it.

Regulatory enforcement can damage working relationships with regulated organizations and make future regulatory detection and interaction more difficult. The response from regulated organizations depends in part on how fair, proportionate and deserved they see the enforcement action to be. Faced by sanctions which, though unwelcome, they recognize as merited by their performance, there will probably be only a short-term deterioration in the relationship. However, when sanctions appear unduly severe, capriciously imposed or plainly undeserved, the effect on the relationship will be more substantial and lasting. Regulated organizations will often respond very negatively even when the sanction is relatively minor because they take issue with the principle of being punished and see it as a symbolic act. They may appeal through the regulator's own processes, go to court to seek redress, or lobby other stakeholders like politicians and government agencies to get the decision changed or to influence the regulator's future behaviour. Moreover, the impact of regulatory enforcement action can be cumulative and a series of minor sanctions can do as much to harm future relationships as fewer, more significant enforcement actions (Braithwaite 1985).

The symbolic importance of regulatory enforcement actions deserves some exploration. Often, regulatory enforcement actions are relatively trivial in relation to the scale of the regulated organization and its activities. Fining a nursing home chain $20,000 when it has a turnover of $100 million a year or more is clearly not that important in financial terms. Publishing a critical report or assessment of a hospital or health plan may result in some short-term adverse publicity, but it is unlikely to do much real harm to its business income or market share. Much regulatory enforcement action is largely of symbolic importance, for the message it conveys to the organization concerned, to the wider community of regulated organizations and to other stakeholders like patients, the media and the general public, and what is or is not acceptable behaviour or performance. Regulatory enforcement serves to mark out the pale, but may not be sufficient deterrent to prevent those organizations which want to go beyond it from doing so.

Approaches to regulatory enforcement

Table 5.9 lists the main approaches to regulatory enforcement, describing and offering some examples of each. It is immediately apparent that most approaches to regulatory enforcement involve the use of sanctions or penalties rather than incentives or rewards. Regulators do have some, limited incentives available to them – for example, many regulatory agencies award some kind of 'accreditation with distinction' status to organizations that perform well, and this carries with it some status and may confer some market advantage. Some of the incentives which regulators may offer are, in effect, the absence of sanctions. For example, it is common for regulatory agencies to give high-performing organizations some exemption or greater freedom from regulatory scrutiny, such as a longer period of licensure or accreditation before their next survey or inspection. A few regulators have – or will have – more significant incentives to offer in return for good performance. For example, the Commission for Health Improvement will determine which NHS trusts are performing best, and they will get increased autonomy from the Department of Health, greater financial freedom over capital developments and their estates and assets, and increased access to the NHS performance fund. In the USA, there have been some experiments with paying nursing homes a higher rate for Medicare or Medicaid patients if they achieve certain quality standards, which, although they have never been extended to the mainstream, may offer another model for regulatory incentivization (Norton 1992; Zinn 1994).

However, most enforcement options available to regulators involve sanctions, penalties or punishments of some kind, and the five main approaches are listed in Table 5.9 in approximate order of scale and severity, in something akin to an enforcement hierarchy. Perhaps the first and most common sanction used is increased regulatory scrutiny. A regulator may choose to return following an inspection for a follow-up visit, or to monitor the organization more closely in other ways. Although these are really forms of regulatory detection, there is no doubt that they are used to persuade regulated organizations to change. They want the regulator 'off their back' and so they comply with the regulator's requirements in the hope that when

Table 5.9 Approaches to regulatory enforcement

Approach	Description	Examples
Incentives and rewards	Provision of positive rewards as an incentive for, or recognition of, good performance. Some rewards are effectively the absence of sanctions (e.g. reduced regulatory scrutiny)	• 'Earned autonomy' in the UK, under which NHS trusts get greater financial freedoms for good performance • Award of accreditation certificates by the National Committee for Quality Assurance (NCQA) and the Joint Commission on the Accreditation of Healthcare Organizations (JCAHO), which organizations then use in their marketing
Increased regulatory scrutiny	Increased level of regulatory detection activities, such as more frequent monitoring or more visits/surveys in response to evidence of poor performance	• Provisional accreditation by JCAHO and NCQA which results in follow-up visits or early reaccreditation • Commission for Health Improvement (CHI) 'fast-track' clinical governance reviews for NHS trusts with apparent problems
Public disclosure	The publication and dissemination of information on regulated organizations' performance	• Publication of reports and findings such as CHI review and investigation reports, JCAHO and NCQA accreditation results, etc. • Websites containing comparative information, such as the NCQA Quality Compass or the Centers for Medicare and Medicaid Services nursing home NHCompare website
Restraints on activities	Restrictions or restraints – either temporary or permanent – placed on the regulated organization's activities	• Block placed on new admissions to US nursing homes, usually temporarily while problem is resolved

Table 5.9—*continued*

Approach	Description	Examples
		• Effective termination of ability to provide certain services (e.g. obstetrics, A&E, paediatrics) in hospitals through withdrawal of recognition of medical staff training posts by medical Royal Colleges in the UK • Ultimately, refusal or removal of state/federal licence to operate, which puts a nursing home, hospital or health plan in the USA out of business
Financial penalties	Imposition of fines – financial penalties for breaking regulatory requirements	• Denial of payment for a patient or patients in Medicare/Medicaid because of problems with care • Imposition of fines or 'civil money penalties' by nursing home regulators in USA or the National Care Standards Commission in UK for breaches of regulatory requirements
Managerial intervention	Direct intervention in the management or leadership of the regulated organization	• Taking over the management of a nursing home in the USA and installing a temporary manager while longer-term solution is sought • Modernization Agency intervention in zero star NHS trusts, providing management support and advice • Replacement of management team for failing NHS trusts through 'franchising'

that is seen to be the case, the increased regulatory scrutiny will be withdrawn.

The next sanction commonly used by regulators is some form of public disclosure or reporting of regulated organizations' performance. For example, the Commission for Health Improvement (CHI) and the National Committee for Quality Assurance (NCQA) both publish their findings more or less in full; CHI in particular makes an effort to get coverage in the local and national media by issuing press releases and providing interviews. In high-profile cases, where CHI has criticized an NHS trust or called into question its performance, the resultant media attention can be intense, if usually short-lived, and can exert considerable pressure on the organization and those who lead it. Some NHS chief executives have effectively been forced to resign by a poor CHI review and its sequelae (Day and Klein 2002). Another way for regulators to use public disclosure, less oriented towards the media and more directed at patients and users of health services, is to provide comparative information through reports, directories or league tables. The internet has made this a much easier and more powerful tool than it was in the past. For example, NCQA's Quality Compass website (www.ncqa.org) allows patients, users and healthcare funders (such as employers) to compare the performance of health plans very easily and to access both the results of accreditation visits and their HEDIS scores. The Centers for Medicare and Medicaid Services (CMS) site, Nursing Home Compare (http://www.medicare.gov/nhcompare/home.asp), provides a similar service for those looking for a nursing home, drawing on data collected through the licensure and certification process by CMS and the state survey agencies.

The three main other forms of sanctions available to regulators are all, on the whole, more direct interventions in the business of the regulated organization. First, regulators may have powers to restrict the future activities of a regulated organization, perhaps by changing or setting the terms of its licence to operate. For example, a hospital could have permission to admit and treat more complex cases requiring intensive care withheld or withdrawn, or could be told that it may not operate in certain specialties or areas, such as cardiac surgery, transplant surgery or neurology. This kind of restraint may be a permanent condition of licensure, reflecting the organization's capacity and capability and preventing small, ill-equipped hospitals from undertaking work that would be better done in a larger, better resourced and equipped facility. Alternatively, restraints on activities may be a temporary sanction, imposed with the intention of producing changes after which the restraint can be released. For example, US nursing home regulators can instruct nursing homes not to accept any new admissions until a problem has been rectified. Because the costs of having empty beds will gradually build, this sanction can provide a powerful incentive to comply with regulatory requirements.

Secondly, a regulator can impose direct financial penalties or fines for non-compliance. These fines can be a simple flat penalty or may be calculated on a sliding scale that takes into account the nature of the infraction and the period of non-compliance. Sometimes, fines are set so that they continue to accumulate until the organization complies with the regulator's directions. Systems of financial sanctions generally require some kind of civil court application in the USA and UK, which can be a slow and laborious process, open to challenge by regulated organizations. The penalties rarely rise above a few thousand pounds or dollars, levels at which they are a significant cost to small regulated organizations but little more than an irritation to larger organizations. They are dwarfed by the costs of other forms of non-regulatory civil action, such as claims for negligence brought by patients and their families, which can be for millions of pounds or dollars.

Thirdly, and perhaps most rarely, a regulator can choose to intervene directly in the management of a regulated organization to support or to change its leadership. Direct intervention can take the form of advice or support to the existing management team, aimed at enabling them to bring the organization into regulatory compliance. For example, the NHS Modernization Agency sends its 'rapid response' unit into zero star NHS trusts to provide a temporary injection of managerial capacity and, hopefully, to transform and develop local management's capacity to deal with future problems. Alternatively, direct intervention can involve changing the management team, a regulatory equivalent of the common response to financial failure, in which administrators are put in to run a company until it is wound up or sold as a going concern. This kind of intervention is usually reserved for urgent and serious problems, such as a failing nursing home, which regulators may take over temporarily (to avoid its closure and the resultant problems for displaced residents) and manage its transition to different ownership. It is essentially a short-term, crisis response – few regulators are equipped to run the organizations they regulate – and there needs to be a clear longer-term strategy for the future management of any organization put into 'regulatory administration'.

Conclusions

Like direction and detection, the nature and style of regulatory enforcement is shaped by the objectives of regulation and the regulatory model adopted by the regulator. However, some general conclusions can be drawn from this analysis of the tools and techniques of regulatory enforcement and the descriptions of their use in Chapters 3 and 4.

It is important that the purpose or intent of regulatory enforcement is clear. Is it intended to punish or to persuade (Braithwaite 1985)? Punishment may be a perfectly legitimate regulatory purpose in the interests of fairness and justice. When most regulated organizations comply, but a few do not, it would be quite unfair if the non-compliant were allowed to profit by their behaviour, and so some form of punishment may be needed both in the name of justice and to deter others from not complying. However, persuasion seems to be the dominant purpose of regulatory enforcement in practice, in which case the value of approaches to enforcement may be judged best in terms of their capacity to bring about changes in behaviour in regulated organizations, without harming future regulatory processes or relationships or making future regulatory compliance less likely. That is not a simple task. Given sufficient regulatory enforcement powers, it is straightforward to make organizations do things through the threat or actual imposition of sanctions, but doing so in a way that actually sustains relationships and promotes future compliance is more difficult.

Two requirements emerge from this analysis. First, regulators need ready access to a wide range of enforcement powers, including both rewards and sanctions. They need the kind of hierarchy of enforcement powers described in Chapter 2 in the discussion of responsive regulation and the capacity to use them when needed. Many regulators have rather limited enforcement powers or too few enforcement options, which makes it difficult to match enforcement to the behaviour of a regulated organization. Some have enforcement powers in theory but are unable or unwilling to use them, and so might as well not have those powers at all.

Secondly, regulators need an intelligent enforcement strategy, in which the likely benefits and costs or harms of regulatory enforcement are considered and thought through for each enforcement action. This means giving regulatory staff considerable discretion and freedom of action in deciding when and how to use regulatory enforcement within agreed principles or guidelines, rather than attempting to prescribe a single approach to be taken in all circumstances. It is likely that effective enforcement strategies will be: demonstrably fair, in the sense that regulated organizations recognize that actions are deserved; proportionate, matching the scale and nature of enforcement actions to the problems of regulatory non-compliance at hand; swift, in that enforcement happens relatively quickly and with a minimum of bureaucracy; and reintegrative, which means they are designed to promote future compliance as well as to resolve the immediate issues of non-compliance (Braithwaite 2002).

6

CONCLUSIONS: THE FUTURE FOR HEALTHCARE REGULATION

We noted in Chapter 1 that one of the advantages of international comparisons in health policy is that they let us examine other ways of organizing, financing or managing healthcare without having to try them out for ourselves. We can, with some caution, use other countries as our laboratory. And, while we can't control events, we can learn a great deal from what happens. Distance can lend objectivity to our observations, making it easier to see what is really going on, and to disentangle the underlying trends from the surface turmoil of change. This chapter summarizes the US and UK experience of regulating healthcare in the hope that each can learn from the other, and that other countries embarking on healthcare regulation might learn from both of them. It then goes on to distil from the US and UK experience some understanding of the determinants of effectiveness in healthcare regulation, in two ways. First, it examines the common causes of regulatory failure and asks to what extent they might be avoidable. Secondly, it draws together emerging ideas on what constitutes effective regulatory policy and practice. In closing, the chapter goes on to discuss how these findings might be brought to bear in improving the design and development of systems of healthcare regulation in both the UK and the USA.

REGULATING HEALTHCARE IN THE USA AND THE UK: A COMPARISON

In both the USA and the UK, healthcare regulation is endemic. There are few areas of healthcare provision which are not regulated, and many healthcare entities face multiple, overlapping forms of regulatory oversight and scrutiny from different directions and for different purposes. There is probably a lot more regulation in the USA, but that may just be a matter of time rather than a sign of any fundamental difference in approach. Healthcare regulation is a rather more recent development in the UK, but it is growing at least as fast as, if not faster than, in the USA. In both countries, the regulatory ratchet appears to ensure that regulatory requirements are rarely relaxed or disestablished, and that each year regulation bites a little more tightly into the work of healthcare providers.

In both the USA and the UK, regulation seems to have an inherent momentum, all of its own, which means that once government or the healthcare industry takes steps to regulate, those actions are very difficult to slow or stop, let alone to roll back or undo. Once a regulatory agency has been established and regulatory powers have been put in place, it is very difficult for anyone to say that it doesn't work and we'd all be better off without it. To do so is often, falsely, equated with saying that the problems which regulation was introduced to solve don't exist or don't matter very much. So, when regulation does not appear to work, the solution turned to by politicians and policy-makers is often more regulation, not less. There are, perhaps, two practical lessons here. First, we should regulate cautiously and carefully, and be hesitant and sceptical about proposals to extend the remit or scope of regulation unless we are really sure that it is necessary and will work. Secondly, we should be much more willing to consider alternative or complementary strategies to regulation, and to compare and test the likely effectiveness of regulatory and non-regulatory approaches to securing the same objectives.

There are few meaningful estimates of the costs of healthcare regulation in either the USA or the UK. In both countries, it is easy to find out what the costs of running healthcare regulatory agencies are, but much more difficult to discover what regulation really costs, because much of the cost falls upon healthcare organizations and is never clearly accounted for. If a hospital quality manager spends all of his time for 6 months preparing for an accreditation visit or a Commission for Health Improvement clinical governance review, that should be counted as a cost of regulation, but it generally is not. Our inability to tell what regulation costs should be the cause of mild alarm, since it's difficult to arrive at any meaningful assessment of the value of regulation without knowing its price. But in both the USA and the UK, our lack of information about costs betokens a regulatory culture in which costs don't really seem to matter very much, and that is a more serious problem. There are few, if any, incentives for regulatory agencies to keep their costs down and quite a few reasons for them to push their costs up. In both countries, regulatory systems are not designed to promote parsimony or to control or limit regulatory costs.

It is striking that regulation appears to find a place and a purpose in two such different healthcare systems as those of the USA and the UK. In the USA, which is as close to a market-based healthcare economy as you will find in any developed country, regulation seems to play an important part in governing the healthcare market, controlling its worst excesses and enabling it to function and to serve some non-market social and political objectives. It buffers and constrains market behaviours which would be socially damaging or politically unacceptable, and so allows the system to continue to function. Paradoxically, it appears likely that without the mediating effects of healthcare regulation, America's market-based healthcare economy could not function for long, because it would be brought down by its own excesses and the consequent public and political reaction – something which those who call for less regulation in the USA would do well to remember.

In the UK, which is more or less as close to a wholly state-funded and -provided healthcare system as can be found in the developed world, regulation serves a profoundly different purpose. Rather than being a tool to constrain the healthcare market, regulation is being used to replace direct state ownership and government management of healthcare provision with a more indirect and distanced form of state control. When the UK NHS was being run as a vertically integrated bureaucratic monolith, with a direct managerial line of control from the Secretary of State in Whitehall to every hospital, clinic and healthcare worker, there was little perceived need for regulation as a way to get things done. However, as the NHS becomes more diverse with a variety of NHS, not-for-profit and commercial entities involved in healthcare provision, and a much less direct connection between these entities and the Department of Health, new mechanisms are needed to sustain accountability and strategic coherence. Paradoxically, the granting of greater freedom from Whitehall and increased local autonomy and devolved decision-making have been accompanied by the growth of new ways for central government to direct and intervene, primarily through regulation. In political terms, the transfer of responsibility to regulatory agencies like the National Institute for Clinical Excellence and the Commission for Health Improvement seems to allow ministers to distance themselves from awkward decisions by claiming that it's all a matter for the regulator, while continuing to wield considerable influence behind the scenes.

In the USA, a deep-seated cultural antipathy towards government and a preference for private sector solutions has shaped the development of the healthcare system. In the UK, equally deeply entrenched beliefs in the importance of a publicly funded and provided healthcare system and a profound distrust of commercial involvement in healthcare provision have shaped the creation and subsequent development of the NHS. Yet in both countries, regulation appears to work most effectively at the interface between the governmental and non-governmental worlds. Private sector regulation by itself is often toothless and ineffectual; government, when it regulates alone, is prone to imposing bureaucratic rigor mortis while failing to deal with real regulatory problems. It is the hybrid regulators in both countries that appear to make the best regulators – and they, through whatever legislative or administrative devices, combine private sector fleetness and flexibility with governmental authority and enforcement powers.

In conclusion, it is evident from the US and UK experience that healthcare regulation is an uncertain endeavour, prone to a host of unintended consequences and unanticipated effects that can diminish its effectiveness, or mean that while it solves one set of problems it creates others. From this perspective, it is hard to make sense of the enthusiastic willingness to resort to regulation often exhibited by politicians and policy-makers, or the continuing faith which patients, consumers, funders and other stakeholders seem to place in regulation. Unrealistic expectations and over-optimistic predictions of the effectiveness of regulation abound. This does not mean that the nihilistic, ultrasceptical stance should be adopted, which argues that all regulation is inherently destined to fail and we should simply let market forces run their course whenever possible. Rather, it suggests that a more pragmatic, incremental and evaluative approach to regulation could pay dividends.

However, there is a marked absence of what might be called an evaluative culture in healthcare regulation – among policy-makers, regulators, regulated organizations and other stakeholders. Surely, knowing the uncertainties of regulation, they should be motivated to find out more about how regulation works, explore what makes for effective regulation, examine what causes regulatory failures and incorporate that knowledge into future regulatory policy and practice? Yet there is little or no tradition of regulatory experimentation in healthcare, and regulators have shown them-selves to be, with a few notable exceptions, rather cautious about testing the effectiveness or impact of what they do and reluctant to try out new ideas and methods. The regulatory community in health-care has also been slow to see the value of observing and learning from regulation in other settings – whether in healthcare systems in other countries or in other industries and areas of public policy – and has tended towards a kind of exceptionalism and parochialism which emphasizes the 'differentness' of hospitals (or nursing homes, or private healthcare, or the NHS, or whatever). This means we miss out on opportunities to learn from similarities, comparisons and contrasts with regulation elsewhere, or to use ideas and concepts from general regulatory theory. As a result, we have a limited base of empirical and theoretical research into, and analysis of, the structures, processes and outcomes or impacts of healthcare regulation to tell us what makes for effective regulation, and on which to found current and future policy.

The next two sections examine this question of what makes for effective regulation from two perspectives. First, I summarize the common causes or problems of regulatory failure – what often goes wrong with regulation and why. Secondly, I bring together ideas from several sources on the characteristics or traits of 'good' or 'effective' regulation.

UNDERSTANDING REGULATORY FAILURE

There are several reasons for starting by examining the causes of regulatory failure, or the reasons why regulation does not work. Regulation is often seen as a remedy for the well-known problems of market failure, yet we know it may simply substitute a different but perhaps less well understood set of problems (Enthoven 1980). The results of regulation in practice are so often disappointing by comparison with the policy intent or its hypothetical benefits, that it could be argued that some degree of failure is commonplace (Bardach and Kagan 1982; Brennan and Berwick 1996). More positively, understanding the causes of regulatory failure is crucial if they are to be avoided or ameliorated. Table 6.1 sets out a simple categorization of some of the common causes of regulatory failure, drawing on the general regulatory literature.

Examples of each of these forms of regulatory failure can be identi-fied in our reviews of regulation in the UK and USA in Chapters 3

Table 6.1   Some common problems of regulatory failure

Capture	The regulatory process or regulatory agency is 'captured' by particular sectional interests – commonly, but not only those of regulated organizations – which exercise undue influence over decisions about regulatory policy or over the processes of regulation to promote their own self-interest
Goal displacement	The original purposes of regulation are replaced or overlaid with other objectives, often quite different in character. Sometimes, the process of regulation seems to become the purpose itself
Proliferation	The systems of regulation expand and develop over time, increasing in scope, complexity and cost and becoming disproportionately extensive and intrusive. Old or outdated regulatory requirements are not removed or replaced properly and an accretion of layers of regulatory standards and processes develops
Ossification	The systems of regulation inhibit or hinder natural processes of change, innovation and development, both by prescribing and putting in place particular ways of doing things and by focusing organizational capacities on compliance rather than on improvement. Regulatory requirements become outdated and prevent performance improvement rather than promoting it
Unaccountability	The regulatory agency is insufficiently accountable to the political process which created it or the legal system within which it operates, and regulators become unelected and unaccountable arbiters of the 'public interest' who actually serve their own self-interest
Juridification or legalism	Regulation becomes progressively more legalistic in character, style and process, often through the increasing involvement of lawyers at both the regulatory agency and regulated organizations in managing the process of regulation, until it is difficult to distinguish regulatory systems from conventional civil courts

and 4. For example, the problem of *regulatory capture* has long been seen by pro-market economists as an almost inevitable consequence of regulation and an argument for not 'tampering' with the market (Goodman 1980). But while they are largely worried about provider

capture, in healthcare we see examples of capture by healthcare providers, by funders and by government. For example, many would argue that in the USA the Joint Commission on the Accreditation of Healthcare Organizations (JCAHO) is captured by hospital and professional interests who have used it to defend or promote their own interests rather than the public benefit. But, in the same way, the arrangements for nursing home regulation appear to have been captured by government funding agencies who face an equal conflict of interest between their regulatory responsibility for setting quality standards and their financial imperative to control or reduce costs. In the UK, government capture of the regulatory machinery is commonplace, few regulators have the statutory powers and authority of their equivalents in the USA, and most exercise influence through a central government department rather than on their own account.

The problem of *proliferation* is almost universal – in hospital regulation in the USA by federal, state and non-governmental regulators, in nursing home regulation in both the UK and the USA, in health plan regulation in the USA, and almost everywhere else. Regulators seem almost inexorably driven to expand the scope or remit of regulation and to produce ever more detailed and comprehensive statements of their regulatory requirements. This reaches its apotheosis in the JCAHO accreditation manual for hospitals (725 pages, 500 standards) or the Centers for Medicare and Medicaid Services (CMS) *State Operations Manual* (185 standards for nursing homes, several thousand pages long, dozens of appendices). Yet it is possible for regulators to enunciate the principles by which they plan to regulate and to leave their detailed realization to healthcare providers themselves (Braithwaite and Braithwaite 1995).

Although the problem of *ossification* is difficult to quantify, anecdotal examples of regulatory requirements which are outdated and impede high-quality, leading-edge clinical practice are easy to find and suggest that it is commonplace. The CMS standards for hospitals – already a decade out of date – are perhaps the most startling example of regulatory requirements lagging far behind the realities of clinical and organizational practice. However, in areas like nursing home care, it is evident that traditional facility-oriented regulation is often antithetical towards new approaches to caring for the elderly which emphasize independence, mutual support and empowerment (Thomas 1996; Reinhard and Stone 2001). Somehow, regulators all too often fall into the trap of specifying means rather than ends and defining in too much detail how things should be done in areas of care where how things are done changes far more rapidly than the regulations could ever do.

By way of a final example, the problem of *juridification* also appears to be endemic in healthcare regulation, particularly in the USA with its longstanding culture of adversarial legalism in regulation (Kagan and Axelrad 2000). What begins as a direct dialogue between clinical professionals in the regulatory agency and the regulated organization becomes mediated first between the corporate machinery of both and then through legal advisers and representatives. A problem that might be resolved simply and directly, professional to professional, is formalized, documented and officially charged by the regulator in terms that almost inevitably provoke defensiveness and denial from the regulated organization. It is striking that many US healthcare regulatory agencies appear to employ more lawyers than doctors and that the processes of regulation which they put in place are quasi-judicial in nature. This may be a regrettable but understandable necessity, given that hospitals and other healthcare providers are often willing to challenge regulatory decisions through the courts if they do not agree with them, but it is almost certainly harmful to the longer-term aims and objectives of healthcare regulation.

It is striking that none of these problems of regulatory failure is inevitable or unavoidable. For example, the scope for regulatory capture can be reduced if regulatory governance arrangements are designed to involve a wide range of stakeholders in regulation, to prevent any one sectional interest having undue influence, and to build in checks and balances. The likelihood of gradual goal displacement, in which the original purposes of regulation become secondary and the process of regulation becomes to some extent the purpose itself, can be reduced if systems of continuing or periodic evaluation of regulatory performance against those original objectives are used. The proliferation of regulatory standards and systems can be controlled if some kind of prospective regulatory impact analysis of new standards is required, or if the overall numbers or intensity of standards and systems is capped, or if regulatory standards and processes are given automatic 'sunset' dates at which they expire if they are not explicitly updated or renewed. In short, an awareness of the likely problems of regulatory failure can go some way to making such failures less likely.

There are also good reasons to be cautious about using the label of 'failed' regulation at all. First, there is an established academic and political perspective which believes that regulation always fails, and rather prematurely leaps to the conclusion that regulation is to be avoided at almost all costs rather than seeking a more nuanced understanding of how it can be used more effectively (Noll 1985). Secondly, failure is a highly subjective term, and it is important to understand the perspective from which regulatory performance has been assessed. Regulation has, by its nature, diffuse benefits but concentrated costs, which means that opposition to regulation is often stronger than support for it (Hawkins and Thomas 1984). It benefits users, patients, consumers and the public, but the costs fall on regulated organizations – hospitals, health plans, nursing homes and so on. The latter are generally more vociferous in their criticism than the former are in their support, with the result that an unduly negative picture of the performance of regulation can be created.

THE CHARACTERISTICS OF EFFECTIVE REGULATION

It has already been noted that the diversity of purpose and the variation in context or setting for regulation makes it difficult and perhaps unhelpful to identify characteristics of good or effective regulation that are universally applicable. However, some common ground can be established and an empirically based understanding of the determinants of effectiveness can at least help to challenge some of the ways in which regulation is used. For example, two decades ago, Bardach and Kagan (1982) caricatured the commonly accepted view of what constituted effective regulation in the USA – federally operated, comprehensive, using explicit standards, applied rigidly without favour or discretion, with tough penalties and big sanctions for non-compliance – and pointed out that it simply was not borne out by the evidence. Yet the analysis in Chapter 3 suggests that this viewpoint still commands considerable political and public support in US healthcare regulation, and there is still little evidence that it works well.

The principles of responsive regulation – first outlined in Chapter 2 and reviewed in Chapter 5 – seem to provide a useful and well-founded starting point for determining what constitutes effective regulation. If we accept that a responsive approach to regulation is more likely to be effective (and the evidence reviewed in Chapter 5 appears to provide some empirical support for that position in healthcare), then the six key characteristics of responsive regulation – contingency, hierarchy, flexibility, tripartism, parsimony and empowerment – could be used to create a framework for assessing the effectiveness of regulatory regimes. However, these may be a necessary but not a sufficient set of conditions, since there are clearly other aspects of regulatory arrangements that affect regulatory performance.

There have been a number of other attempts to enunciate the principles of good or effective regulation, and they have tended to be relatively congruent with each other and with the principles of responsive regulation discussed above. For example, in the UK, the Better Regulation Unit (part of the Cabinet Office in central government and previously called the Deregulation Unit) has promulgated five principles of good regulation, synthesized from their experience of reviewing regulatory arrangements in a wide range of different fields (Better Regulation Taskforce 1998; Vass 2002). They are that regulation should be transparent, accountable, targeted, consistent and proportionate. To some extent, these principles might appear to be self-evident (since no-one, presumably, would argue for disproportionate, unaccountable or inconsistent regulation). However, they have been influential in shaping ideas internationally about the nature and characteristics of effective regulation (European Commission 2001; National Audit Office 2001).

Based on empirical research on US healthcare regulation and drawing on both the ideas of responsive regulation and the work of the Better Regulation Unit and others, Walshe and Shortell (submitted) propose a framework of ten dimensions or factors that are important to effective regulation in healthcare. They are summarized in Table 6.2 in the form of a series of questions designed to be used in assessments of effectiveness, but need some further explanation.

The first principle is that regulation should be focused on *performance improvement* and that should be the main metric by which regulatory performance is measured and evaluated. This should mean both dealing with poor performance by regulated organizations and promoting improvement even among those who already perform well. The rationale for this principle is simply that all too often, even though performance improvement is meant to be the primary objective of regulation, regulatory means and ends become confused and the process becomes the purpose in itself. Too often, regulatory performance is measured in terms of the regulatory process (numbers of standards set, surveys completed or sanctions issued) rather than in terms of its impact. A continuing focus on the question 'will this regulation bring about a meaningful improvement in healthcare?' seems to be necessary if regulatory direction and intent is to be sustained.

The second principle is that regulation should be *responsive*, incorporating the ideas of responsive regulation outlined earlier and in particular the principle of contingency. It is very clear that 'one size fits all', 'cookie cutter' approaches to regulation produce problems of regulatory mismatch between the needs of the regulated organization and the approach of the regulator, which are wasteful at best and often harmful. Regulators should treat regulated organizations differently according to how they behave and perform – far from being unfair or inconsistent, this is crucial both to reward good performance adequately and to deal properly and effectively with poor performance. It is very difficult for highly prescriptive approaches to regulation to be sufficiently responsive.

The third principle is that regulation should be *proportionate*, in the sense that major problems receive a substantial regulatory response but minor issues attract less attention, and in the sense that regulatory resources are targeted on areas or organizations where major problems exist. Disproportion results in over-regulation, which wastes regulatory resources and provokes a defensive and adversarial reaction from regulated organizations who understandably and rightly resent the imposed costs of regulatory scrutiny which seem to produce limited benefits. The converse problem of under-regulation can also be found, and is likely to mean that needed performance improvements in regulated organizations happen slowly or do not happen at all. Essentially, regulatory resources are always limited and they need to be targeted and used proportionately to get the greatest improvement from them.

The fourth principle is that regulatory methods – especially those used in regulatory direction and detection – should be demonstrably *rigorous and robust*. In simple terms, there should be a rigorous process for developing and testing regulatory standards and measures which ensures they conform with accepted scientific requirements of validity, reliability and general utility. This process should be transparent, in the sense that regulated organizations and other stakeholders should be able to see how standards and measures have been produced, and look behind them to see the underlying evidence and research on which they have been based. Too often, regulatory direction appears to be based on untested assumptions about what constitutes good performance or acceptable practice, and too much reliance is placed on regulatory detection methods that are subjective and unreliable.

The fifth principle is that regulatory arrangements should aim to balance *flexibility and consistency* in their regulatory approach. It

Table 6.2 Some principles for effective regulation

Improvement focus	• Is performance improvement the explicitly stated, primary objective of the regulatory process? • Are the regulatory arrangements directed at promoting performance improvement, or are there ways in which they might hinder or slow improvement?
Responsiveness	• Does the regulator have access to and make prompt and timely use of a wide range of different direction, detection and enforcement mechanisms? • Does the regulator adapt or tailor its approach to individual regulated organizations, making its use of regulatory mechanisms contingent on the response or behaviour of the organization?
Proportionality and targeting	• Is the level and scope of regulatory intervention appropriately matched to the size and importance of the performance problem or issue? • Are regulatory resources focused on or directed towards those organizations or areas where performance problems are known or suspected to exist?
Rigour and robustness	• Are regulations or standards developed through a rigorous process which takes full account of available evidence? • Are regulatory methods, especially those for measurement, developed and tested rigorously and do they achieve adequate validity and reliability in use?
Flexibility and consistency	• Do the regulatory arrangements allow sufficient flexibility for regulatory staff to use appropriate discretion in matching regulatory interventions and actions to individual circumstances or contexts? • Is the consistency of regulatory practice maintained, through careful monitoring and comparison of the work of regulatory staff, while taking into account the need for flexibility?
Cost-consciousness	• Is the regulator aware of the full costs of regulation, including costs both to the regulatory agency and to regulated organizations? • Does the regulator undertake a proper comparison of the costs and benefits of regulatory interventions, especially when new regulatory interventions are being developed? • Does the regulator take steps to minimize the interaction and compliance costs for regulated organizations when it can do so?

Openness and transparency	• Is information about the design regulatory process freely available, so that all stakeholders are informed about how systems for regulation are developed and set up? • Is information about the regulatory process itself freely available, so that all stakeholders are informed about the work programme of the regulator and plans and time-scales for its regulatory interventions? • Are the results of regulation, including the findings and decisions about individual regulated organizations, freely available to all stakeholders, including the public?
Enforceability	• Does the regulator have access to and make prompt and timely use of a wide range of both incentives and sanctions with which it can influence regulated organizations and promote change? • Does the regulator use the minimum enforcement action needed to secure change? • Are improvement and good performance recognized and rewarded by the regulator? • When persistent or serious problems of poor performance are identified, are they dealt with promptly and fully by the regulator, and are the most serious sanctions (such as delicensing) used if they are needed?
Accountability and independence	• Is there a mechanism for holding the regulator accountable for its actions to those with an interest in the area being regulated (including patients and the public, healthcare funders and payors, healthcare providers, and health policy-makers)? • Do the governance arrangements for the regulator maintain a balance between different interest groups or stakeholders and avoid any one group being dominant? • Does the regulator have sufficient independence of action from stakeholders or interest groups to be able to take actions which may not be welcomed by some such groups?
Formative evaluation and review	• Does the regulator have systems in place to monitor and formatively evaluate how its systems of regulation work and to assess their impact on performance? • Are the results of evaluation reviewed and used to modify systems of regulation where necessary?

Source: Walshe and Shortell (in press).

would appear that attempts to ensure consistency and to be fair and just to regulated organizations often lead to a highly prescriptive and constrained style of regulation in which there is little flexibility or scope for regulatory discretion and professional judgement. Yet some degree of flexibility is essential for effective regulation. Regulators sometimes assume, mistakenly, that to be fair and consistent they need to treat all regulated organizations in the same way, whereas in fact fairness demands that those who perform differently should be treated differently. Regulatory discretion is essential to effective regulation, but regulators have to be trusted to use their discretion wisely and fairly and need to be held accountable for their actions.

The sixth principle is that regulators and others should be *cost-conscious* – that is, be aware of and sensitive to the full, real costs of regulatory arrangements. Often, it seems that the costs of regulation are underestimated or ignored and that important costs (especially those incurred by regulated organizations) are hidden and unmeasured. Regulators are prone to discount the cost consequences of regulatory design decisions and to focus only on the costs to themselves, and there are few incentives for regulatory agencies to be efficient in the use of other people's resources. There are some well-established methods for assessing the impact of regulatory requirements which attempt to quantify the costs and benefits (Froud *et al.* 1998; National Audit Office 2001). Some regulators are required to do regulatory impact analyses when developing any new regulations, but the process is often treated as a hurdle to be overcome rather than as a useful and productive exercise for testing and shaping regulatory design. Cost-consciousness is more a cultural than a technical requirement – regulators need to be genuinely committed to minimizing the full costs of regulation while still pursuing their regulatory mission.

The seventh principle is that regulatory arrangements should generally be *open and transparent*. When regulation is conducted behind closed doors, there is an understandable suspicion among many stakeholders, including regulated organizations, that the process is corrupt or unfair. To build trust and general support for the purposes of regulation, it is important that, wherever possible, systems of regulation should be open to public scrutiny and be transparent, in the sense that all parties can see how regulatory processes work as well as what they produce. Three areas where openness is particularly important are the development of regulatory standards, the publication of findings from regulatory detection mechanisms such as surveys and inspections, and the implementation of regulatory enforcement. Having said that, there may be times when public scrutiny would make it more difficult to achieve the purposes of regulation – for example, when dealing with difficult and sensitive performance problems in an individual regulated organization – and there needs to be some provision for privacy, especially in the bilateral dealings between the regulator and individual regulated organizations.

The eighth principle is that a *wide range of enforcement strategies* is needed. Regulators often have significant enforcement powers in theory but can make little or no use of them in practice, for a variety of reasons discussed in Chapter 5. Some regulators have few direct powers and are too reliant on persuasion or exhortation, or the actions of others, to secure compliance. Regulatory enforcement should make use of incentives as well as sanctions, and the minimum enforcement action that will secure compliance should be used, but regulators need to be willing and able to escalate enforcement action swiftly when faced with real non-compliance. Ultimately, regulation needs to be backed up by a wide range of enforcement strategies or actions that can be deployed flexibly to respond appropriately to the behaviour and performance of regulated organizations.

The ninth principle concerns the *accountability and independence* of the regulatory agency. The regulator needs to be held to account for its own performance. However, it also needs sufficient space and independence to undertake its regulatory role, that can mean it doing things that are unpopular or unwelcome among some stakeholders at times. If the lines of accountability to elected politicians or others are too tightly drawn, regulated organizations and others will lobby to get them to influence regulatory policy, and the regulator is likely to become cautious about doing anything that might upset any stakeholders. However, if there are no clear mechanisms for regulatory accountability, the regulator may become too inward-looking and driven by regulatory self-interest, and take too little account of the legitimate views of others. A balance is needed, giving the regulator considerable freedom of action but still holding it ultimately to account for its actions. There is also a need to ensure that the accountability mechanisms for the regulator are not dominated by any single sectional interest – regulated organizations, consumers, government and so on. That kind of dominance, however well-intentioned the dominant interest group may be, sets up the conditions for regulatory capture and fatally compromises the independence of the regulatory agency.

Finally, the tenth principle is that the regulator should be committed to *evaluation and review*. New regulatory policies and approaches
should be piloted and tested before being introduced, the impact
and effectiveness of regulatory activities should be evaluated, and
the results of evaluation research should be used to modify and
improve systems of regulation. This may seem like common sense,
but it rarely happens in practice. Regulation is often a politicized and
contested domain, in which powerful interest groups seek to protect
their own interests and gain some advantage, and it can be difficult to
bring evidence to bear in the design and development of systems of
regulation.

THE FUTURE FOR HEALTHCARE REGULATION IN THE USA AND THE UK

If the current systems of healthcare regulation in the USA and the
UK are examined against the principles of good or effective regulation set out in the last section, they are found wanting in many ways.
Regulation in practice often seems a long way from the high ideals
or good intentions evinced when systems of regulation were first
established. There is clearly plenty of room for improvement in the
way both countries use regulation in healthcare.

In the USA, after three decades of increasingly intensive and
intrusive healthcare regulation, the costs of regulation often appear
to outweigh the benefits. The complex, bureaucratic, overlapping
and duplicative systems of regulation described in Chapter 3 mirror
the fragmented and costly nature of the healthcare system itself. In
both cases, the managerial and organizational logic for some kind
of rationalization is strong, but the political context makes change
a slow and difficult process and there are many groups with vested
interests in maintaining the *status quo*. In addition, the uniquely
adversarial culture of public life in the USA produces a legalistic,
rule-obsessed style of regulation which is manifestly inefficient and
ineffective to most outsiders' eyes, but which fits perfectly well into
the wider cultural and social milieu in that country. Only an optimist
would predict much will change in the near future.

In the UK, healthcare regulation is a rather newer phenomenon
and there is perhaps a greater opportunity to shape its development and learn the lessons of experience elsewhere. Our regulatory
tradition – in healthcare and in other areas – is much more consensual and collaborative, but even so there are already early signs

that some of the problems of regulation familiar from the US experience in healthcare and from regulation elsewhere are emerging. British healthcare regulation already seems somewhat fragmented, the costs of regulation appear to be increasing rapidly and there is remarkably little empirical evidence of its benefits.

In both countries, however, the future of healthcare regulation seems assured. Despite some misgivings about the effectiveness of regulation, there is little real appetite for its removal and few ideas on what else to put in its place. The 'regulatory ratchet' makes it far easier to regulate than to deregulate and, if anything, we might expect that the scope and intensity of healthcare regulation in both countries will increase in the future. Pragmatically, the debate should therefore probably centre on how best to regulate healthcare organizations, rather than whether to regulate them at all. The ideas of responsive or smart regulation, and the principles for effective regulation set out above, provide, at the very least, a starting point for that kind of debate.

There are, perhaps, two key conclusions to draw from this book. First, more thought and effort should be invested in designing and developing new systems of regulation in healthcare, with a view to preventing some of the problems of regulatory failure that have been identified. The experience of the USA and the UK suggests that the initial design of systems of regulation is crucial to their subsequent effectiveness, but that decisions about regulatory design are often not well thought through and nor are they properly informed by a theoretical and practical understanding of the processes of regulation. Once systems of regulation have been established, changing them through reform becomes much more difficult even if regulation is not working well, which means it is even more important to get the right regulatory design first time around. Secondly, a more evaluative culture and climate in healthcare regulation is needed, in which regulatory experimentation and change are encouraged rather than penalized and the impact of regulation on organizational performance is assessed. Developing stronger empirical foundations for regulatory practice through research and evaluation could help to produce greater consensus among stakeholders in regulation about its future direction, and more support for the aims and methods of regulation among key groups, particularly regulated organizations.

The history of healthcare regulation in the UK and the USA could be construed as the continuing triumph of hope over experience. Stakeholders in regulation – politicians, policy-makers, the public, regulated organizations and others – ask regulators to tackle problems of performance that are often longstanding and intractable in nature, and they create a regulatory environment and systems of regulation which restrict the regulatory agency's effectiveness. Then, when regulation does not work, they all too often blame the regulator. But the experience does not stop them reaching for regulatory solutions again in the future. The need for regulation is so strong that it will always be with us, even if there was overwhelming evidence that its costs and harms far outweighed its benefits. However, the conclusion of this book is more positive than that. There is plenty of evidence for the efficacy of regulation in bringing about performance improvement (that it *can* work), even though the evidence on its effectiveness (whether it *does* work) is very mixed. At its best, healthcare regulation can be a powerful force for improvement in healthcare organizations, and both regulatory theory and practice offer some important lessons in how to make regulation work better.

REFERENCES

ABT Associates (1998). *Study of Private Accreditation: Deeming of Nursing Homes, Regulatory Incentives and Non-regulatory Initiatives, and Effectiveness of the Survey and Certification System*, Vols 1–4. Washington, DC: HCFA.

Administration on Aging (1999). *Long Term Care Ombudsman Report for 1998*. Washington, DC: Administration on Aging.

Altman, S.H., Reinhardt, U.E. and Shactman, D. (eds) (1999). *Regulating Managed Care: Theory, Practice and Future Options*. San Francisco, CA: Jossey-Bass.

American Health Care Association (1999). *Facts and Trends 1999: The Nursing Facility Sourcebook*. Washington, DC: AHCA.

American Health Care Association (2001). *Staffing of Nursing Services in Long Term Care: Present Issues and Prospects for the Future*. Washington, DC: AHCA.

American Health Quality Association (1999). *A Pillar of Quality: The Medicare Peer Review Organization/Quality Improvement Organization Program*. Washington, DC: AHQA.

American Health Quality Association (2000). *A Measure of Quality: Improving Performance in American Health Care*. Washington, DC: AHQA.

American Hospitals Association (2001). *Patients or Paperwork: The Regulatory Burden Facing America's Hospitals*. Chicago, IL: AHA.

Anderson, G.F. and Hussey, P.S. (2000). *Multinational Comparisons of Health Systems Data, 2000*. New York: Commonwealth Fund.

Association of California Life and Health Insurance Companies (2001). *Statutory and Regulatory Overview of California Preferred Provider Organization (PPO) Industry*. Sacramento, CA: ACLHIC.

Ayres, I. and Braithwaite, J. (1992). *Responsive Regulation: Transcending the Deregulation Debate*. Oxford: Oxford University Press.

Baldwin, R. and Cave, M. (1999). *Understanding Regulation: Theory, Strategy and Practice*. Oxford: Oxford University Press.

240   Regulating healthcare

Bardach, E. and Kagan, R. (1982). *Going by the Book: The Problem of Regulatory Unreasonableness*. Philadelphia, PA: Temple University Press.

Barron, B.A. (1999). *Outsmarting Managed Care*. New York: Random House.

Bernstein, M.N. (1955). *Regulating Business by Independent Commission*. Princeton, NJ: Princeton University Press.

Berwick, D.M. (1988). Toward an applied technology for quality measurement in healthcare. *Medical Decision Making*, 8(4): 253–8.

Berwick, D.M. (1989). Continuous improvement as an ideal in health care. *New England Journal of Medicine*, 320(1): 53–6.

Berwick, D.M. (1996). A primer on leading the improvement of systems. *British Medical Journal*, 312: 619–22.

Berwick, D.M. and Wald, D.L. (1990). Hospital leaders' opinions of the HCFA mortality data. *Journal of the American Medical Association*, 263(2): 247–9.

Best, L., Stevens, A. and Colin-Jones, D. (1997). Rapid and responsive health technology assessment: the development and evaluation process in the South and West region of England. *Journal of Clinical Effectiveness*, 2(2): 51–6.

Better Regulation Taskforce (1998). *Principles of Good Regulation*. London: Cabinet Office.

Blumenthal, D. and Kilo, C.M. (1998). A report card on continuous quality improvement. *Milbank Quarterly*, 76(4): 625–48.

Braithwaite, J. (1985). *To Punish or Persuade: Enforcement of Coal Mine Safety*. Albany, NY: State University of New York Press.

Braithwaite, J. (2002). *Restorative Justice and Responsive Regulation*. New York: Oxford University Press.

Braithwaite, J. and Braithwaite, V. (1995). The politics of legalism: rules versus standards in nursing home regulation. *Social and Legal Studies*, 4: 307–41.

Braithwaite, J. and Drahos, P. (2000). *Global Business Regulation*. Cambridge: Cambridge University Press.

Brennan, T.A. and Berwick, D.M. (1996). *New Rules: Regulation, Markets and the Quality of American Health Care*. San Francisco, CA: Jossey-Bass.

Breyer, S.G. (1982). *Regulation and Its Reform*. Cambridge, MA: Harvard University Press.

Brook, R.H., McGlynn, E.A. and Shekelle, P.G. (2000). Defining and measuring quality of care: a perspective from US researchers. *International Journal for Quality in Health Care*, 12(4): 281–95.

Brown, L.D. (1980). Regulation, healthcare and mismatch. In R.S. Gordon (ed.) *Issues in Health Care Regulation*. New York: McGraw-Hill.

Brown, L.D. (1998). Exceptionalism as the rule? U.S. health policy innovation and cross-national learning. *Journal of Health Politics, Policy & Law*, 23(1): 35–51.

Burgner, T. (1996). *The Regulation and Inspection of Social Services.* London: Department of Health/Welsh Office.

Commission for Health Improvement (2001a). *A Guide to Clinical Governance Reviews in NHS Acute Trusts.* London: CHI.

Commission for Health Improvement (2001b). *Service Problems in the NHS: How CHI and Others Work Together.* London: CHI.

Commission for Health Improvement (2002). *Holding a Mirror Up to Ourselves: CHI's Annual Report and Accounts 2000–2001.* London: CHI.

Cook, K., Shortell, S.M., Conrad, D.A. and Morrisey, M. (1983). A theory of organizational response to regulation: the case of hospitals. *Academy of Management Review,* 8(2): 193–205.

Cookson, R., McDaid, D. and Maynard, A. (2001). Wrong SIGN, NICE mess: is national guidance distorting allocation of resources? *British Medical Journal,* 323: 743–5.

Copeland, C. and Pierron, W.L. (1999). ERISA and the regulation of group health plans. In S.H. Altman, U.E. Reinhardt and D. Shactman (eds) *Regulating Managed Care: Theory, Practice and Future Options.* San Francisco, CA: Jossey-Bass.

Crossman, R. (1977). *The Diaries of a Cabinet Minister,* Vol. III. London: Hamilton Cape.

Dame, L. and Wolfe, S. (1996). *The Failure of Private Hospital Regulation: An Analysis of the Joint Commission on Accreditation of Healthcare Organizations' Inadequate Oversight of Hospitals.* Washington, DC: Public Citizen Publications.

Davies, H.T.O. and Marshall, M.N. (2000). UK and US healthcare systems: divided by more than a common language. *Lancet,* 355: 336.

Davis, K. (2001). Universal coverage in the United States: lessons from experience of the 20th century. *Journal of Urban Health,* 78(1): 46–58.

Day, P. and Klein, R. (1987). *Accountabilities: Five Public Services.* London: Tavistock.

Day, P. and Klein, R. (1990). *Inspecting the Inspectorates.* York: Joseph Rowntree Memorial Trust.

Day, P. and Klein, R. (2001). *Auditing the Auditors: Audit in the National Health Service.* London: The Stationery Office/Nuffield Trust.

Day, P. and Klein, R. (2002). Who knows best? *Health Service Journal,* 112: 26–9.

Day, P., Klein, R. and Tipping, G. (1988). *Inspecting for Quality: Services for the Elderly.* Bath: Centre for the Analysis of Social Policy, University of Bath.

Dent, T.H.S. and Sadler, M. (2002). From guidance to practice: why NICE is not enough. *British Medical Journal,* 324: 842–5.

Department of Health (1997). *The New NHS: Modern, Dependable.* London: Department of Health.

Department of Health (1998). *A First Class Service: Quality in the New NHS.* London: Department of Health.

Department of Health (1999). *Faster Access to Modern Treatment: How NICE Appraisal will Work*. London: Department of Health.

Department of Health (2000a). *An Organisation with a Memory: Report of an Expert Group on Learning from Adverse Events in the NHS Chaired by the Chief Medical Officer*. London: The Stationery Office.

Department of Health (2000b). *The NHS Plan: A Plan for Investment, A Plan for Reform*. London: The Stationery Office.

Department of Health (2001). *Shifting the Balance of Power within the NHS: Securing Delivery*. London: The Stationery Office.

Department of Health (2002). *The NHS Plan: Next Steps for Investment, Next Steps for Reform*. London: The Stationery Office.

Department of Health and Social Security (1969). *Report of the Committee of Inquiry into Allegations of Ill-treatment of Patients and Other Irregularities at the Ely Hospital, Cardiff*. London: HMSO.

Department of Managed Health Care (2001). *Strategic Business Plan 2000/ 2001*. Sacramento, CA: DMHC, State of California.

Derrett, S., Devlin, N. and Harrison, A. (2002). Waiting in the NHS, part 2 – a change of prescription. *Journal of the Royal Society of Medicine*, 95(6): 280–3.

Devlin, N., Harrison, A. and Derrett, S. (2002). Waiting in the NHS, part 1 – a diagnosis. *Journal of the Royal Society of Medicine*, 95(5): 223–6.

Donelan, K., Blendon, R.J., Schoen, C. *et al.* (1999). The cost of health system change: public discontent in five nations. *Health Affairs*, 18(3): 206–16.

Dunlop, J.T. (1980). The limits of legal compulsion. In R.S. Gordon (ed.) *Issues in Health Care Regulation*. New York: McGraw-Hill.

Eisner, M.A. (1994). Economic regulatory policies: regulation and de-regulation in historical context. In D.H. Rosenbloom and R.D. Schwartz (eds) *Handbook of Regulation and Administrative Law*. New York: Marcel Dekker.

Enthoven, A. (1980). Match, mismatch, competition and regulation. In R.S. Gordon (ed.) *Issues in Health Care Regulation*. New York: McGraw-Hill.

European Commission (2001). *Mandelkern Group on Better Regulation: Final Report*. Brussels: European Commission.

Feachem, R.G., Sekhri, N.K. and White, K.L. (2002). Getting more for their dollar: a comparison of the NHS with California's Kaiser Permanente. *British Medical Journal*, 324: 135–41.

Feldman, S.E. and Rundall, T.G. (1993). PROs and the health care quality improvement initiative: insights from 50 cases of serious medical mistakes. *Medical Care*, 50(2): 123–52.

Ferlie, E. and Shortell, S.M. (2001). Improving the quality of health care in the United Kingdom and the United States: a framework for change. *Milbank Quarterly*, 79(2): 281–315.

Ferlie, E., Pettigrew, A., Ashburner, L. and Fitzgerald, L. (1996). *The New Public Management in Action*. Oxford: Oxford University Press.

Finkelstein, R., Hurwit, C. and Kirsch, R. (1995). *The Managed Care Consumers' Bill of Rights: A Health Policy Guide for Consumer Advocates.* New York: Public Policy and Education Fund for New York.

Francis, J.G. (1993). *The Politics of Regulation: A Comparative Perspective.* Oxford: Blackwell.

Froud, J., Boden, R., Ogus, A. and Stubbs, P. (1998). *Controlling the Regulators.* London: Macmillan.

Fuchs, B.C. (1997). *Managed Health Care: Federal and State Regulation.* Washington, D.C: Congressional Research Service, Library of Congress.

General Accounting Office (1999a). *Nursing Homes: Additional Steps Needed to Strengthen Enforcement of Federal Quality Standards,* GAO/ HEHS-99-46. Washington, DC: GAO.

General Accounting Office (1999b). *Nursing Homes: Complaint Investigation Processes Often Inadequate to Protect Residents,* GAO/HEHS-99-80. Washington, DC: GAO.

General Accounting Office (1999c). *Nursing Homes: Proposal to Enhance Oversight of Poorly Performing Homes has Merit,* GAO/HEHS-99-157. Washington, DC: GAO.

General Accounting Office (1999d). *Nursing Home Care: Enhanced HCFA Oversight of State Programs Would Better Ensure Quality,* GAO/HEHS-00-6. Washington, DC: GAO.

General Accounting Office (2000). *Nursing Homes: Sustained Efforts are Essential to Realize Potential of the Quality Initiatives,* GAO/HEHS-00-197. Washington, DC: GAO.

General Accounting Office (2001). *Private Health Insurance: Federal Role in Enforcing New Standards Continues to Evolve.* Washington, DC: GAO.

Goodman, J.C. (1980). *The Regulation of Medical Care: Is the Price Too High?* San Francisco, CA: Cato Institute.

Gordon, R.S. (ed.) (1980). *Issues in Health Care Regulation.* New York: McGraw-Hill.

Greenberg, W. (1991). *Competition, Regulation and Rationing in Health Care.* Chicago, IL: Health Administration Press.

Greer, S. (2001). *Divergence and Devolution.* London: The Nuffield Trust.

Gunningham, N., Grabosky, P. and Sinclair, D. (1998). *Smart Regulation: Designing Environmental Policy.* Oxford: Clarendon Press.

Hackey, R.B. (1998). *Rethinking Health Care Policy: The New Politics of State Regulation.* Washington, DC: Georgetown University Press.

Hadley, T.R. and McGurrin, M.C. (1988). Accreditation, certification and the quality of care in state hospitals. *Hospital and Community Psychiatry,* 39(7): 739–42.

Ham, C. (1999). Improving NHS performance: human behaviour and health policy. *British Medical Journal,* 319: 1490–2.

Hancher, L. and Moran, M. (eds) (1989). *Capitalism, Culture and Regulation.* Oxford: Oxford University Press.

Harrington, C. and Carrillo, H. (1999). The regulation and enforcement of federal nursing home standards 1991–1997. *Medical Care Research and Review*, 56(4): 471–94.

Harrington, C., Carrillo, H., Thollaug, S., Summers, P. and Wellin, V. (2000). *Nursing Facilities, Staffing, Residents, and Facility Deficiencies, 1991–99*. Report prepared for the Health Care Financing Administration. San Francisco, CA: University of California.

Harrison, S. and Wood, B. (1999). Designing health service organisation in the UK, 1968 to 1998: from blueprint to bright idea and 'manipulated emergence'. *Public Administration*, 77(4): 751–68.

Hawes, C. (1996). *The History and Impact of Federal Standards in OBRA-87*. New York: Commonwealth Fund.

Hawes, C. (1997). Regulation and the politics of long term care. *Generations*, 21(4): 5–9.

Hawkins, K. and Thomas, J. (1984). The enforcement process in regulatory bureaucracies. In K. Hawkins and J. Thomas (eds) *Enforcing Regulation*. Boston, MA: Kluwer-Nijhoff.

HCIA/JCAHO (1993). *Comparing Quality and Financial Performance of Accredited Hospitals*. Oakbrook Terrace: JCAHO.

Health Care Financing Administration (2000). *Medicaid Nursing Facilities: State Operations Manual. Provider Certification*. Baltimore, MD: HCFA.

Health Select Committee, House of Commons (1999). *Fifth Report: The Regulation of Private and Other Independent Healthcare*. London: The Stationery Office.

Health Service Ombudsman for England (2001a). *Annual Report 2000–01*. London: The Stationery Office.

Health Service Ombudsman for England (2001b). *Business Plan for 2002*. London: Health Service Ombudsman for England.

Health Service Ombudsman for England (2002). *Investigations Completed August–November 2001*. London: The Stationery Office.

Heffler, S., Levit, K., Smith, S. *et al.* (2001). Health spending growth up in 1999: faster growth expected in the future. *Health Affairs*, 20(2): 193–203.

Henkel, M., Kogan, M., Packwood, T., Whitaker, T. and Youll, P. (1989). *The Health Advisory Service: An Evaluation*. London: King's Fund.

Higgins, J. (2001). The listening blank. *Health Service Journal*, 111: 22–5.

Higgs, R. (ed.) (1995). *Hazardous to Our Health? FDA Regulation of Health Care Products*. Oakland: The Independent Institute.

Hood, C., James, O., Jones, G. *et al.* (1998). Regulation inside government: where new public management meets the audit explosion. *Public Money and Management*, 18(2): 61–8.

Hood, C., Scott, C., James, O. *et al.* (1999). *Regulation Inside Government*. Oxford: Oxford University Press.

Hume, C. (2001). The National Care Standards Commission: what it means for nurses. *Nursing Standard*, 8(5): 8–10.

Iglehart, J.K. (1996). The National Committee for Quality Assurance. *New England Journal of Medicine*, 335(13): 995–9.

Iglehart, J.K. (1999a). The American healthcare system: expenditures. *New England Journal of Medicine*, 340(1): 70–6.

Iglehart, J.K. (1999b). The American healthcare system: Medicare. *New England Journal of Medicine*, 340(4): 327–32.

Iglehart, J.K. (1999c). The American healthcare system: Medicaid. *New England Journal of Medicine*, 340(5): 403–8.

Iglehart, J.K. (2001). The Centers for Medicare and Medicaid Services. *New England Journal of Medicine*, 345(26): 1920–4.

Ignagni, K. (1999). The managed care industry: balancing market forces and regulation. In S.H. Altman, U.E. Reinhardt and D. Shactman (eds) *Regulating Managed Care: Theory, Practice and Future Options*. San Francisco, CA: Jossey-Bass.

Institute of Medicine (1986). *Improving the Quality of Care in Nursing Homes*. Washington, DC: National Academy Press.

Institute of Medicine (1990). *Medicare: A Strategy for Quality Assurance*. Washington, DC: National Academy Press.

Institute of Medicine (1995). *Real People, Real Problems: Evaluation of the Long Term Care Ombudsman Program of the Older Americans Act*. Washington, DC: National Academy Press.

Institute of Medicine (1999). *The National Round-table on Health Care Quality: Measuring the Quality of Care*. Washington, DC: National Academy Press.

Institute of Medicine (2000). *To Err is Human: Building a Safer Health System*. Washington, DC: National Academy Press.

Institute of Medicine (2001). *Improving the Quality of Long Term Care*. Washington, DC: National Academy Press.

International Society for Quality in Health Care (1997). *International Standards and Accreditation for Health Care: Feasibility Paper*. Victoria, Australia: ISQua.

Isles, V. and Sutherland K. (2001). *Organisational Change: A Review for Health Care Managers, Professionals and Researchers*. London: NCCSDO.

Jencks, S.F. and Wilensky, G.R. (1992). The health care quality improvement initiative: a new approach to quality assurance in Medicare. *Journal of the American Medical Association*, 268(7): 900–3.

Jessee, W.F. and Schranz, C.M. (1990). Medicare mortality rates and hospital quality: are they related? *Quality Assurance in Health Care*, 2(2): 137–44.

Johnson, H. and Broder, D.S. (1996). *The System: The American Way of Politics at the Breaking Point*. Boston, MA: Little, Brown.

Joint Commission for the Accreditation of Healthcare Organizations (1996). *Comprehensive Accreditation Manual for Hospitals*. Oakbrook Terrace: JCAHO.

Joint Commission for the Accreditation of Healthcare Organizations (2000). *White Paper on Future of Accreditation*. Oakbrook Terrace: JCAHO.

Jost, T.S. (1990). Regulation of the quality of nursing home care in the United States. *Quality Assurance in Health Care*, 1(4): 223–8.

Jost, T.S. (ed.) (1997). *Regulation of the Healthcare Professions*. Chicago, IL: Health Administration Press.

Kagan, R.A. (1984). The 'criminology of the corporation' and regulatory enforcement strategies. In K. Hawkins and J.M. Thomas (eds) *Enforcing Regulation*. Boston, MA: Kluwer-Nijhoff.

Kagan, R. and Axelrad, L. (eds) (2000). *Regulatory Encounters: Multinational Corporations and American Adversarial Legalism*. Berkeley, CA: University of California Press.

Kane, R.L. (1998). Assuring quality in nursing home care. *Journal of the American Geriatrics Society*, 46(2): 232–7.

Kapp, M.B. (2000). Quality of care and quality of life in nursing facilities: what's regulation got to do with it? *McGeorge Law Review*, 31: 707–31.

Kennedy I. (2001). *Bristol Royal Infirmary Inquiry: Learning from Bristol*. London: The Stationery Office.

Kerrison, S.H. and Pollock, A.M. (2001). Caring for older people in the private sector in England. *British Medical Journal*, 323: 566–9.

Klazinga, N. (2000). Re-engineering trust: the adoption and adaption of four models for external quality assurance of health care services in western European health care systems. *International Journal for Quality in Health Care*, 12(3): 183–9.

Klein, R. (1987). The regulation of nursing homes: a comparative perspective. *Milbank Quarterly*, 65(3): 303–47.

Klein, R. (2001a). What's happening to Britain's National Health Service? *New England Journal of Medicine*, 345(4): 305–8.

Klein, R. (2001b). *The New Politics of the National Health Service*, 4th ed. Harlow: Prentice Hall.

Klein, R. and Scrivens, E. (1993). The bottom line. *Health Service Journal*, 103: 24–6.

Klein, R., Day P. and Redmayne, S. (1996). *Managing Scarcity: Priority Setting and Rationing in the National Health Service*. Buckingham: Open University Press.

Komaroff, A. (1978). The PSRO quality assurance blues. *New England Journal of Medicine*, 298(21): 1194–6.

Kuttner, R. (1999a). The American healthcare system: health insurance coverage. *New England Journal of Medicine*, 340(2): 163–8.

Kuttner, R. (1999b). The American healthcare system: employer sponsored health coverage. *New England Journal of Medicine*, 340(3): 248–52.

Latimer, J. (1997). The essential role of regulation to assure quality in long term care. *Generations*, 21(4): 10–14.

Levin, A. (1980). *Regulating Health Care: The Struggle for Control*. New York: Academy of Political Science.

Leyerle, B. (1994). *The Private Regulation of American Healthcare*. New York: M.E. Sharpe.

Light, D.W. (1998). Is NHS purchasing serious? An American perspective. *British Medical Journal*, 316: 217–20.

Lipsky, M. (1983). *Street Level Bureaucracy*. London: Russell Sage Foundation.

Little Hoover Commission (1998). *Review of Governor's Reorganisation Plan #1 of 1998*. Sacramento, CA: Little Hoover Commission.

Locock, L. (2001). *Maps and Journeys: Redesign in the NHS*. Birmingham: HSMC, University of Birmingham.

Luft, H.S. (1985). Competition and regulation. *Medical Care*, 23(5): 383–400.

Maddock, S. (2002). Making modernisation work: new narratives, change strategies and people management in the public sector. *International Journal of Public Sector Management*, 15(1): 13–43.

Majone, G. (1994). The rise of the regulatory state in Europe. *West European Politics*, 17(3): 77–101.

Marshall, M.N., Shekelle, P.G., Leatherman, S. and Brook, R.H. (2000). The public release of performance data: what do we expect to gain? A review of the evidence. *Journal of the American Medical Association*, 283(14): 1866–74.

Martin, J.P. (1984). *Hospitals in Trouble*. Oxford: Blackwell.

Medicare Payment Advisory Commission (2000). *Report to Congress: Selected Medicare Issues*. Washington, DC: MedPAC.

Mendelson, M.A. (1974). *Tender Loving Greed*. New York: Vintage Books.

Merry, M.D. (1991). Can an external quality review system avoid the inspection model? *Quality Review Bulletin*, 17(10): 315–19.

Midwinter, A. and McGarvey, N. (2001). In search of the regulatory state: evidence from Scotland. *Public Administration*, 79(4): 825–49.

Mills, S.Y. (2001). Regulation in complementary and alternative medicine. *British Medical Journal*, 322: 158–9.

Modernization Agency (2001). *The Work of the Agency: Information for NHS Organisations*. London: NHS Modernization Agency.

Moran, M. (1999). *Governing the Health Care State: A Comparative Study of the United Kingdom, the United States, and Germany*. Manchester: Manchester University Press.

Moran, M. and Prosser, T. (1994). *Privatization and Regulatory Change in Europe*. Buckingham: Open University Press.

Moran, M. and Wood, B. (1993). *States, Regulation and the Medical Profession*. Buckingham: Open University Press.

Moss, F. and Halamandaris, V. (1977). *Too Old, Too Sick, Too Bad: Nursing Homes in America*. Germandtown, MD: Aspen.

National Audit Office (2001). *Better Regulation: Making Good Use of Regulatory Impact Assessments*. London: The Stationery Office.

National Care Standards Commission (2002a). *Care Homes for Older People: National Minimum Standards, Care Home Regulations*. London: The Stationery Office.

National Care Standards Commission (2002b). *Independent Health Care: National Minimum Standards Regulations*. London: The Stationery Office.

National Committee for Quality Assurance (2000). *The State of Managed Care Quality Report 2000*. Washington, DC: NCQA.

National Committee for Quality Assurance (2001). *The State of Managed Care Quality Report 2001*. Washington, DC: NCQA.

National Committee for Quality Assurance (2002a). *NCQA Overview: Measuring the Quality of America's Health Care*. Washington, DC: NCQA.

National Committee for Quality Assurance (2002b). *Standards for the Accreditation of Managed Care Organizations*. Washington, DC: NCQA.

Nazarko, L. (1997). A question of inspection. *Nursing Times*, 93(46): 40–2.

Netten A., Forder, J. and Knight, J. (1999). *Costs of Regulating Care Homes for Adults*. Canterbury: PSSRU, University of Kent at Canterbury.

Newdick, C. (2001). Strong words. *Health Service Journal*, 111: 26–7.

NHS Confederation (2002). *Reviewing the Reviewers: NHS Experience of CHI Clinical Governance Reviews*. London: NHS Confederation.

Noll, R. (1985). Government regulatory behaviour: a multidisciplinary survey and synthesis. In R. Noll (ed). *Regulatory Policy and the Social Sciences*. Berkeley, CA: University of California Press.

Norton, E. (1992). Incentive regulation of nursing homes. *Journal of Health Economics*, 11(2): 105–28.

Nutley S.M. and Smith, P.C. (1998). League tables for performance improvement in healthcare. *Journal of Health Services Research and Policy*, 3(1): 50–7.

O'Donoghue, P. (1974). *Evidence about the Effects of Health Care Regulation: An Evaluation and Synthesis of Policy Relevant Research*. Denver, CO: Spectrum Research.

Office of Inspector General, Department of Health and Human Services (1999a). *The External Review of Hospital Quality: A Call for Greater Accountability*. Washington, DC: OIG.

Office of the Inspector General, Department of Health and Human Services (1999b). *Nursing Home Survey and Certification: Deficiency Trends*. OEI-02-98-00350. Washington, DC: OIG.

Office of the Inspector General, Department of Health and Human Services (1999c). *Quality of Care in Nursing Homes: An Overview*. OEI-02-99-00060. Washington, DC: OIG.

Ogus, A. (1994). *Regulation: Legal Form and Economic Theory*. Oxford: Clarendon Press.

Pollack, R.F. (1999). Regulation from a consumer's perspective. In S.H. Altman, U.E. Reinhardt and D. Shactman (eds) *Regulating Managed Care: Theory, Practice and Future Options*. San Francisco, CA: Jossey-Bass.

Power, M. (1997). *The Audit Society: Rituals of Verification*. Oxford: Oxford University Press.

Raftery, J. (2001). NICE: faster access to modern treatments? Analysis of guidance on health technologies. *British Medical Journal*, 323: 1300–3.

Randall, A. (2002). Take the wheel. *Health Service Journal*, 112: 29.

Reinhard, S. and Stone, R. (2001). *Promoting Quality in Nursing Homes: The Wellspring Model*. New York: Commonwealth Fund.

Reinhardt, U.E. (1992). The United States: breakthroughs and waste. *Journal of Health Politics, Policy and Law*, 17(4): 637–66.

Reiss, A.J. (1984). Selecting strategies of social control over organisational life. In K. Hawkins and J.M. Thomas (eds) *Enforcing Regulation*. Boston, MA: Kluwer-Nijhoff.

Rhodes, G. (1981). *Inspectorates in British Government: Law Enforcement and Standards of Efficiency*. London: Allen & Unwin.

Roberts, J.S., Coale, J.G. and Redman, R.R. (1987). A short history of the Joint Commission on Accreditation of Hospitals. *Journal of the American Medical Association*, 258(7): 936–40.

Robinson, J.C. (1999). *The Corporate Practice of Medicine: Competition and Innovation in Health Care*. Berkeley, CA: University of California Press.

Robinson, J.C. (2001a). The end of managed care. *Journal of the American Medical Association*, 285(20): 2622–8.

Robinson, J.C. (2001b). Physician organization in California: crisis and opportunity. *Health Affairs*, 20(4): 81–96.

Robinson, R. and Steiner, A. (1998). *Managed Health Care*. Buckingham: Open University Press.

Rockwell, D.A., Pelletier, L.R. and Donnelly, W. (1993). The cost of accreditation: one hospital's experience. *Hospital and Community Psychiatry*, 44: 151–5.

Rosenbloom, D.H. (1994). The evolution of the administrative state and transformations of administrative law. In D.H. Rosenbloom and R.D. Schwartz (eds) *Handbook of Regulation and Administrative Law*. New York: Marcel Dekker.

Rosenthal, M.B., Frank, R.G., Buchanan, J.L., and Epstein, A.M. (2001). Scale and structure of capitated physician organizations in California. *Health Affairs*, 20(4): 109–19.

Sanazaro, P.J. (1974). Medical audit: experience in the USA. *British Medical Journal*, i: 271–82.

Sanazaro, P.J. and Worth, R.M. (1978). Concurrent quality assurance in hospital care: report of a study by Private Initiative in PSRO. *New England Journal of Medicine*, 298(21): 1171–7.

Schyve, P.M. and O'Leary, D.S. (1998). The Joint Commission's agenda for change and beyond. In C. Caldwell (ed.) *Handbook for Managing Change in Healthcare*. Milwaukee: ASQ Quality Press.

Scott, C. (2001). *Public and Private Roles in Health Care Systems*. Buckingham: Open University Press.

Scrivens, E. (1995). *Accreditation: Protecting the Professional or the Consumer?* Buckingham: Open University Press.

Sculpher, M., Drummond, M. and O'Brien, B. (2001). Effectiveness, efficiency and NICE. *British Medical Journal*, 322: 943–4.

Selznick, P. (1985). Focusing organisational research on regulation. In

R. Noll (ed.) *Regulatory Policy and the Social Sciences*. Berkeley, CA: University of California Press.

Sheldon, T. and Chalmers, I. (1994). The UK Cochrane Centre and the NHS Centre for Reviews and Dissemination. *Health Economics*, 3: 201–3.

Shortell, S.M., O'Brien, J.L., Carman, J.M. *et al.* (1995). Assessing the impact of continuous quality improvement/total quality management: concept versus implementation. *Health Services Research*, 30(2): 377–401.

Shortell, S.M., Gillies, R. and Anderson, D.A. (2000). *Remaking Healthcare in America: The Evolution of Integrated Delivery Systems*. San Francisco, CA: Jossey-Bass Wiley.

Singer, S.J. and Enthoven, A.C. (1999). California's struggle with regulation. In S.H. Altman, U.E. Reinhardt and D. Shactman (eds) *Regulating Managed Care: Theory, Practice and Future Options*. San Francisco, CA: Jossey-Bass.

Smith, P.C. (ed) (2002). *Measuring Up: Improving Health System Performance in OECD Countries*. Paris: OECD Publications.

Social Services Inspectorate (2001). *Safe Enough? Inspection of Health Authority Registration and Inspection Units 2000*. London: Department of Health.

Stacey, M. (1992). *Regulating British Medicine: The General Medical Council*. Buckingham: Open University Press.

Thomas, W.H. (1996). *Life Worth Living: How Someone You Love Can Still Enjoy Life in a Nursing Home*. Acton, MA: Vanderwyk & Burham.

Vass, P. (2002). The principles of better regulation: separating rules and responsibility. Paper presented at the *Centre for Regulation and Competition International Workshop*, Manchester, 4–6 September.

Vladeck, B. (1980). *Unloving Care: The Nursing Home Tragedy*. New York: Basic Books.

Walsh, N. and Walshe, K. (1998). *Accreditation in Primary Care*. Birmingham: Health Services Management Centre, University of Birmingham and Royal College of General Practitioners.

Walshe, K. (ed). (1995). *Evaluating Clinical Audit: Past Lessons, Future Directions*. London: Royal Society of Medicine.

Walshe, K. (1998). Evidence based healthcare: what progress in the NHS? *Journal of the Royal Society of Medicine*, 91(suppl. 35): 15–19.

Walshe, K. (1999). Improvement through inspection? The development of the new Commission for Health Improvement in England and Wales. *Quality in Health Care*, 8(3): 191–6.

Walshe, K. (2000a). Adverse events in healthcare: issues in measurement. *Quality in Healthcare*, 9: 47–52.

Walshe, K. (2000b). *Clinical Governance: A Review of the Evidence*. Birmingham: Health Services Management Centre, University of Birmingham.

Walshe, K. (2001a). Regulating nursing homes in the United States: are we learning from experience? *Health Affairs*, 20(6): 128–44.

Walshe, K. (2001b). Don't try this at home: health policy lessons for the NHS from the United States. *Economic Affairs*, 21(4): 31–5.

Walshe, K. (2002). The rise of regulation in the NHS. *British Medical Journal*, 324: 967–70.

Walshe, K. and Ham, C. (1997). *Acting on the Evidence: Progress in the NHS*. Birmingham: NHS Confederation.

Walshe, K. and Harrington, C. (2002). The regulation of nursing facilities in the US: an analysis of the resources and performance of state survey agencies. *The Gerontologist*, 42: 475–87.

Walshe, K. and Higgins, J. (2002). The use and impact of inquiries in the NHS. *British Medical Journal*, 325: 895–900.

Walshe, K. and Offen, N. (2001). A very public failure: lessons for quality improvement in healthcare organisations from the Bristol Royal Infirmary. *Quality in Health Care*, 10: 250–6.

Walshe, K., Walsh, N., Schofield, T. and Blakeway Philips, C. (eds) (1999). *Accreditation in Primary Care: Towards Clinical Governance*. Oxford: Radcliffe Medical Press.

Walshe, K., Wallace, L., Latham, L., Freeman, T. and Spurgeon, P. (2001). The external review of quality improvement in healthcare organisations: a qualitative study. *International Journal of Quality in Health Care*, 13(5): 367–74.

Walshe, K. and Shortell, S.M. (submitted). The impact of social regulation on the performance of healthcare organizations in the United States.

Wanless, D. (2002). *Securing Our Future Health: Taking a Long Term View*. London: HM Treasury.

Webster, C. (1998). *National Health Service Reorganisation: Learning from History*. London: Office of Health Economics.

Weiner, J.P., Lewis, R. and Gillam, S. (2001). *US Managed Care and PCTs: Lessons to a Small Island from a Lost Continent*. London: King's Fund.

Wiener, C.L. (2000). *The Elusive Quest: Accountability in Hospitals*. New York: Aldine de Gruyter.

Wilson, J.Q. (1980). *The Politics of Regulation*. New York: Basic Books.

World Health Organization (2000). *The World Health Report 2000*. Geneva: WHO.

Zinn, J.S. (1994). Market competition and the quality of nursing home care. *Journal of Health Politics, Policy and Law*, 19(3): 555–82.

FURTHER READING

General regulation – theory and practice

Ayres, I. and Braithwaite, J. (1992). *Responsive Regulation: Transcending the Deregulation Debate*. Oxford: Oxford University Press. Seminal work which sets out the ideas of responsive regulation, such as escalating pyramid of strategies and intervention/sanction, use of delegation in regulation, approach of 'the benign big gun', enforced self-regulation and partial regulation.

Baldwin, R. and Cave, M. (1999). *Understanding Regulation: Theory, Strategy and Practice*. Oxford: Oxford University Press. General overview of regulation theory, with a focus on the British utilities/public sector. Describes theories and concepts of regulation, then goes on to describe development of regulation in the UK.

Baldwin, R., Scott, C. and Hood, C. (1998). *A Reader on Regulation*. Oxford: Oxford University Press. Compilation of papers published in a variety of journals on aspects of regulation, including origins and development, standard-setting and rule definition, regulatory styles and techniques, and accountability and evaluation of regulation.

Bardach, E. and Kagan, R. (1982). *Going by the Book: The Problem of Regulatory Unreasonableness*. Philadelphia, PA: Temple University Press. Seminal and very readable account of the problems of regulation, with a particular focus on regulatory 'unreasonableness'. Chapters focusing on the management of regulatory agencies and the inspection function, and a wider discussion of regulatory design.

Bardach, E. and Kagan, R. (eds) (1982). *Social Regulation: Strategies for Reform*. San Francisco, CA: Institute for Contemporary Studies. Edited volume resulting from a conference of regulatory policy-makers and researchers, focused on issues of regulatory reform in the light of 1970s US regulatory experience and the Reagan reforms of the 1980s.

Black, J. (1997). *Rules and Regulators*. Oxford: Clarendon Press. Study of the theory and practice of rule-making in regulation, with range of practical examples drawn mainly from the financial services sector. Illustrates the problems and challenges of good rule-making and draws together key lessons.

Braithwaite, J. (1985) *To Punish or Persuade: Enforcement of Coal Mine Safety*. Albany, NY: State University of New York Press. Study of major mining disasters in USA, UK and elsewhere, which shows the impact of regulation on mine safety and explores the different advantages of deterrence- and compliance-based approaches.

Breyer, S.G. (1982). *Regulation and Its Reform*. Cambridge, MA: Harvard University Press. Classic description of the theory and practice of regulation in industry/markets. Sets out main justifications for regulation and a number of regulatory approaches/strategies and their problems – mainly focused on economic regulation. Describes use of regulation in several settings and outlines approaches to regulatory reform.

Froud, J., Boden, R., Ogus, A. and Stubbs, P. (1998). *Controlling the Regulators*. London: Macmillan. Results of ESRC-funded study of regulatory impact assessment/evaluation; describes a variety of methodologies and identifies advantages and disadvantages and impact on regulatory behaviour.

Gunningham, N., Grabosky, P. and Sinclair, D. (1998). *Smart Regulation: Designing Environmental Policy*. Oxford: Clarendon Press. Comprehensive account of the development of regulation in environmental policy, with focused sections on the chemical and agriculture sectors. Promotes idea of smart regulation (cf. responsive regulation) and the use of a complementary mix of regulatory methods.

Hawkins, K. and Thomas, J. (eds) (1984). *Enforcing Regulation*. Boston, MA: Kluwer-Nijhoff. Edited collection of contributions on approaches to enforcement, including chapters on how enforcement works, the behaviour of regulatory inspectorates, the economics of enforcement, and examples in occupational health and safety and mining.

Howard, P.K. (1994). *The Death of Common Sense: How Law is Suffocating America*. New York: Warner Books. Short, polemical book focused on exposing the extremes of US regulatory regimes and the adverse effects of regulation and especially of adversarial legalism in regulation. Suggests a need to reform regulation to move away from rules-based approaches to a more flexible, outcome-driven, principled approach.

Kagan, R. and Axelrad, L. (eds) (2000). *Regulatory Encounters: Multinational Corporations and American Adversarial Legalism*. Berkeley, CA: University of California Press. Edited collection of research studies on the use of regulation in same areas across different countries – USA, Europe and Japan mainly. Provides good evidence of the unique US focus on adversarial legalism in regulation and of its limited benefits and considerable costs.

Noll, R.G. (ed.) (1985). *Regulatory Policy and the Social Sciences*. Berkeley, CA: University of California Press. Edited volume of contributions on the place of regulation from a range of social sciences/disciplines. Includes good comprehensive overview of the field by Noll.

Ogus, A. (1994). *Regulation: Legal Form and Economic Theory*. Oxford: Clarendon Press. Comprehensive and detailed summary of the theory and practice of regulation, from a primarily legal and economic perspective. Chapters on the theory and ideas of regulation and on forms of economic and social regulation.

Power, M. (1997). *The Audit Society: Rituals of Verification*. Oxford: Oxford University Press. Pioneering analysis of the ritual use of audit (in variety of techniques/forms) in modern society and the transfer of trust from people/institutions to audit methodologies.

Rosenbloom, D.H. and Schwartz, R.D. (eds) (1994). *Handbook of Regulation and Administrative Law*. New York: Marcel Dekker. Edited volume on development of administrative law and regulatory processes with relevant contributions on regulatory rule-making, enforcement and agency management.

Health and social care regulation

Abbott, T.A. (ed.) (1995). *Health Care Policy and Regulation*. Norwell, MA: Kluwer. Collection of papers from a conference on health care reform and regulation. Its main focus is on economics/price regulation and there is a section on quality regulation concerned with quality improvement methods.

Allsop, J. and Mulcahy, L. (1996). *Regulating Medical Work: Formal and Informal Controls*. Buckingham: Open University Press. Overview of a variety of UK mechanisms for regulation in its widest sense, including complaints, litigation, professional licensure, disciplinary procedures, etc.

Altman, S.H., Reinhardt, U.E. and Shactman, D. (eds) (1999). *Regulating Managed Care: Theory, Practice and Future Options*. San Francisco, CA: Jossey-Bass. Edited volume of papers from a RWJ sponsored conference, discussing the development of regulation in managed care and its impact on the future growth/shape of managed care.

Brennan, T.A. and Berwick, D.M. (1996). *New Rules: Regulation, Markets and the Quality of American Health Care*. San Francisco, CA: Jossey-Bass. Overview of the use of regulation and its impact, especially on quality, in healthcare in the USA. Gives comprehensive historical account of the evolution of quality assurance, development of regulation, and places in context current thinking on continuous quality improvement (CQI). Offers suggested improvements to regulation, linked to CQI ideas and the concept of responsive regulation (cf. Ayres and Braithwaite 1992).

Clough, R. (ed.) (1994). *Insights into Inspection: The Regulation of Social Care*. London: Whiting & Birch. Edited volume of contributions describing and in part analysing the systems for inspection/regulation in social care (including both residential and non-residential services for the elderly, children and others) in the UK. Describes development of local authorities as regulators/inspectors as well as providers.

Day, P. and Klein, R. (1987). *Accountabilities: Five Public Services*. London: Tavistock. Exploration of the concepts of accountability in public services and how they are carried through in practice, using case studies in five settings (health, education, social services, police, water). A thoughtful discussion of the ideas and issues, setting them in the context of differences between case study organizations.

Day, P. and Klein, R. (1990). *Inspecting the Inspectorates*. York: Joseph Rowntree Memorial Trust. Report of research undertaken into the roles of inspectorates in health and social care, focusing on case studies in ten organizations and the roles of three regulators – Social Services Inspectorate, Audit Commission and Health Advisory Service.

Day, P. and Klein, R. (2001). *Auditing the Auditors: Audit in the National Health Service*. London: Nuffield Trust/The Stationery Office. Study of the role of the Audit Commission and its impact on the NHS, which also looks at the relationship with, and role of, the National Audit Office and the new Commission for Health Improvement.

Day, P., Klein, R. and Tipping, G. (1988). *Inspecting for Quality: Services for the Elderly*. Bath: Centre for Analysis of Social Policy, University of Bath. Short evaluation of the Health Advisory Service, concluding that it had a flawed and ineffectual approach to its role, which lacked focus, explicit standards and proper implementation/action follow-up.

Dingwall, R. and Fenn, P. (eds) (1992). *Quality and Regulation in Health Care*. London: Routledge. Short edited volume on quality in healthcare, containing contributions on litigation/tort, complaints, medical discipline, medical error and health legislation/politics.

Freddi, G. and Bjorkman, J.W. (1989). *Controlling Medical Professionals: The Comparative Politics of Health Governance*. London: Sage. Edited volume containing a series of mainly country-based chapters, each describing the development of the health system and the place of medical professionals within it (covers USA, Sweden, France, Germany, Italy, UK, etc.).

Goodman, J.C. (1980). *The Regulation of Medical Care: Is the Price Too High?* San Francisco, CA: Cato Institute. Monograph on regulation and competition in US healthcare, arguing that free market and its benefits have been prevented by the American Medical Association and professional/producer lobbies, and what is needed now is not more regulation, but less.

Gordon, R.S. (1980). *Issues in Health Care Regulation*. New York: McGraw-Hill. Edited volume of essays/papers on regulation in healthcare, with some highly original and still relevant contributions from Enthoven, Breyer, Feldman and others. Product of a Harvard/Kennedy School of Government conference.

Greenberg, W. (1991). *Competition, Regulation and Rationing in Health Care*. Chicago, IL: Health Administration Press. Health economist's exploration of the use of regulation and competition in the health sector;

largely descriptive but with some discussion of the effects of regulation/competition.

Hackey, R.B. (1998). *Rethinking Health Care Policy: The New Politics of State Regulation*. Washington, DC: Georgetown University Press. Exploration of how a number of states have approached the task of regulating healthcare and health services, covering both the policy process/politics and the nature, content and effects of regulation.

Harrison, S. and Pollitt, C. (1994). *Controlling Health Professionals: The Future of Work and Organization in the NHS*. Buckingham: Open University Press. General text on the changing relationships between professionals and managers in the UK health service, focusing on the growing managerialism and the co-option of professionals to managerial aims and roles.

Higgs, R. (ed.) (1995). *Hazardous to Our Health? FDA Regulation of Health Care Products*. Oakland: The Independent Institute. A polemical critique of the role of the FDA as regulator of pharmaceuticals and medical devices, and a call for much reduced regulatory oversight.

Hopkins, G. (2000). *An Inspector Calls: A Practical Look at Social Care Inspection*. Lyme Regis: Russell House. Practical handbook on the process of inspection for residential homes for children and the elderly in the UK. Presents results of surveys of inspectors and providers and discusses good practice in preparing for and undertaking inspections.

Levin, A. (1980). *Regulating Health Care: The Struggle for Control*. New York: Academy of Political Science. Edited collection of papers on the role of regulation in healthcare across a range of areas, from pharmaceuticals and insurance to hospital costs and quality.

Leyerle, B. (1994). *The Private Regulation of American Healthcare*. New York: M.E. Sharpe. Polemical critique of the development of managed care and the growth of the accountability and performance measurement functions in American healthcare, with detailed discussion of peer review organizations and other regulators.

Moran, M. (1999). *Governing the Health Care State: A Comparative Study of the United Kingdom, the United States, and Germany*. Manchester: Manchester University Press. Political science perspective on the growth of the healthcare industry/system and its relationship with the state and society. Analyses systems in place for governance, areas of consumption, technological innovation and professions.

Moran, M. and Wood, B. (1993). *States, Regulation and the Medical Profession*. Buckingham: Open University Press. A comparison of systems of regulation and relationships between the state and the medical profession in three countries – the UK, USA and Germany. It examines professional entry, pay and competition and the effect of regulation on doctors, patients and funders.

O'Donoghue, P. (1974). *Evidence about the Effects of Health Care Regulation: An Evaluation and Synthesis of Policy Relevant Research*. Denver, CO: Spectrum Research. A collation of literature reviews on the use of regulation in health care, including regulation aimed at professionals and organizations and regulation of both cost and quality. Mainly of historical interest, demonstrating that issues have been discussed and debated for many years.

Scrivens, E. (1995). *Accreditation: Protecting the Professional or the Consumer?* Buckingham: Open University Press. General overview of the development of accreditation in the USA, Canada, Australia and the UK, with a focus on reporting and describing accreditation programmes in the UK.

Wiener, C.L. (2000). *The Elusive Quest: Accountability in Hospitals.* New York: Aldine de Gruyter. Sociological exploration of the growing call/ requirement for accountability in US healthcare, with a wide-ranging historical perspective. Discusses growth of accreditation, with a particular focus on JCAHO, but also covers indicators/disclosure, etc.

Health professions and professional regulation

Jost, T.S. (ed.) (1997). *Regulation of the Healthcare Professions.* Chicago, IL: Health Administration Press. Edited volume with chapters summarizing the development of licensure and recertification in the USA, systems for discipline, scope of practice and self-regulation.

Stacey, M. (1992). *Regulating British Medicine: The General Medical Council.* Buckingham: Open University Press. Extensive account of the development of the General Medical Council (GMC) and its role in self-regulation from its foundation in 1858 through to the early 1990s. Argues the case for continuing and extending reforms already started, and prefigures much of subsequent changes to the GMC.

Public sector and government regulation

Blackie, J. (1970). *Inspecting the Inspectorate.* London: Routledge & Kegan Paul. Account of the development of HM Inspectorate of Schools from 1840 to 1966 by a former senior inspector. Of mainly historical interest.

Foster, C.D. (1992). *Privatisation, Public Ownership and the Regulation of Natural Monopoly.* Oxford: Blackwell. A comprehensive study of privatization under the Conservative administration, which contrasts the legal and economic systems of regulation in the USA with the rather looser approach taken in the UK, and sets out the mechanisms and controls needed when public utilities and natural monopolies are transferred to private hands.

Henkel, M. (1991). *Government, Evaluation and Change.* London: Jessica Kingsley. Based on an ESRC study of the development of new public management approaches and the growth of evaluation in government. Discusses case studies of Audit Commission, use of consultants, Social Services Inspectorate and Health Advisory Service.

Hood, C., Scott, C., James, O. *et al.* (1999). *Regulation Inside Government.* Oxford: Oxford University Press. Overview of the growth of regulation in the public sector over recent years, based on an ESRC study of regulation in the UK. Discusses theory and practice of regulation and offers a number of frameworks for categorizing regulators and their activities, and has descriptive chapters on regulation in different areas.

Moran, M. and Prosser, T. (1994). *Privatization and Regulatory Change in Europe.* Buckingham: Open University Press. Discussion of the process and impact of privatization of state or nationalized industries in the UK, Europe and former Soviet bloc countries, focused on political and social implications of transfer of ownership and control.

Rhodes, G. (1981). *Inspectorates in British Government: Law Enforcement and Standards of Efficiency.* London: Allen & Unwin. SSRC-funded study of the development of inspection in the UK, with a strong descriptive and historical content. Covers schools, trading standards, factories/mines, etc. Finishes with more theoretical/analytical perspective on future development of inspection.

Wilcox, B. and Gray, J. (1996). *Inspecting Schools: Holding Schools to Account and Helping Schools to Improve.* Buckingham: Open University Press. Comprehensive review of the development of inspection in school education, focused on the 1990s and the establishment of OFSTED. Reviews evidence on inspection methods, processes and impacts.

INDEX

THE EUROPEAN PATIENT OF THE FUTURE

Angela Coulter and Helen Magee (Eds.)

Health care is changing fast and patients' experiences and expectations are also changing. Developments in information technology and biotechnology are already having a profound influence on the way health services are delivered and the organization of health care is under reform in most countries. Patients no longer see themselves as passive recipients of care: increasingly they expect to be involved in all decisions that affect them.

This book reports the results of a major study carried out in eight different European countries to look at health policy dilemmas through the eyes of the patient. Drawing on literature reviews, focus groups and a survey of 1,000 people in each of the eight countries, the book addresses the following questions:

- Why might the patients of the future be different?
- What will patients and citizens expect from health systems?
- Will the public be willing to pay more for better health care?
- What kind of value trade-offs are people prepared to make, for example between prompt access and continuity of care, or between choice and equity?
- How will patients access information, advice and treatment?
- How should policy-makers and providers react to patients' desire for greater autonomy?
- How can public confidence in health systems be maintained in the future?

The European Patient of the Future is a clear, jargon-free text which will be a key resource for all health service professionals, health policy analysts and patient advocates.

Contents
Series Editor's introduction – Introduction – Health services in the different countries – Germany – Italy – Poland – Slovenia – Spain – Sweden – Switzerland – United Kingdom – Communication, information, involvement and choice – Key Issues for European patients – Appendix – Index.

224pp   0 335 21187 9 (Paperback)   0 335 21188 7 (Hardback)

REASONABLE RATIONING
INTERNATIONAL EXPERIENCE OF PRIORITY SETTING IN HEALTH CARE

Chris Ham and Glenn Robert (Eds.)

Reasonable Rationing is must reading for those interested in how to connect theory about fair rationing processes to country-level practices. The five case studies reveal a deep tension between political pressures to accommodate interest group demands and ethically motivated efforts to improve both information and institutional procedures for setting fair limits to care. The authors frame the issues insightfully.

Professor Norman Daniels, Harvard School of Public Health

- How are different countries setting priorities for health care?
- What role does information and evidence on cost and effectiveness play?
- How are institutions contributing to priority setting?
- What are the lessons for policy makers?

Priority setting in health care is an issue of increasing importance. Choices about the use of health care budgets are inescapable and difficult. A number of countries have sought to strengthen their approach to priority setting by drawing on research-based evidence on the cost and effectiveness of different treatments. This book brings together leading experts in the field to summarize and analyse the experience of priority setting in five countries: Canada, The Netherlands, New Zealand, Norway and the United Kingdom. Drawing on literature from a range of disciplines, it makes a significant contribution to the debate on the role of information and institutions in priority setting.

Reasonable Rationing has been written with a broad readership in mind. It will be of interest to policy makers, health care professionals and health service managers, as well as students of health and social policy at advanced undergraduate and postgraduate levels.

Contents
Introduction – International experience of rationing – New Zealand – Canada – United Kingdom – Norway – The Netherlands – Conclusions – References – Index.

192pp   0 335 21185 2 (Paperback)   0 335 21186 0 (Hardback)